Also covers the new English GCSE

AQA GCSE

Series editor: Steve Davies

English

Language & Literature

FOUNDATION

Authors:
John Clare
Helen Clyde
Steve Davies
Mike Devitt
Shelley Etheridge
Sarah Forrest
Robert Francis
Joanna Haffenden
Chris Hawkes
Linda Hill
Sharon McCammon
Kathryn Simpson

The Publishers would like to thank the following for permission to reproduce copyright material:
Photo credits **Unit 1 image:** © Niels Poulsen DK / Alamy; **page 2:** © Imagestate Media Partners Limited - Impact Photos / Alamy**; page 4:** © Ingram Publishing Limited**; page 5 and APPLE image throughout:** © Ingram Publishing Limited**; Unit 2 image:** © David Hancock / Alamy; **page 7:** © Rex Features; **page 9:** © Design Pics Inc. / Alamy; **page 10 and 90:** © Geoffrey Robinson / Rex Features; **page 11:** © Christopher Furlong/Getty Images; **page 13:** © 1997 Doug Menuez / Photodisc / Getty Images**; page 14:** © Russell Illig / Photodisc / Getty Images; **page 18:** © Peter M. Fisher/ Corbis; **Unit 3 image:** © Bernhard Lang / Riser / Getty Images; **page 29:** © Steve Davies; **Unit 4 image:** © Larry Lilac / Alamy; **page 38:** © Ingram Publishing Limited; **page 40:** © Keystone/Getty Images; **Unit 5 image:** © Steven Lam / Stone / Getty Images; **page 55:** © Design Pics Inc. / Alamy; **page 56:** © Kevin Peterson / Photodisc / Getty Images; **page 57:** © OJO Images / Rex Features; **Unit 6 image:** © Daniel Kerek / Alamy; **page 65:** © The Granger Collection, NYC / TopFoto; **page 66:** © National Army Museum, London/ The Bridgeman Art Library; **page 69 (left):** © Ullstein Bild / TopFoto; **(right):** © Popperfoto/Getty Images; **page 71 (left):** © ERIK C PENDZICH / Rex Features; **(right):** © Neville Elder/Corbis; **(top):** © Jess Alford / Photodisc / Getty Images AP/Press Association Images; **page 73:** © Kevin Peterson/Photodisc/Getty Images; **Unit 7 image:** © Mira / Alamy; **page 77:** © Design Pics Inc. / Alamy; **page 78:** © Jess Alford / Photodisc / Getty Images; **page 79 and 80:** © Steve Connolly; **page 81:** © OJO Images / Rex Features; **page 84:** © Design Pics Inc. / Alamy **Unit 8 image:** © CreativeAct - Emotions series / Alamy; **page 85 (top):** With kind permission by Facebook, Inc.; **(bottom):** © Fremantle Media; **page 86:** © Ingram Publishing Limited; **page 88:** © Purestock; **page 89:** © Design Pics Inc / Rex Features; **page 91 (top):** © Blend Images / Alamy; **(middle):** © Image Source Pink / Alamy; **(bottom):** © Photofusion Picture Library / Alamy; **Unit 9 image:** © Margarita Sarri / Flickr / Getty Images; **page 93:** © AA World Travel Library/TopFoto; **page 95 (left):** © Britain On View/VisitBritain; **(right):** © Bryan & Cherry Alexander Photography / Alamy; **page 99:** © John Springer Collection/Corbis; **page 100 and 122 (right):** © Peter Cade / Iconica / Getty Images; **page 102 (left):** © Olivia Edward/Photographer's Choice/Getty Images; **(middle):** © Tanya Constantine/Blend Images/Getty Images; **(right):** © Alex Segre / Rex Features; **Unit 10 image and page 106:** © The London Art Archive / Alamy; **page 105:** © akg-images / British Library; **page 107 and 108:** © Richard Caton Woodville/The Bridgeman Art Library/Getty Images; **page 109:** © Florence Nightingale Museum, London, UK/ The Bridgeman Art Library; **Unit 11 image:** © Will Stanton / Alamy; **page 113 and 114:** © Paramount / Everett / Rex Features; **page 117:** © Stephane Cardinale/People Avenue/Corbis; **Unit 12 image:** © Mohamed Sadath / Alamy; **page 119 (top):** © 1997 Steve Mason / PhotoDisc Inc./ Getty Images; **(bottom):** © Hulton Archive / Getty Images; **page 121:** © Ross Fraser / Alamy; **page 122 (left):** © Design Pics Inc. / Alamy; **page 124:** © Jules Frazier / Photodisc / Getty Images; **Unit 13 image:** © Harriet Cummings / Alamy; **page 127:** © Tate, London 2009 / © Estate of the Artist c/o Lefevre Fine Art Ltd, London; **page 129:** © Clive Barda/ArenaPAL/TopFoto; **page 131 (top):** © Donald Cooper / Rex Features; **(bottom):** With kind permission by www.marlboroughplayers.co.uk; **Unit 14 image:** © BE&W agencja fotograficzna Sp. z o.o. / Alamy; **page 135:** © THE KOBAL COLLECTION / 20TH CENTURY FOX / MORTON, MERRICK; **page 139:** © Rex Features; **page 141:** © Geraint Lewis / Rex Features; **Unit 15 image:** © Peter Cavanagh / Alamy; **page 143 (top):** © Sipa Press / Rex Features; **(bottom):** © David Fisher / Rex Features; **page 144:** © 1997 Karl Weatherly / PhotoDisc Inc. / Getty Images; **page 145 (all):** © Kevin Peterson / Photodisc / Getty Images; **page 147:** © Jonathan Hordle / Rex Features; **page 148:** © Stephane Masson/Kipa/Corbis; **page 149:** © Image Source / Rex Features; **page 150:** © World Illustrated/Photoshot. All rights reserved; **Unit 16 image and page 43:** © Corbis. All Rights Reserved; **page 152:** © Janine Wiedel Photolibrary / Alamy; **page 154:** © Design Pics Inc. / Alamy; **page 157:** © BBC; **Unit 17 image:** © Richard Newstead / Lifesize / Getty Images; **page 159:** © Design Pics Inc / Rex Features; **page 161:** © Alex Segre / Alamy; **page 162 and 163:** © zak/istockphoto.com; **page 165:** © Comstock Images / Photolibrary Group Ltd; **page 166:** © Markku Ulander / Rex Features.
Acknowledgements **Page 4:** extract from *Of Mice and Men* by John Steinbeck (Penguin 2000), copyright © John Steinbeck, 1937,1965, reproduced by permission of Penguin Books Ltd; **page 7:** 'History of Crufts', extract from www.crufts.org.uk/history-crufts (2009), copyright The Kennel Club, reproduced with their permission; **page 11:** 'You and Your Dog in the Countryside' from www.countrysideaccess.gov.uk/dog/ reproduced by permission of Natural England; **page 13:** dog food advert from www.uk.pedigree.com/our-product-promises.aspx, reproduced by permission of Mars Petcare UK; **page 14:** 'Part Friend, Part Family' article from www.improvementaudio.com/dogcareguide.htm; **page 19:** Richard Savill, 'Springer spaniels recruited as rescue dogs by police' from *Daily Telegraph* (October 1st, 2009), © Telegraph Media Group Limited 2009, by permission of the publisher; **page 20:** extract from *All Creatures Great and Small* by James Herriot (Michael Joseph, 1975), reproduced by permission of David Higham Associates; **pages 21–24:** Avon Fire & Rescue leaflets, www.avonfire.gov.uk/Avon/ (2009); **page 25:** 'Things to know about Sanday' from www.sandayorkney.co.uk/leaflet.php (2007), reproduced by permission of Sanday Tourism Association; **page 26:** Lewisham Council, 'Re-Cycling - Why Bother?' from *Lewisham Life* (June/July 2003); Viking worksheet from www.parents.dfes.uk/discover, reproduced by permission of Qualifications & Curriculum Development Agency; **page 28:** *Sprocket Man* from http://www.cpsc.gov/CPSCPUB/PUBS/341.pdf, reproduced by permission of U.S. Consumer Product Safety Commission; **page 30:** front cover of *Lewisham Life* magazine (April 2007 edition), reproduced by permission of Lewisham Council; 'Safe driving for life – it's all about attitude!' (2009), reproduced by permission of The Big Red L Company; **page 32:** Children's Workforce Development Council, 'Do you want someone to be there for you?' from http://www.newcastlechildrenservices.org.uk; **page 34:** 'Who Do You See?' (2009), reproduced by permission of Wyre Community Safety Partnership; **page 36:** Disneyland Resort Paris leaflet, reproduced by permission of Holiday Discount Centre; **page 38:** reproduced by permission of the Irish Heart Foundation, (24/06/2009); **page 44:** Change4Life leaflet (2008), reproduced by permission under Click-Use PSI Licence C2009002464; Tessa Jowell, letter to David Currie (2009), reproduced by permission under Click-Use PSI Licence C2009002464; **page 46:** Department of Health, smokefree leaflet (2009), reproduced by permission under Click-Use PSI Licence C2009002464; **page 51:** Drug Driving leaflet, reproduced by permission of Department for Transport; **page 53 and 101:** extracts from *A Kestrel for a Knave* by Barry Hines (Michael Joseph, 1968), copyright © Barry Hines, 1968, reproduced by permission of Penguin Books Ltd; **page 54:** road safety information, reproduced by permission of Brake; **page 59:** Kent County Council flooding leaflet, reproduced by permission of Environment Agency; **page 75:** Simon Armitage, 'I am very bothered' from *Book of Matches* (Faber & Faber, 2001); **page 78:** 'Brendon Gallacher' by Jackie Kay, from *Two's Company* (Blackie, 1992), copyright © Jackie Kay, 1992, reproduced by permission of Penguin Books Ltd; **page 79:** 'Nettles' by Vernon Scannell from *The Guardian* (28 June 2008), reproduced by permission of The Estate of Vernon Scannell; **page 81:** 'The Falling Leaves' by Margaret Postgate Cole, 1915, from *Minds at War: the Poetry and Experience of the First World War*, edited by David Roberts (Saxon Books, 1999), reproduced by permission of David Higham Associates; **page 84:** 'A Good Poem' by Roger McGough from *Collected Poems* (Penguin, 2004); **page 87:** extract from *Boy: Tales of Childhood* by Roald Dahl (Jonathan Cape, 1994), reproduced by permission of David Higham Associates; **page 89:** extract from *Notes from a Small Island* by Bill Bryson (Doubleday, 1995), reproduced by permission of The Random House Group Ltd; **page 98:** extract from *New Moon* by Stephenie Meyer (Atom, 2007), copyright © 2006 Stephenie Meyer, reproduced by permission of Little, Brown & Company; extract from *Private Peaceful* by Michael Morpurgo (HarperCollins Children's Books, 2004), reproduced by permission of HarperCollins Publishers Ltd; **page 111:** review of *Public Enemies* by Simon Thompson from http://www.heartlondon.co.uk (2009), reproduced by permission of the author; **page 112:** review of *Up* by Jonathan Romney from http://www.uncut.co.uk (2009); **page 114:** review of *Transformers: Revenge of the Fallen* by Peter Bradshaw from *The Guardian* (19 June 2009), copyright Guardian News & Media Ltd 2009, reproduced by permission of the publisher; **page 117:** *Twilight* review from http://eshed.net (2009); **Unit 13:** extracts from *An Inspector Calls* by J. B. Priestley, (Heinemann, 1992), © J. B. Priestley, 1988, reproduced by permission of PFD (www.pfd.co.uk) on behalf of The Estate of J. B. Priestley; extracts from *Of Mice and Men* by John Steinbeck (Penguin 2000), © John Steinbeck, 1937, 1965, reproduced by permission of Penguin Books Ltd; **page 148:** 'Unrelated Incidents – No. 3' by Tom Leonard, reproduced by permission of the author, © Tom Leonard from *outside the narrative: poems 1965–2009*, (Etruscan/WordPower 2009); **page 156:** extract from Waterloo Road reproduced by permission of and © Shed Productions (WR) Limited.

Every effort has been made to trace all copyright holders, but if any have been inadvertently overlooked the Publishers will be pleased to make the necessary arrangements at the first opportunity.

Although every effort has been made to ensure that website addresses are correct at time of going to press, Hodder Education cannot be held responsible for the content of any website mentioned in this book. It is sometimes possible to find a relocated web page by typing in the address of the home page for a website in the URL window of your browser.

Hachette UK's policy is to use papers that are natural, renewable and recyclable products and made from wood grown in sustainable forests. The logging and manufacturing processes are expected to conform to the environmental regulations of the country of origin.

Orders: please contact Bookpoint Ltd, 130 Milton Park, Abingdon, Oxon OX14 4SB. Telephone: (44) 01235 827720. Fax: (44) 01235 400454. Lines are open 9.00 – 5.00, Monday to Saturday, with a 24-hour message answering service. Visit our website at www.hoddereducation.co.uk

Clare, Clyde, Davies, Devitt, Etheridge, Forrest, Francis, Haffenden, Hawkes, Hill, McCammon, Simpson © 2010

First published in © 2010 by
Hodder Education,
An Hachette UK Company
338 Euston Road
London NW1 3BH

Impression number 5 4 3 2 1
Year 2014 2013 2012 2011 2010

All rights reserved. Apart from any use permitted under UK copyright law, no part of this publication may be reproduced or transmitted in any form or by any means, electronic or mechanical, including photocopying and recording, or held within any information storage and retrieval system, without permission in writing from the publisher or under licence from the Copyright Licensing Agency Limited. Further details of such licences (for reprographic reproduction) may be obtained from the Copyright Licensing Agency Limited, Saffron House, 6–10 Kirby Street, London EC1N 8TS.

Cover photo from Jens Lucking / Jupiter Images
Illustrations by Andrew Roberts and Julian Molesdale
Typeset in Garamond 11pt by 2idesign Ltd
Printed in Italy

A catalogue record for this title is available from the British Library

ISBN: 978 1444 108 682

Contents

Introduction to your book

Exam Units

Controlled Assessment Units

8 Creating a Personal Voice

This unit will help you prepare for the Creative Writing Controlled Assessment Tasks. You will learn how to write in an interesting way about people, places and events from your life.

AQA spec link:
This unit will help you prepare for:
- GCSE English – Unit 3 Creative Writing: Prompts and Me. Myself. I.
- GCSE English Language – Unit 3 Creative Writing: Commissions

Approx teaching time: 4–6 hours

9 Creating Characters, Mood and Atmosphere

This unit will help you prepare for the Creative Writing Controlled Assessment Tasks. You will learn how to create mood and atmosphere in your writing and create effective characters.

AQA spec link:
This unit will help you prepare for:
- GCSE English – Unit 3 Creative Writing: Moving Images and Prompts and Me. Myself. I.
- GCSE English Language – Unit 3 Creative Writing: Commissions and Re-Creations

Approx teaching time: 4–6 hours

10 Re-creations

This unit will help you prepare for the Creative Writing Controlled Assessment Tasks. You will learn how to transform one text into another.

AQA spec link:
This unit will help you prepare for:
- GCSE English – Unit 3 Creative Writing: Prompts and Re-Creations
- GCSE English Language – Unit 3 Creative Writing: Re-Creations

Approx teaching time: 4–6 hours

11 Linking Words and Images

This unit will help you prepare for the Creative Writing Controlled Assessment Tasks. You will learn about the typical features of a review, and the skills and understanding you need to write a good review.

AQA spec link:
This unit will help you prepare for:
- GCSE English Language – Unit 3 Creative Writing: Moving Images

Approx teaching time: 4–6 hours

12

Themes and Ideas – Family Relationships

This unit will help you prepare for the Reading and Literature Controlled Assessment Tasks. Using three William Wordsworth poems, you will learn about the key things you need to comment on when analysing themes in poetry.

AQA spec link:
This unit will help you prepare for:
- GCSE English and GCSE English Language – Unit 3 Understanding Written Texts: Themes and Ideas
- GCSE English Literature – Unit 3 The significance of Shakespeare and the English Literary Heritage: Themes and Ideas

Approx teaching time: 4–6 hours

13

Presenting People

This unit will help you prepare for the Reading and Literature Controlled Assessment Tasks. You will consider the techniques that writers use to create character and learn how to explain how a character is presented to a reader or audience.

AQA spec link:
This unit will help you prepare for:
- GCSE English and GCSE English Language – Unit 3 Understanding Written Texts: Characterisation and voice
- GCSE English Literature – Unit 3 The significance of Shakespeare and the English Literary Heritage: Characterisation and voice

Approx teaching time: 4–6 hours

14

Genres and Form – Openings

This unit will help you prepare for the Reading and Literature Controlled Assessment Tasks. Using the opening scenes from two Shakespeare plays, you will look at themes, ideas, characters and language used.

AQA spec link:
This unit will help you prepare for:
- GCSE English and GCSE English Language – Unit 3 Understanding Written Texts: Themes and Ideas
- GCSE English Literature – Unit 3 The significance of Shakespeare and the English Literary Heritage: Themes and Ideas

Approx teaching time: 4–6 hours

15

Attitudes to Spoken Language

This unit will help you prepare for the Spoken Language Controlled Assessment Tasks. You will think about attitudes to how we speak and learn some of the important terms we use to describe language.

AQA spec link:
This unit will help you prepare for:
- GCSE English Language – Unit 3 Spoken language study: Social attitudes to spoken language

Approx teaching time: 4–6 hours

16

Speech Types and Genres

This unit will help you prepare for the Spoken Language Controlled Assessment Tasks. You will think learn about some of the factors which influence spoken language.

AQA spec link:
This unit will help you prepare for:
- GCSE English Language – Unit 3 Spoken language study: Spoken genres language

Approx teaching time: 4–6 hours

17

Impact of Technology on Language Use

This unit will help you prepare for the Spoken Language Controlled Assessment Tasks. You will find out how language is changed by the use of technology.

AQA spec link:
This unit will help you prepare for:
- GCSE English Language – Unit 3 Spoken language study: Multi-modal talk

Approx teaching time: 4–6 hours

Doing Well in the English and English Language Exam

This section is full of practical advice from a Senior Examiner on how to achieve success in the exams. You will learn tips for preparing for the exams and advice on how to boost your marks.

Grammar

This section breaks down key concepts of grammar, such as word classes, phrases, clauses and sentences, and punctuation. You will see how you can use grammar to improve your reading and writing.

Concept Bank

A glossary of key terms and concept words used throughout the book.

Introduction to your book

Welcome! It is with excitement that the writing team presents this book to you. We set ourselves two challenges when writing it …

The first challenge was to write a book that prepared you for whichever of the AQA GCSE English courses you decide to follow – English, or English Language and/or English Literature. Over the next 17 units, we have provided material that will allow you to achieve the best results, whichever course you have chosen.

The units which help you with your exams

After **Unit 1** – which tunes you into reading and writing at GCSE level – the book moves on to **Units 2–5** which support you in getting ready for the English and English Language exams. **Units 6 and 7** will help you in the GCSE Literature exam – in particular the poetry sections. For further exam guidance, the section Doing Well in the English and English Language Exam (pages 167–72) gives you advice about how to boost your marks in the exam.

The units which help you with your Controlled Assessment Tasks

Units 8–17 support the Controlled Assessment Tasks that your teacher will choose for you. They cover the Creative Writing tasks for English and English Language; the Reading and Literature tasks for English, English Language and English Literature; and the Spoken Language Investigation tasks for English Language.

Features of the book

You will notice that we have explained important words in the **Concept Banks** at the side of the page (these are collected together at the end of the book in the Concept Bank for easy reference, pages 182–84). We have also included some Grammar Links throughout. These link to a section at the end of the book – Grammar (page 173–81) – which gives you help with grammar and punctuation.

The second challenge we set ourselves was as important – we wanted the activities and tasks to be demanding but always do-able; we wanted the tasks to involve all sorts of ways of learning, and we wanted the work you will be doing to be interesting and fun. You will find role-play, drama, discussion, image and media study, and writing and reading of all kinds of texts. We hope this variety keeps you interested, makes your learning fun and gives you the confidence, skills and understanding to go for those good grades in your exams and Controlled Assessment Tasks.

Enjoy the journey!

Steve Davies

Learning aim

In this unit you will look at some text types and their features that you may already know and make sure you understand them. You will then learn how to look at texts and write about them. You will see how to write texts of your own.

(i) Concept bank

Text: What we think of as a text is changing. Once, the word 'text' meant simply longer writing such as novels. Now we have all kinds of texts, including images and film as well as written and spoken texts. Some texts do not have words at all.

1.1 What do we mean by text?

You will learn that there are many different types of text.

⊃ For starters

You will write – and write about – many text types throughout your GCSE course. Look at these materials, 1, 2, and 3, and decide which are **texts**. Give reasons for your choices.

1

Riding a bike.

- First make sure that the saddle is at the right height.
- Check that your feet are flat on the floor.
- Now find a flat area without obstacles that you might ride into.
- Begin by pushing yourself along with your feet.
- Do not try using the pedals at this stage.
- Try out the brakes and test out your steering.

2

3

'… guaranteed to keep the reader flipping through the pages.'
The Guardian

All three are texts, with a particular audience and purpose in mind. Text 1 is instructional, text 2 is an information text and text 3 is a review.

⊃ Task

1 Who do you think the audience is for each text? What might the purpose of each text be?
2 Note as many text types and their features as you can in two columns.

⊃ Taking it further

Look carefully at text 1 on how to ride a bike. It is an instructional text. How does it get its message across (e.g. think about the verbs it uses, and the way it is set out on the page)?

1.2 Context and purpose

You will learn that writers need to write texts that fit their purpose. You will see that authors need to use different features to keep the audience's attention.

ⓘ Concept bank

Context: the situation, purpose or audience for a text. The language, structure and presentation of a text affects, and is affected by, context.

Similes: comparing one thing with another using 'as' or 'like'.

🔗 Grammar link

The first person singular uses 'I' and 'me'. Persuasive texts often use the second person: 'you' and 'your'.

⟲ For starters

Think about your journey to school. You will have passed several texts displayed as signs or symbols on your way. You are so used to seeing some of them that you will hardly have noticed them. Try to remember as many as you can and note how they have been made. Think about:

- size, shape and colour
- position and **context**
- image and language
- audience and purpose
- effect and impact.

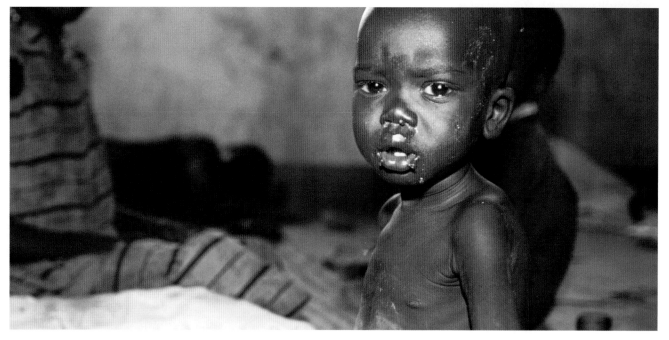

⬆ *A starving child in Africa*

⟲ Task

Look at the image above.

1. Write a description of the image so that a reader could imagine it in the mind's eye. Use two **similes** (using 'as' or 'like') in your description.
2. How does this image affect you as a 'reader' of the text? What emotions does it create in you?
3. What effect or impact do you think the text's author wanted to create in the reader or viewer?

⟲ Taking it further

1. Do you think this image is effective? Say why or why not.
2. How might you feel if you were the parent of the child? Give reasons for your response. Remember to use the first person ('I').
3. Prepare a short speech to persuade an advertising company that using this type of image is not appropriate. Share your ideas with the class.

The World of Texts

1.3 Fiction texts – audience and reader

You will learn how writers of fiction try to keep their reader's interest. You will look at writing from the past.

⊃ For starters

Read this opening to a story:

> There are not many people – and as it is desirable that a story-teller and a story-reader should establish a mutual understanding as soon as possible, beg it to be noticed that I confine this observation neither to young people nor to little people, but extend it to all conditions of people: little and big, young and old: yet growing up, or already growing down again – there are not, I say, many people who would care to sleep in a church.

🔗 Grammar link

The first person singular uses 'I' and 'me'. You have already seen how non-fiction texts can use the first and second person. Although many novels are written in the third person ('he', 'she', 'it', 'they'), many are written in the first person.

1 Reading the text, what kind of story do you think it is introducing?
2 How does the text try to attract the reader's attention? How good is it at gaining your interest? Explain your answers.
3 When do you think this passage might have been written? What features of the text give you a clue that this was written in the past?
4 Rewrite the story opening above in as few words as possible.

⊃ Task

Read the extract on the right from a modern children's novel.

1 Reading the text, what kind of story do you think it is introducing?
2 How does the text try to attract the reader's attention? How good is it at gaining your interest? Explain your answers.
3 Terry Pratchett uses some short, powerful sentences. Choose one short sentence and explain why it grabs the reader's attention.
4 Why is 'Perspicacia Tick' a good name for a witch?
5 How does this modern text differ from the old text above?

⊃ Taking it further

Write your own story-starter imitating Terry Pratchett's opening, including some short sentences, a description of the weather and a simile. Read it to a friend and see if it 'grabs their interest'.

> Some things start before other things.
>
> It was a summer shower but didn't appear to know it, and it was pouring rain as fast as a winter storm.
>
> Miss Perspicacia Tick sat in what little shelter a raggedy hedge could give her and explored the universe. She didn't notice the rain. Witches dried out quickly.
>
> From *The Wee Free Men* by Terry Pratchett (2003)

1.4 Fiction texts – form and genre

You will learn about different fiction genres and practise recreating a text in different styles.

⊃ For starters

1 Look at the two text outlines on the right. What **genres** are they likely to be?

2 Were you right? Check with your teacher. Note down the features that gave you a clue. These features are the **form** of the text.

⊃ Task

Analysing form and genre means you need to look at the shape of a text on the page, the types of sentences in it and the actual words used to create those sentences.

1 Read this short extract from *Of Mice and Men,* an American novel written in 1937.

> Lennie dabbled his big paw in the water and wiggled his fingers so the water arose in little splashes; rings widened across the pool to the other side and came back again. Lennie watched them go. 'Look, George. Look what I done.'

2 The genre of this novel is sometimes called 'Naturalism' – it describes everyday events in a down-to-earth, 'realistic' way. What features of the text show that this is a 'naturalistic' novel?

3 Find two words or phrases in the text which tell us that Lennie is not very bright. Explain the effect of the word or phrase. Write a paragraph about how the text portrays Lennie.

⊃ Taking it further

1 Imagine you are going to change this extract into a science fiction text. Write the next two or three sentences that would signpost the science fiction genre to the reader. Make sure you include references to science or technology, such as spaceships. You may want to include an alien, or set the story in space or on another planet.

2 Now imagine you are going to change the extract into a horror text. Write the next two or three sentences that would signpost the horror genre to the reader. The weather and night often play a role in horror, so you might like to set the story in a storm or the dark.

ⓘ Concept bank

Genre: style or type. There are genres of fiction, like *Of Mice and Men*, and non-fiction, such as newspapers.

Form: the way in which subject matter is presented; the shape of the text on the page.

⊞ Grammar link

Nouns identify a person, an object such as a book, or a thing such as a thought.

Adjectives qualify or say more about a noun. For example: a 'big book' – 'book' is the noun and 'big' is the adjective.

Verbs describe an action done by a person or thing. For example: 'He threw the big book.'

The World of Texts

4

1.5 Non-fiction texts – purpose, audience and intention

> You will learn a checklist of features to use when you analyse or plan a range of non-fiction texts.

⊃ For starters

One of the things you need to remember about non-fiction texts, even those with **facts** in them, is that they are not always true or reliable. You may have seen a TV advert that claims that 8 out of 10 cats prefer a particular type of cat food, but it is doubtful that every cat has been asked! The writer's purpose and intention affect the way facts are used, but facts are included to make a text more believable.

Using a 'fact', write a sentence to inform new students at your school about an aspect of school life. Be as creative as you can. For example, you might tell them that 8 out of 10 students always complete their homework the night it is set.

⊃ Task

One checklist for analysing or writing non-fiction that you might find helpful is to think of an apple.

A **Audience** – who are you writing for?
P Purpose – why are you writing? What message is being communicated?
P Presentation – what features, images or layout should this text type have?
L Language – what vocabulary and sentence structure suits it best?
E Effect – has the writing achieved the purpose for the audience?

Using the **APPLE** checklist, plan an **argument text** for parents and carers about whether school uniform should be compulsory in all schools. You can work with a partner.

⊃ Taking it further

1 Now try writing the argument text. Remember that an **argument** text looks at both sides of a subject. To make sure you balance your argument, copy and complete the table below before you start.

Arguments for school uniform	Arguments against school uniform

2 Share your writing with a partner and identify two positive features and one aspect that could be better.

> ### ⓘ Concept bank
>
> **Fact:** a statement that can be checked and proved to be true or false.
>
> **Audience:** the intended readership of a particular piece of writing.
>
> **Argument text:** presents different sides to a debate and comes to a conclusion.
>
> **Argument:** a logical statement in support of a point, backed up with relevant facts and figures.

1.6 Spoken texts – style and register

You will learn the terms 'style' and 'register'. You will begin to use the right style and register for different speaking activities.

⊃ For starters

Look at the **style** of these greetings:

> Good morning. I am most pleased to make your acquaintance. I do hope you are well.

> Hello. Very nice to meet you. How are you?

> Wotcha 'kay?

You can see that these greetings become less formal. We dress in different styles for different occasions – such as jeans for a trip to town but a suit for a job interview. In the same way, we need to use the right style for speaking occasions too.

⊃ Task

1 Using the right level of formality, write a response to each greeting in the correct style.
2 Practise the most formal example with a partner. It may feel very strange to start with!
3 Copy the table below and suggest some vocabulary to create an appropriate **register** for each situation. There are some examples to get you started:

Situation	Vocabulary for the situation
Attending a job interview	*experience, application form*
A teacher telling off a student	*responsible*
Two 15-year-old girls gossiping	*yeah*

ⓘ Concept bank

Style: the choices about words and sentences that a writer or speaker makes, such as the level of formality of a text.

Register: the way a text sounds to its readers or listeners. This could be formal or informal, bossy, amusing, friendly or cold … or many other registers.

⊃ Taking it further

With a partner, devise and act out a short drama, using an appropriate style and the right register for the situation. Choose **one** of these situations:

- trying to persuade a parent to let you go to a party
- reporting student views about lunches to the Headteacher
- complaining about a faulty MP3 player in a shop.

Learning aim

This unit will prepare you for Section A of the English or English Language examination, which will ask you to show that you can understand and analyse texts.

S	skim – let your eyes travel quickly across it to get an idea of what the text is about
3Q	three questions – say in your head what you think are the three main questions the text is trying to answer
R	read the text carefully to see how it answers those questions.

2.1 Reading information texts

You will learn how to approach a non-fiction text you have never seen before and how to analyse a non-fiction text. You will also learn the three features of a good non-fiction text.

↻ For starters

The best way to 'get to grips' with a new text is to use the **S3QR** checklist on the left.

1 Use this **S3QR** checklist to read the Crufts text below.
2 Discuss the text as a whole class – what are its main points?

History of Crufts Dog Show

Crufts is named after its founder, Charles Cruft. The first Crufts show in that name was booked into the Royal Agricultural Hall, Islington in 1891. This was the first in a long series of shows there. During this era it was possible for individuals to run shows for personal profit, an aspect that appealed mightily to Charles Cruft, and he ran his shows with considerable profit to himself. Today there are no privately owned dog shows and permission to hold shows is granted by the Kennel Club, which licenses only non-commercial organisations. 5

In 1938 Charles Cruft died and his widow ran the 1939 show. Three years later Mrs Cruft felt the responsibility for running the show too demanding so she asked the Kennel Club to take it over and it was sold to them; 1948 was the first show under the Kennel Club auspices. Held at Olympia, it proved an immediate success with both exhibitors and the public. Since then Crufts has increased in stature year by year. In 1979 it was decided to change the venue from Olympia to Earls Court as the increasing entries had the show bursting at the seams. In 1982 the show ran for three days and in 1987 for four days to accommodate the increasing numbers. 1991 saw the Crufts Centenary Show being held at the Birmingham National Exhibition Centre, the first time the show had moved from London. 10 15

↻ **Task**

It is one thing to understand what a text is saying, but you also need to be able to judge its value. Is it a trustworthy source giving information or advice we can act on? Or is it full of errors or, worse, is it written to mislead and brainwash us?

To answer this, we must analyse the text. **Analysis** means thinking about a text and explaining how it is written, and how it tries to influence the reader.

Here is another checklist – **FIFAT** – that will help you to analyse a text:

F How factual is it – is it packed with **facts**, or is it full of unproved **opinions**?

I How **impersonal** is it – is the author standing back and trying to give a fair and **balanced** view of the topic? Or is it very **personal**, full of 'my' and 'I', and perhaps **biased**?

F How **formal** is it – is the language chatty and full of everyday slang (**informal**), or is it 'academic' in tone, and written in **Standard English**?

A How authoritative is it – is the writer obviously an expert, or just a 'man in the street' sounding off?

T How trustworthy is it – think about why the author was writing, and what the author wanted you to come away thinking.

ⓘ Concept bank

Analysis: thinking about a text and explaining how it is written, and how it tries to influence the reader.

Factual	Full of true facts		Full of unproved claims and opinions	**Opinionated**
Impersonal	Balanced, fair		Biased	**Personal**
Formal	Academic tone, Standard English	Somewhere in between	Chatty, full of street slang	**Informal**
Authoritative	Obviously written by an expert, in the know		Obviously written by a crank who knows nothing	**Unreliable**
Trustworthy	Truthful, reliable		An attempt to deceive and brainwash	**Untrustworthy**

Use the **FIFAT** checklist to explain why the second paragraph of the Crufts text seems to be an informative, reliable text. Organise your ideas in five sections:

• how Factual it is
• how Impersonal it is
• how Formal it is
• how Authoritative it is
• how Trustworthy it is.

ⓘ Concept bank

Fact: a statement that can be checked and proved to be true or false.

Opinion: one person's thoughts or feelings about something– other people may not agree.

Impersonal: where the language of a text is dispassionate, as though the author is completely detached from the subject.

Balanced: where the approach is unbiased and based on the facts.

Personal: where the author is emotionally involved – the opposite of 'impersonal'.

Biased: where the text is affected by the author's personal feelings and beliefs.

Formal text: uses academic English as in a textbook, for example.

Informal text: uses everyday words, as in a telephone conversation, for example.

Standard English: writing or speaking that is generally accepted as grammatically correct.

⊃ Taking it further

People write information texts to tell us things. We read them to find things out. We want to do this quickly and easily. Here are three rules for writing a good text:

- **K**eep **I**t **S**traightforward – not complicated
- **K**eep **I**t **S**hort – not longer than it needs to be
- **K**eep **I**t **S**tructured – set out in a sensible order.

We call these the 'three kisses'.

1 In pairs, consider the Crufts text on page 7 and discuss whether it deserves 'three kisses' – has the writer followed the three rules for a good text? Then discuss this as a whole class.

2 Get hold of a newspaper and find:
- a news report
- a comment by the editor
- a letter to the editor
- a job advert.

Use **S3QR**, **FIFAT** and the three kisses to read, analyse and judge each text. Compare your results with another group.

3 Working on your own, choose the most interesting of your texts and:
- write a very short paragraph stating what the text is about
- use **FIFAT** to write an analysis of the text in five short paragraphs
- finish with a conclusion in which you use the three kisses to judge whether it is a good text, and say why. (Tip: Begin your conclusion with: 'Therefore …').

2.2 Reading advice texts

You will learn how to recognise ten features of an advice text. You will also learn three features which give an advice text its register.

(i) Concept bank

Register: the way a text sounds to its readers or listeners. This could be formal or informal, bossy, amusing, friendly or cold … or many other registers.

↻ For starters

1 Work with a partner. Take it in turns to tell each other about a hobby or a sport you do.
   You have just *informed* your partner about your hobby.

2 Now, working with the same partner, suggest things they could do to get better at their hobby.
   You have just *advised* your partner about their hobby.

3 What difference was there between giving information and giving advice? Discuss what you said, but also about how you said it. Share your ideas as a whole class.

4 Look at the list on page 11 telling you the 'Ten features of an advice text'. How many things on the list did you use when you advised each other on how to improve? Give yourself a score out of 10!

↻ Task

1 Read Text A below about looking after your dog if you visit the seaside. Read it using **S3QR**. How many of the ten features of an advice text can you spot in it?

S3QR stands for: **S**kim it, ask what **3 Q**uestions it is answering, then **R**ead it carefully.

Text A

If you do decide to take your dog away with you, there are many considerations that have to be made to ensure that your dog is safe and happy. We hope that this factsheet helps you to have a safe and enjoyable break with your best canine friend …

At the seaside

Unfortunately some coastal towns have banned dogs from their beaches in order to gain clean-beach awards and some may allow dogs only at certain times of the year (usually October to April).

- **Check with the local authority or tourism office before booking your holiday** to make sure that there will be a dog-friendly beach nearby.
- **Be careful of beaches with strong tides or undercurrents**. If there is a swimming ban or warning signs for human swimmers, then do not allow your dog to swim either.
- **Be careful if you are throwing a ball** for your dog to retrieve on sand, as he may ingest a large amount of sand and become ill.
- **Keep your dog under control** – especially in the presence of children. Always remember to pick up your dog's poop …

If you choose the right holiday for you and your dog, a great time can be had by all, with many happy memories to remember for months to come.

Ten features of an advice text

Structure:

- starts by saying that the advice will be useful
- sets out its ideas in a logical order – often as a list
- tells the reader the good results of doing as it says
- includes what the reader should not do
- ends by recommending the advice to the reader.

Register:

- uses second person – 'you' and 'your'
- uses instructions – 'You should …'
- authoritative – knows what it is talking about
- includes specialist words
- includes facts and examples.

2 Here is part of an advice leaflet called *You and Your Dog in the Countryside*. Read it using **S3QR**. How many of the ten features of an advice text can you spot in it?

Text B

You and Your Dog in the Countryside

Hello! I'm John the sheepdog from the Countryside Code, and I just love the countryside. I'll guide you through this leaflet to help you have an enjoyable time by being responsible with your dog in the countryside, and help protect the landscape, wildlife and people that make it so special.

Whether ambling along leafy lanes, rambling through forests, or exploring new access land, the countryside is a great place for you and your dog to explore and enjoy.

Six steps to worry-free 'walkies' by following the Countryside Code

- By law, you must control your dog so that it does not scare or disturb farm animals or wildlife. On most areas of open country and common land, known as 'access land', you must keep your dog on a short lead between 1 March and 31 July – and all year round near farm animals.
- You do not have to put your dog on a lead on public paths, as long as it is under close control. But as a general rule, keep your dog on a lead if you cannot rely on its obedience. By law, farmers are entitled to destroy a dog that injures or worries their animals.
- If a farm animal chases you and your dog, it is safer to let your dog off the lead – do not risk getting hurt by trying to protect it.

- Take particular care that your dog does not scare sheep and lambs, or wander where it might disturb birds that nest on the ground – eggs and young will soon die without protection from their parents.
- Everyone knows how unpleasant dog mess is and it can cause infections, so always clean up after your dog and get rid of the mess responsibly. Also, make sure your dog is wormed regularly to protect it, other animals and people.
- At certain times, dogs may not be allowed on some areas of access land or may need to be kept on a lead. Please follow any official signs.

You can also find out more about these rules from www.countrysideaccess.gov. uk, by emailing openaccess@ naturalengland.gov.uk or calling 0845 100 3298.

Wherever you go, following these steps will help keep your pet safe, protect the environment, and show you are a responsible dog owner.

Text B – *You and Your Dog in the Countryside* tells you to do many things. But did you feel that it was bossing you about? Probably not, because of the way in which it was written.

When they are analysing advice texts, teachers often use the term 'register'. A text's register is the 'tone of voice' it is written in.

A text's register is affected by three things (**WAS**):

W Words – Lots of specialist words, **facts** and examples will make it sound authoritative (as if it knows what it is talking about). Words like 'must' and 'ought' might make it sound bossy.

A Address – 'I' feels personal or reflective; 'you' is direct and can be challenging; 'we' is friendly and persuasive; 'it' and 'they' feel formal and fair.

S Sentence-types – Short sentences can feel powerful and authoritative. Longer sentences often feel more reasonable. Commands can seem bossy. Questions allow the readers to make up their own minds.

The register of Text B – *You and Your Dog in the Countryside* is 'firm but friendly'.

3 Using the **WAS** checklist, explain why the text is firm but friendly by answering these questions:
- Find a word (or short phrase) which makes the text sound friendly; how does it make it sound friendly?
- Find a word (or short phrase) which makes the text sound firm; how does it make it sound firm?
- Find an example of the word 'I'; how does this make the text sound?
- Find an example of the word 'you' or 'your'; how does this make the text sound?
- Find a short sentence, and explain how it makes the text sound 'firm'.
- Find a command, and explain how it makes the text sound 'firm'.

⟳ Taking it further

1 Look back at Text A about taking your dog to the seaside on page 10. How would you describe that text's register? Using the **WAS** checklist, write three paragraphs to explain why you feel that way about it.

2 Using the **WAS** checklist to guide your ideas, rewrite the introduction to Text A so that it is either:
- extremely bossy
- chatty and friendly

or
- pleading and begging.

Explain to a friend how you chose your Words, Address and Sentence-types to achieve the intended effect.

ⓘ Concept bank

Fact: a statement that can be checked and proved to be true or false.

🔗 Grammar link

Person: an author might write in the first person ('I' or 'we'), in the second person ('you'), or in the third person ('he', 'she', 'it' or 'they').

2.3 Reading persuasive writing

You will learn about the different writing techniques persuasive texts use to influence the reader.

⊃ For starters

Imagine you overhear your younger sister trying to persuade your mum to let her get a puppy. She uses all the persuasive techniques listed on the right. Think of some of the things (facts, opinions, claims, etc ...) she might have said to your mum.

⊃ Task

Persuasive techniques

Persuasive texts try to make us do what the author wants us to do. Take, for instance, this text from a web page about a brand of dog food:

ⓘ Concept bank

Argument: a logical statement in support of a point, backed up with relevant facts and figures.

Fact: a statement that can be checked and proved to be true or false.

Our 8 Product Promises

For good healthy food

Making our products healthier and tastier is a never-ending job. We've put 60 years of research into our latest recipes so they have the right balance of vitamins, fibre and protein for healthier digestion. Dogs also find them more tail-thumpingly delicious than ever. But we believe that research alone isn't enough.

Something else that helps make our products naturally delicious are our eight product promises. They make sure that quality is always our first, second, third, fourth, fifth, sixth, seventh and eighth priority.

---

1 What is the text trying to do?
2 Copy the list of eight persuasive techniques at the top of this page. For each technique, can you find an example in the web page where the author has used that technique? Copy and complete a table like this to help you:

Technique	Example from text
Arguments	we've put 60 years of research into our recipes so they have the right balance of vitamins, fibre and protein ...
Facts	

ⓘ Concept bank

Opinion: one person's thoughts or feelings something certain way. not a...

Which persuasive techniques does the text not use?

3 Read the text below using the **S3QR** checklist on the right.

4 For each of the eight persuasive techniques you learned on page 13, can you find an example in the text where the author has used that technique?

S3QR stands for: **S**kim it, ask what **3 Q**uestions it is answering, then **R**ead it carefully.

Part Friend, Part Family
Taking Care of Your Dog Safely and Naturally

Are You Ready to Transform Your Dog Into an Obedient and Composed 'Poised Pooch' That Will Follow Your Every Command and Behave Under ANY Circumstances? If so, Then I've Got GREAT News ...

For the First Time Ever, The Impenetrable Canine Mind Has Been 'Cracked!' – Take This Exclusive Opportunity to Peek Inside It and Discover Expert Training Tactics and Techniques That Are Guaranteed to Tame Even the Rowdiest, Most Unruly Dog! Keep Reading to Learn How to Raise and Train a Dog From Any Age!   5

Dear friend,

Let's be honest with ourselves here, everyone obviously knows that dogs – however cute, lovable and playful they may be at times – can be (sometimes extremely!) difficult at others!

It doesn't matter whether you are trying to raise your puppy into a healthy dog ...   10

Or matter whether you've tried to train and discipline your dog so that it responds to your commands and learns the behaviours you want it to (and it won't!) ...

Or whether you are simply curious and want to learn everything there is to know about dogs – how to look after them, care for them, tend to their needs (and even how to understand 'dog language') the right way – like a true dog lover should ...   15

None of that really matters right now. That is, until you place yourself in the 'inner circle' of dog-training knowledge containing secrets and tricks that allow experts to charge CRAZY fees – for nothing more than implementing proven principles. You will learn all of that above and tons more.

And yes, you bet, the PROVEN principles I'll be talking about are the EXACT ones that you'll be learning today so ...   20

'... I Suggest You Cancel Your Next Appointment With Your Personal Dog Trainer IMMEDIATELY ...'

... because you certainly won't be needing him or her once you're 'in the know'.

And it's absolutely true – because that's what you will be learning – how to train your dog ... including every nitty gritty little detail the dog trainers know off by heart. Within ᵗʰᵉ next couple of minutes, you WILL pick up on information that you probably thought ᵗᵒ be possible to obtain so easily.   25

ʳᵃⁿᵍᵉ of tips, tricks and techniques, so honed, and so fine-tuned, ᵖᵉʳsonal dog trainer at $50–100 PER HOUR or more to stop ᵒʳ she would NOT reveal them!   30

14

⊃ Taking it further

Persuasive texts also use **register** and **rhetorical devices** to persuade readers.

Register

1 The *Part Friend, Part Family* advert on page 14 has a very enthusiastic and convincing register. Analyse the register of this text using the **WAS** checklist on the right to explain how it sounds enthusiastic and convincing. Discuss with a friend how its register helps to persuade the reader to buy the audiobook.

Rhetorical devices

Very persuasive language is called **rhetorical language** – it can persuade you just by the emotional power of the words it uses. It uses many 'devices' (tricks) to 'get to' your feelings. Here are four examples of rhetorical devices:

- **List of three** – repeating an idea or argument three times in slightly different ways.
- **Rhetorical questions** – where a writer or speaker makes a point, but puts it as a question (not expecting an answer).
- **Colloquialisms** – where the writer suddenly abandons the formal register and uses an everyday word or turn of phrase for effect. For example: 'So I suggest that you need to *get with it*.'
- **Hyperbole** – exaggeration. For example: 'I've told you a million times not to exaggerate.'

2 Find an example of each of these four rhetorical devices in the *Part Friend, Part Family* advert on page 14. For each device, discuss with a friend how it helps to persuade the readers to buy the audiobook.

3 Write an essay in three long paragraphs about how the text *Part Friend, Part Family* persuades its readers:

- Start the first paragraph: 'The first way it persuades the reader is by the arguments it uses.' Then write about how it uses a few 'facts', some logical arguments, and lots of emotive claims, promises and opinions. For each, remember to give an example from the text, and to explain how it helps to persuade the reader to buy the audiobook.
- Start the second paragraph: 'The second way it persuades the reader is by the register it uses.' Then use the **WAS** checklist to write about how it uses words, address and different sentence-types. For each, remember to give an example from the text, and to explain how it helps to persuade the reader to buy the audiobook.
- Start the third paragraph: 'The third way it persuades the reader is by the rhetorical devices it uses.' Then write about the rhetorical devices it uses. For each, remember to give an example from the text, and to explain how it helps to persuade the reader to buy the audiobook.

WAS stands for:

Words – how do the words make it sound?

Address – how does it address the reader?

Sentence style – long and detailed, or short and powerful? Does it use statements, questions or commands?

ⓘ Concept bank

Register: the way a text sounds to its readers or listeners. This could be formal or informal, bossy, amusing, friendly or cold ... or many other registers.

Rhetorical devices: language tricks writers use to have an emotional effect on the reader.

Rhetorical language: very persuasive language that uses emotional words.

List of three: when a writer or speaker repeats an idea or argument three times in slightly different ways.

Rhetorical questions: are addressed to the reader but do not require an answer.

Colloquialisms: informal words or phrases, including slang.

Hyperbole: exaggeration.

2.4 Reading argument writing

> You will learn how to extract information, summarise information, and infer meaning from an argument text.

⊃ For starters

1 Think of ideas to support or oppose the view that 'Owners of stray dogs should be heavily fined'.
2 Argue your case with a partner who takes the opposite view.

⊃ Task

1 Read this **argument text** using **S3QR** – **S**kim it, think of **3 Q**uestions it is trying to answer, and then **R**ead it carefully.

NIGHT-TIME NO-GO AREA

Our town centre is going to the dogs and the council needs to act now, writes
Mark Philips, a Middlesfield street cleaner who has had enough.

Have you been into the town centre of an evening? When the crowds have staggered home, the last bus has picked up its kebab-spattered yobs, and the police are chasing the car thieves? I have and it's not pleasant. 5
You'll not have seen me and the team. We're the ones driving those brush-trucks cleaning up the day's mess. So what's the problem? More pay? Shorter hours? No. What we want is to do our jobs – doing other folks' 10
dirty work – without fear for our safety. Too much to ask? Apparently so for this town council!

In the last year, six street cleaners from Middlesfield have been attacked by stray dogs 15
whilst carrying out their work. Bad luck? No. The result of a council that asks its workers to battle through grime and garbage whilst being growled at by angry strays, and does nothing to protect us. 20

Since 2008, the number of dogs loose on the streets of Middlesfield has risen by 28%, according to the RSPCA. Middlesfield General Hospital reports that the number of patients treated for dog bites has more 25
than doubled in the past year and no one will have missed the recent story of Hannah

Wishcombe, the Frinley girl savaged by a stray whilst on her way home from school. After countless stitches and tetanus jabs, 30
Hannah has made a remarkable recovery – but next time? The next victim may not be quite so lucky. Middlesfield Council has yet to act decisively to stamp out this threat.

What can be done about it? It'll cost more 35
and those costs will have to come out of council tax. Fewer schools. Libraries closed. Uncared for old folk! Nonsense. Under the 1990 Environmental Protection Act, every council has the legal responsibility to 40
'deal with dogs straying on any land where the public have access'. We simply want tougher penalties for dog owners who fail to secure their pets. Too drastic? Tell that to Steve Coombes, a 42-year-old Cranton street 45
cleaner, still in hospital after an attack from a rottweiler. Steve was clearing your streets of gum, litter and beer bottles.

How many more council workers will suffer before something is done? In a country 50
happy to stump up millions for the 2012 Olympics, it's criminal to ask street cleaners to risk their wellbeing when there are easy and affordable solutions.

Extract, **summarise** and **infer**: you might have to use all three of these skills in your exam, so it is best if you clearly understand what they are and how to do them.

Extract information

This is where you find surface information (**facts** or **opinions**) in the text. You can answer 'extract' questions simply by taking words or phrases from the text – copying them or rewriting them in your own words.

2 Look again at the *Night-Time No-Go Area* text by Mark Philips and answer these 'extract' questions:
  * What does the 1990 Environmental Protection Act say?
  * What does Philips say about the 2012 Olympics?
  * Which two cases does Philips mention to support his argument?

Summarise a text or paragraph

This is where you write the main points the writer has made in your own words. The skill is to be able to sum up, in a few words, what the text is about – its subject matter and the author's views or 'angle', for example.

A good summary will also include a short quote from the passage, followed by an explanation of the meaning and effect of the quote.

3 Copy the table below and use it to summarise – paragraph by paragraph – the points Mark Philips makes. The first row has been done for you and some others have been started to help you. Then write up *one* of the rows from your table as a proper paragraph.

ⓘ Concept bank

Argument text: presents different sides to a debate and comes to a conclusion.

Extract: find and state information from a text.

Summarise: state a text's main ideas in a concise way, using a small number of words.

Infer: to read 'between the lines' – to see what a writer is 'getting at' even though it is not openly stated in the text.

Fact: a statement that can be checked and proved to be true or false.

Opinion: one person's thoughts or feelings about something – other people may not agree.

Evidence: a piece of information used by a writer to make a point – for example, anecdotes (stories), personal experiences, statistics or statements by 'experts'.

Paragraph number	Points Mark Philips makes	Quote from the text to use as evidence	Meaning and effect of the quote
1	Philips introduces his argument by saying that the town council is not taking proper care of the safety of its workers.	He writes: 'What we want is to do our jobs – doing other folks' dirty work – without fear for our safety.'	Here he emphasises that: • he wants to work • it is a nasty job • the problem – he is afraid of being bitten by a dog.
2	A second paragraph develops his argument by telling the reader ...	'six street cleaners have been attacked by stray dogs'	Here he emphasises ...
3	In the third paragraph ...		
4			
5			

Infer opinions, feelings and meanings

This is where you, as a reader, can see what the writer thinks, feels or means, even though it may not be openly stated in the text.

To 'infer' meaning, first state what the writer is 'getting at', next find one or two quotes which show this, and then explain the meaning and effect of the quote.

4 Copy the table below and use it to answer the following questions. To help you, the first one has been done.

  a How does the reader know that Philips is angry at the council which employs him?

  b How does Philips feel about some dog owners?

  c What does the text suggest about Middlesfield Council?

Use your table to write up *one* of the questions as a proper paragraph.

	Points Mark Philips makes	Quote from the text to use as evidence	Meaning and effect of the quote
a	Philips is angry that the council is not doing enough to keep its workers safe from dogs.	He writes: 'In a country happy to stump up millions for the 2012 Olympics, it is criminal to ask street cleaners to risk their wellbeing when there are easy and affordable solutions.'	This shows that he thinks that the council: • does not care about its workers • has wrong spending priorities • could easily do something • is in the wrong ('criminal').
b			

↻ Taking it further

Another question in your exam will ask you how the author uses language to influence the reader. In this unit you have learned to recognise a number of language devices (see the list on the right) which you could draw on to answer this question.

1 Read the *Night-time No-Go Area* text on page 16 again.

2 Discuss the text, using the skills you have learned in this unit to:

• analyse its language using **FIFAT** – turn to page 8 if you need to check what **FIFAT** stands for

• analyse its register using **WAS** – see page 12

• find rhetorical devices in the text – see page 15

• judge the text using the three kisses – see page 9.

3 Use the ideas which come out of your discussion to write up, in four paragraphs, an answer to this question:

> How does Philips use language to convince the reader that his claims are correct?

Language devices

• Formal or informal?

• Impersonal or personal?

• Facts or opinions?

• Authoritative?

• Trustworthy?

• Words (especially verbs and adjectives)

• Address

• Sentence-types

• Lists of three

• Rhetorical questions

• Colloquialisms

• Hyperbole

2.5 Exam practice for reading non-fiction

You will practice for the exam by answering some exam-style questions.

Exam practice

Time allowed: 45 minutes (for questions 1–4)

Read Text A – *Springer spaniels recruited as rescue dogs by police*, and answer the question below.

1 Give four reasons from Text A why the Devon and Cornwall Police have replaced German Shepherd dogs with Springer spaniels as rescue dogs. (4 marks)

Text A

Telegraph.co.uk

Springer spaniels recruited as rescue dogs by police

A police force has recruited Springer spaniels as rescue dogs because they are less frightening than German Shepherds.

By Richard Savill, Published: 7:00AM BST 01 Oct 2009.

Devon and Cornwall Police said it was the first force in the country to train the breed, which will be used in search operations.

The three Springer spaniels began work in July and have now been considered a success, a spokesperson said.

Traditionally, the force has deployed German Shepherd dogs which have a range of specialist search skills but are used mainly for tracking criminals.

Insp. Andrew Lilburn said the spaniels were ideally suited to Devon and Cornwall's rural terrain.

The force dog inspector added: 'Our existing general-purpose dogs are fantastic at what they do but vulnerable people are often scared when confronted by a German Shepherd dog.

'These lost-person search dogs have no other skills and are pure specialists in finding people who are lost.'

The police force obtained the dogs as puppies from local breeders and trained them to recognise human scent.

Insp. Lilburn said they could be used to find walkers lost in bad weather, vulnerable young people who have run away or people who are intent on harming themselves.

'We are most often called out to find elderly people with dementia who have wandered off from home and the dogs are invaluable in these instances,' he said.

The dogs have already taken part in a number of rescues, including that of a vulnerable young man found in open countryside at night after he ran away from home.

'These dogs are a real asset to the force,' Insp. Lilburn added.

The spaniels are trained to bark when they find someone; they run backwards and forwards between the person and their handler, eventually leading the handler to their find.

19

Exam practice

Now read Text B – *All Creatures Great and Small*, and answer the following questions.

2 Choose and explain two quotes from Text B which tell the reader that Mrs Pumphrey pampered Tricki Woo. (4 marks)

3 What can you tell from Text B about how James Herriot felt about Mrs Pumphrey? (8 marks)

4 In Text B:

a Find two examples from the passage where the writer uses language to amuse readers. Explain how each example is amusing. (6 marks)

b Find two different examples from the passage where the writer uses language to make his readers like the character of 'James Herriot'. Explain how each achieves this effect. (6 marks)

Text B

All Creatures Great and Small

Mrs Pumphrey was an elderly widow. Her late husband, a beer baron whose breweries and pubs were scattered widely over the broad bosom of Yorkshire, had left her a vast fortune and a beautiful house on the outskirts of Darrowby. Here she lived with a large staff of servants, a gardener, a chauffeur and Tricki Woo. Tricki Woo was a Pekingese and the apple of his mistress' eye. 5

Standing now in the magnificent doorway, I furtively rubbed the toes of my shoes on the backs of my trousers and blew on my cold hands. I could almost see the deep armchair drawn close to the leaping flames, the tray of cocktail biscuits, the bottle of excellent sherry. Because of the sherry, I was always careful to time my visits for half an hour before lunch …

'Oh, Mr Herriot,' Mrs Pumphrey said, looking at her pet anxiously. 'I'm so glad you've come. 10
Tricki has gone flop-bot again.'

This ailment, not to be found in any textbook, was her way of describing the symptoms of Tricki's illness …

I hoisted the little dog on the table … noticing the increased weight, the padding of extra flesh over the ribs. 'You know, Mrs Pumphrey, you're overfeeding him again. Didn't I tell you to cut 15
out all those pieces of cake and give him more protein?'

'Oh yes, Mr Herriot,' Mrs Pumphrey wailed. 'But what can I do? He's so tired of chicken.'

I shrugged; it was hopeless. I allowed the maid to lead me to the palatial bathroom where I always performed a ritual handwashing after the operation.

Then I returned to the drawing room, my sherry glass was filled and I settled down by the fire to 20
listen to Mrs Pumphrey. It couldn't be called a conversation because she did all the talking, but I always found it rewarding …

'Oh, Mr Herriot, I have the most exciting news. Tricki has a pen pal!'

From *All Creatures Great and Small* by James Herriot (1975)

Unit **3** Understanding Presentational Devices

Learning aim

In this unit you will prepare for the question in Section A of the English and English Language exam which asks you to write about how texts use presentational devices and to compare the devices used in two different texts. You will learn what presentational devices are and how to analyse their use.

3.1 Introducing presentational devices

(i) Concept bank

Presentational devices: features of presentation, design and organisation that help a text communicate its information, ideas and feelings. These devices include choice of font, selection of pictures and use of colour.

You will look at how writers and text designers use different presentational devices to make texts easier to read, navigate and understand.

↺ For starters

Look at this text from a leaflet for babysitters by Avon Fire Service.

Text A

Living safely. Safety advice for babysitters. When you are babysitting make sure you do not create any fire hazards. All fires should have a secure fireguard. Do not leave a child alone in a room where there is a fire. Don't let children play too close to fires as their clothing may catch light. Keep matches and lighters out of the sight and reach of children. Never leave children alone with lighted candles. If you have been given permission to smoke while babysitting always make sure that any cigarettes are out and cold before you empty the ashtray. Never leave smoker's materials where a child can reach them. Don't leave ashtrays on upholstered furniture. Never leave the kitchen when you have cooking on the stove. If you have to answer the door or phone turn the heat off or down. Make sure that children can't reach the saucepan handles. If the children in your care are in bed when you are in the house make sure that you know what the family's fire action plan is. (Ask the adults responsible for the children about this before they leave). Do you have an emergency contact telephone number? Is there a trusted family friend or neighbour you can contact? Do you know where the nearest telephone outside the house is? Do you know what the smoke alarm sounds like? If clothing catches fire: Stop – don't run the flames will get worse. Drop – get on the ground or floor. Roll – back and forward quickly until the flames are smothered. You can help by covering the casualty with clothing or blankets and patting to extinguish the flames. Make sure you protect your own hands before attempting this. If there is a fire: Raise the alarm – don't investigate, get everyone up and out of the building. If it's smoky, stay low, crawl if you have to. Once you are outside stay there! Call 999 – Stay calm and ask for the Fire Service. Website: www.avonfire.gov.uk e-mail: community.safety@avonfire.gov.uk tel: 0117 926 2061 in case of fire call 999 Avon fire & rescue preventing protecting responding

⊃ Task

The advice in Text A is important, but if you received it in the post, it would probably go straight in the bin! In pairs, discuss why the design of this piece of information text is so poor. The following words might help: cluttered, dense, overwhelming, confusing, crowded, dull, organisation, layout, presentation, design.

Text B

LIVING SAFELY

SAFETY ADVICE FOR BABYSITTERS

WHEN YOU ARE BABYSITTING MAKE SURE YOU
DO NOT CREATE ANY FIRE HAZARDS.

All fires should have a secure fireguard. Do not leave a child alone in a room where there is a fire. Don't let children play too close to fires as their clothing may catch light.

Keep matches and lighters out of the sight and reach of children. Never leave children alone with lighted candles.

If you have been given permission to smoke while babysitting always make sure that any cigarettes are out and cold before you empty the ashtray. Never leave smoker's materials where a child can reach them. Don't leave ashtrays on upholstered furniture.

Never leave the kitchen when you have cooking on the stove. If you have to answer the door or 'phone, turn the heat off or down. Make sure that children can't reach the saucepan handles.

If the children in your care are in bed when you are in the house, make sure that you know what the family's fire action plan is. (Ask the adults responsible for the children about this before they leave).

- Do you have an emergency contact telephone number?
- Is there a trusted family friend or neighbour you can contact?
- Do you know where the nearest telephone outside the house is?
- Do you know what the smoke alarm sounds like?

If clothing catches fire:
STOP – don't run – the flames will get worse.
DROP – get on the ground or floor.
ROLL – back and forward quickly until the flames are smothered. You can help by covering the casualty with clothing or blankets and patting to extinguish the flames. Make sure you protect your own hands before attempting this.

IF THERE IS A FIRE:
- Raise the alarm – don't investigate, get everyone up and out of the building.
- If it's smoky, stay low, crawl if you have to.
- Once you are outside stay there!
- Call 999 – stay calm and ask for the Fire Service.

website: www.avonfire.gov.uk e-mail: community.safety@avonfire.gov.uk

TEL: 0117 926 2061
IN CASE OF FIRE CALL 999

AVON FIRE & RESCUE
PREVENTING PROTECTING RESPONDING

Text presentational devices

- Logos show who has published the information and give it authority.
- Slogans put across a key message in a clever way.
- Headings and subheadings organise the information and break it into manageable 'chunks'.
- CAPITAL letters and large, **bold** or *italic* text emphasise certain words or phrases.
- Bulleted or numbered lists make large amounts of information easier to take in.
- Different fonts make the text more effective:
  - Serif fonts (such as Times New Roman) are easy to read, and look traditional and authoritative.
  - Sans-serif fonts (such as **Arial**) look modern and simple.
  - 'Gimmick' fonts such as *Old English*, CURLY or **BROADWAY** look fun and create a 'mood'.
  - Handwriting fonts look informal and feel 'friendly'.

Text B uses the same text as Text A, but a teacher has added some text presentational devices.

1 Working with a partner, find *four* different text presentational devices in Text B.

2 Explain *how* each device makes the text easier to read, navigate and understand.

Next, here is the same text professionally designed for Avon Fire Service.

Text C

LIVING SAFELY

SAFETY ADVICE FOR BABYSITTERS

WHEN YOU ARE BABYSITTING MAKE SURE YOU DO NOT CREATE ANY FIRE HAZARDS.

All **fires** should have a secure fireguard.
Do not leave a child alone in a room where there is a fire.
Don't let children play too close to fires as their clothing may catch light.

Keep **matches** and **lighters** out of the sight and reach of children.
Never leave children alone with lighted **candles.**

If you have been given permission to **smoke** while babysitting always make sure that any cigarettes are out and cold before you empty the ashtray. Never leave smoker's materials where a child can reach them. Don't leave **ashtrays** on upholstered furniture.

Never leave the kitchen when you have cooking on the stove. If you have to answer the door or 'phone turn the heat off or down. Make sure that children can't reach the saucepan handles.

If the children in your care are in bed when you are in the house make sure that you know what the family's **fire action plan** is. (Ask the adults responsible for the children about this before they leave).

• Do you have an emergency contact telephone number?
• Is there a trusted family friend or neighbour you can contact?
• Do you know where the nearest telephone outside the house is?
• Do you know what the **smoke alarm** sounds like?

If clothing catches fire:
STOP - don't run the flames will get worse.
DROP - get on the ground or floor.
ROLL - back and forward quickly until the flames are smothered. You can help by covering the casualty with clothing or blankets and patting to extinguish the flames. Make sure you protect your own hands before attempting this.

IF THERE IS A FIRE
• Raise the alarm - don't investigate, get everyone up and out of the building.
• If it's smoky, stay low, crawl if you have to.
• Once you are outside stay there!
• **Call 999** - Stay calm and ask for the Fire Service.

website: www.avonfire.gov.uk
e-mail: community.safety@avonfire.gov.uk

TEL: 0117 926 2061
IN CASE OF FIRE CALL 999

AVON FIRE & RESCUE
PREVENTING PROTECTING RESPONDING

3 Why do you think the designer puts the word 'LIVING' in large, italic capitals?

4 Why is the phone number so big?

5 Choose *three* text presentational devices from page 22, and write an essay about how Text C uses text presentational devices to make it easier to read, navigate, and understand.

• Start with the sentence: 'Safety Advice for Babysitters uses text presentational devices to make it easier to read, navigate, and understand.'

• Then write three paragraphs (one for each device) using this structure:

    One device the leaflet uses is ... The effect of this is ... The designer has done this to ...

⊃ Taking it further

Designers do not use presentational devices only to make the text clearer; they want to affect the reader emotionally. This is also true of the pictures which the designer uses. You will see immediately from the picture of the teddy and the building-brick house on the cover of the *Safety Advice for Babysitters* leaflet that it is aimed at babysitters.

1   Think about each of the following text presentational devices. Suggest *what effect* each device has and why the designer chose to use it:
    - The 'Living Safely' heading in the top left
    - The *Safety Advice for Babysitters* title underneath
    - The Avon Fire & Rescue logo
    - The three-word Avon Fire & Rescue slogan 'Preventing Protecting Responding'.

2   Collect a number of newspapers, magazines and leaflets. Find examples of designers using the different text presentational devices listed on page 22. Explain *what effect* each presentational device has, and suggest *why* the designer has chosen to use each device in that place. The following words might help: emphasise, draw attention to, attractive, stand out, easy-to-read, organise.

3.2 Analysing visual devices

You will learn about different kinds of visual presentational devices, and why they are used.

⊃ For starters

1   Take a sheet of paper and write the word 'PICTURES' in the middle. Working in a group of three or four, spend two minutes thinking of all the situations at school where you come across diagrams, graphics and pictures. Write your ideas on the sheet.
2   Now spend a further two minutes thinking about *why* they are used in those situations.

⊃ Task

Below and on page 26 are four examples of designers using visual presentational devices.

Text A

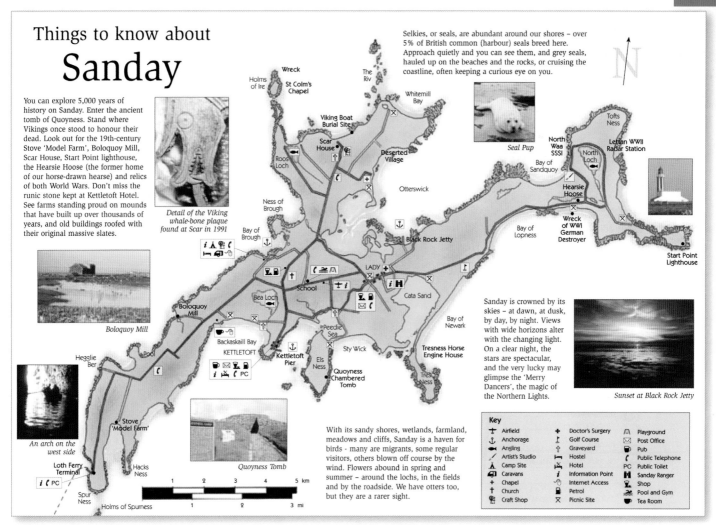

↑ *A tourist leaflet about the island of Sanday*

Text B

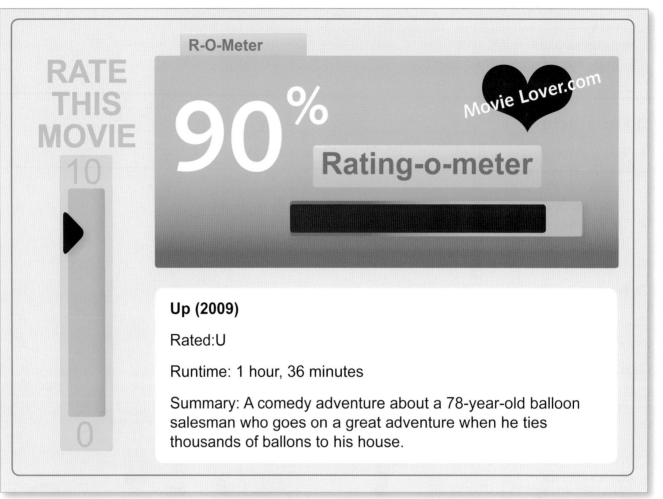

Up (2009)

Rated:U

Runtime: 1 hour, 36 minutes

Summary: A comedy adventure about a 78-year-old balloon salesman who goes on a great adventure when he ties thousands of ballons to his house.

⬆ *A review of the film* Up, *from a website*

Text C

The rubbish in your wheelie bin looks like this. **92%** can be removed if you *reduce, reuse, recycle.*

Lewisham has 55 recycling centres including Landmann Way Recycling and Waste Reception Centre and 60,000 properties have a kerbside paper collection for recycling.

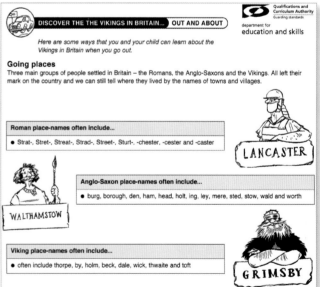

- **27%** Kitchen & garden waste *
  This can also be composted at home
- **23%** Paper & card *
- **7%** Glass bottles & jars *
- **5%** Drink & food cans *
- **5%** Clothes & shoes *
- **19%** Plastic *
- **6%** Nappies - *use reusable nappies*
- **8%** Miscellaneous

* This waste can be recycled in LEWISHAM

⬆ *An illustration from a magazine article* Re-Cycling – Why Bother?

Text D

DISCOVER THE THE VIKINGS IN BRITAIN... **OUT AND ABOUT**

Qualifications and Curriculum Authority
Guarding standards

department for
education and skills

Here are some ways that you and your child can learn about the Vikings in Britain when you go out.

Going places
Three main groups of people settled in Britain – the Romans, the Anglo-Saxons and the Vikings. All left their mark on the country and we can still tell where they lived by the names of towns and villages.

Roman place-names often include...
● Strat-, Stret-, Streat-, Strad-, Street-, Sturt-, -chester, -cester and -caster

LANCASTER

Anglo-Saxon place-names often include...
● burg, borough, den, ham, head, holt, ing, ley, mere, sted, stow, wald and worth

WALTHAMSTOW

Viking place-names often include...
● often include thorpe, by, holm, beck, dale, wick, thwaite and toft

GRIMSBY

⬆ *An information sheet on the Vikings for the parents of 7–11 year olds*

1 The texts on pages 25–26 use a number of visual presentational devices. Use a table like the one below to record which devices are used in each text.

	Photo	Cartoon/ drawing	Map	Graphic	Diagram	Logo
Text A						
Text B						
Text C						
Text D						

Uses of pictures in texts

Pictures are used for five different reasons in texts:

Function	Effect
Illustration: where a picture is used just to let us see what something the author has mentioned looks like.	'This *lets us see* what the actor looks like …'
Demonstration: where a picture is used to help the author make a point about something in the text.	'The picture *shows us* how …'
Explanation: where a picture is used to give a visual explanation, or a simplified version of something in the text.	'The diagram *helps us* understand how oxygen …'
Information: where a picture is used to present additional information (not in the written text) to the reader.	'The pie chart *tells us* that …'
Substantiation: where a picture is used to help convince us of a claim made or to prove something the writer is saying.	'This *supports* the claim that it …'

2 In pairs, find a picture in Texts A–D which fulfils each function in the table above: for example, the photos in Text A are *illustrations* of things to see in Sanday.

When you analyse the use of a picture, you need to think about:
* *What?* – what sort of picture it is and what it shows.
* *What effect?* – the function of the picture for the reader.
* *Why?* – why the designer has chosen to use that picture (relate it to the purpose of the text).

If you had to analyse Text A, you might write a paragraph like the one on the right.

3 Write an analysis of the picture in Text C, using the example on the right as a template:

> Text C is a … of … This diagram is for …; it helps us understand … Text C is …, and the designer is trying to … by ….

Text A shows a photo of a mill. This photo is for illustration; it lets us see what one of the buildings on Sanday looks like. Text A is a tourist leaflet, and the designer is trying to attract tourists by showing them an interesting building.

⊃ Taking it further

Text E

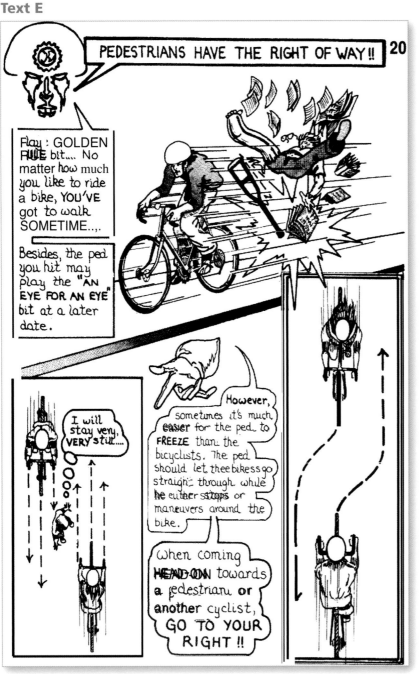

⬆ *A page from an American bicycle safety booklet called* Sprocket Man

1. Choose one of the pictures from Text E, and write an analysis of it, explaining:
   - *What?* – what sort of picture it is and what it shows
   - *What effect?* – the function of the picture for the reader
   - *Why?* – why the designer has chosen to use that picture (relate it to the purpose of the text).

2. Link this paragraph to the paragraph you wrote about the picture in Text C by joining the two with the **discourse marker** 'By contrast'. You have just written a comparison of two pictures.

ⓘ Concept bank

Discourse marker: a word or phrase which helps a reader understand how a writer's argument is organised in a text. For example, paragraphs might start with the discourse markers 'Firstly', 'Secondly', etc. Connectives such as 'In addition' and 'By contrast' are used as discourse markers to warn the reader of a change of idea or emphasis.

3.3 Code-breaking

You will look at how presentational devices can create ideas and feelings in readers' minds.

⊃ For starters

When designers include pictures, they are trying to do much more than simply illustrate or explain a point in the text. Pictures have the power to affect the reader emotionally. Look at these three photos of a lakeside tourist 'hotspot' in Austria called Hallstatt. Which would make the best postcard?

Photo A

Photo B

Photo C

List as many differences between Photos A–C as you can find. Think about:
- the content (what the photos show)
- the **shot**
- the **editing**.

ⓘ Concept bank

Shot: the way in which a photographer chooses to show the subject in a photo. It may be a *long shot* or a *close-up, portrait* or *landscape, low angle* (looking up) or *high angle* (looking down). A *colour filter* may be fitted (to make a sunset appear more golden, for example).

Editing: changing a photo to increase the emotional impact of the picture. It may be *cropped, retouched* or *softened*. The colour properties of the photo may be changed to increase the colour *saturation* (how 'heavy' the colours are in the picture).

⟳ Task

Text A   **Text B**

⬆ *An image used in a driving school's website*   ⬆ *The cover of a local magazine* Lewisham Life, *produced by Lewisham council*

Texts A and B show young adults. The pictures have been carefully designed to create feelings in the reader and to get across a message.

Before you start analysing the photos and their meaning, think about the purpose of the publications:

1   Text A is an advert for a driving school. What impressions of driving might it want to create? Why?
2   Text B is promoting a summer school for young people. Who is it aimed at? What impressions of the summer school will it want to create for its target audience?

Colours have a strong psychological effect on us. Designers use colours to create thoughts and feelings in the reader. Here are some **connotations** of different colours:

Red – sexy, dangerous, 'wicked', 'stop'

Purple (children's favourite colour) – excitement

Green – good, healthy, ecological, 'go'

Yellow – warm, happy, lively

White – pure, clean

Pink – girlie, cute

Brown – earthy, wholesome, traditional

Gold – luxurious

Orange – fun

Black – mysterious, forbidding

Blue and **grey** are neutral colours, often used simply to create a background.

ⓘ Concept bank

Connotation: the idea or meaning suggested by a word, image or colour. For example, red has a connotation of danger.

When you analyse the 'meaning' of a picture, you can think about these *three* aspects of the picture to give you ideas:
- the way the subject of the picture has been presented
- the shot and editing
- the use of colour.

3 Working in pairs, analyse Text A on page 30. Use this table to guide your thinking. In each section there is an example to help you. Try to find at least one other point for each section.

Aspect	**What?** (What presentational device do you notice?)	**What effect?** (What is the function of the device?)	**Why?** (What message is the designer trying to get across?)
How the young people are shown	They are both smiling.	It makes them look happy.	That driving lessons will make you happy.
The shot and editing	They have been cropped and dropped onto a coloured background.	We know no details of them or their lives.	That these driving lessons are for *everyone*
The colours used	They are standing on a red block of colour.	Red stands for danger.	Driving is dangerous – so you need driving lessons.

Share your thoughts as a whole class. You must come up with at least *three* additional points.

4 Now write *three* paragraphs (one for each point), using this frame:

> A presentational feature used in the picture is ... . The effect of this is that ... . The designer is trying to get across the message that ... .

The marks in this question depend on good explanations, so be sure you explain as thoroughly as you can *why* the picture creates its impression.

⊃ Taking it further

1 Working on your own, analyse Text B by thinking about:
- the way the subject of the picture has been presented
- the shot and editing
- the use of colour.

Write *three* paragraphs (one for each point), again using this frame:

> A presentational feature used in the picture is ... . The effect of this is that ... . The designer is trying to get across the message that ... .

2 Link this paragraph to the paragraph you wrote about Text A by joining the two with the discourse marker 'By contrast' or 'Similarly'. You have just written a comparison of two pictures.

3.4 Exam practice for understanding presentational devices

You will review your understanding of how to analyse visual presentational devices, and you will learn how to compare the presentational devices used in two texts. You will complete an exam-style question.

↻ For starters

You now know a range of different presentational devices, and you know that, for each one, you must be able to write about:

- *What?* – what you notice about the presentational device
- *What effect?* – the effect on the reader
- *Why?* – what the designer is trying to do, what message they were trying to get across, and how this relates to the purpose of the publication.

Text A is a poster which is trying to attract young people to trust the CAF scheme. It uses a range of presentational devices.

Text A

↑ *A poster advertising the Common Assessment Framework (CAF), a government scheme to help young people with special needs who are worried about their future*

1. Look back at your checklist of text presentational devices on page 22. Identify *two* text presentational devices in Text A, explain their effect and suggest why the designer uses them.

2. Look back at how to analyse the meaning of a picture on pages 29–31. Describe the main photo in the poster, and suggest the message the designer is trying to get across.

3. Look back at your checklist of the meaning of colours on page 30. Choose *two* colours the designer uses, and suggest why.

↻ Task

Now you are able to analyse a text's presentational devices, you are almost ready to do the exam question which asks you to compare how two texts use presentational devices, for example (see right):

To gain high marks for this question, you need to compare three or more presentational devices. You should write your essay in three paragraphs:

- Paragraph 1: compare the text devices you notice.
- Paragraph 2: compare the pictures.
- Paragraph 3: compare the way the two texts use colours.

In each paragraph, write about the first text, then the second text. To show the examiner that you are comparing the texts, use a comparison discourse marker such as 'By contrast' or 'Similarly'.

This table will help you plan your essay.

> Choose **two** texts and compare them using these headings:
>
> - The way the text is presented
> - The way the pictures are presented.

	Text 1	Discourse marker	Text 2
Paragraph	In each paragraph, write about:	In each paragraph, choose from:	In each paragraph, write about:
Text presentational devices	• What? • What effect? • Why?	**If different:** • By contrast • Alternatively • On the other hand • However • Yet	• What? • What effect? • Why?
Picture devices	• What? • What effect? • Why?		• What? • What effect? • Why?
Colour	• What? • What effect? • Why?	**If similar:** • Similarly • Likewise • Equally • In the same way • Also	• What? • What effect? • Why?

↻ Taking it further

Now try this exam-style question. Text A is the poster you looked at on page 32 and Text B is the poster on page 34.

Exam practice

Compare the way Texts A (on page 32) and B (on page 34) use presentational devices, using these headings:

- The use of different fonts
- The pictures and colours. (12 marks)

Time allowed: 15 minutes

If you'd like to help young people try something new and make a positive contribution to the local community then contact the Young Transformer Wyre Project on:

Telephone: 01234 567890
Email: Youngtransform@webaddress.org
Text: WYTME to 012345 567890

www.youngtransformerwyre.webaddress.org

Young Transformers WYRE

WHO DO YOU SEE?

Troublemaker, Thug, Hoody? or DJ, Stylist, Chef?

It all depends on your point of view doesn't it?

We see the potential that people have if they are given the chance.

That's where you can help.

The Young Transformer Wyre Project is providing grants of up to £2,500 for organisations to deliver training courses, classes and activities that can give young people aged between 7 to 25 years a chance to change their lives.

WYRE   Wyre Borough Council   Community Foundation

⬆ *A poster produced by Wyre Borough Council in the North of England. It is advertising a council-run training scheme aimed at young people.*

! Examiner's tip

Always start your essay with:

Both texts use text presentational devices, pictures and colour to present their content effectively, and to create an emotional impact upon the reader.

4 Changing Minds – Arguing and Persuading

Learning aim

This unit will help you to produce effective persuasive and argumentative work. It will help you to write in a convincing, persuasive manner, to write an effective argument, and to give engaging, persuasive and argumentative presentations.

ⓘ Concept bank

Adjective: a word which describes a noun (a thing, object or person). Examples: 'brilliant', 'massive', 'awesome'.

4.1 Persuasive writing – adverts

You will explore advertising techniques and write your own effective advertisement.

↻ For starters

1 Where do you see writing that is persuasive every day in your life? Write a list of examples you can think of.
2 Feed back your list to the rest of the class.

↻ Task

1 Look at the advertisement for Disneyland Paris on page 36. What is its purpose?

The information you are given is skilfully controlled by the writer to tell you what you need to know at important moments.

2 Look at the section of the advert titled 'Disneyland Park'. Pick out the **adjectives** used to persuade you to go.

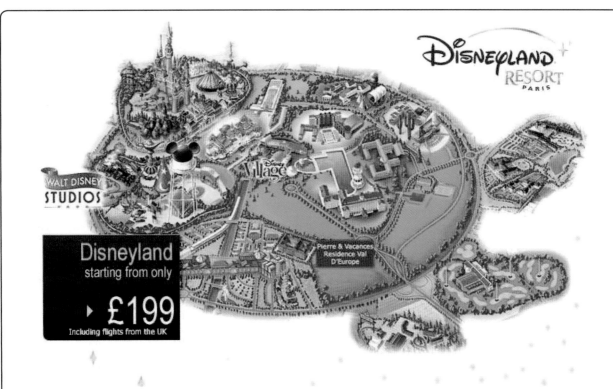

Disneyland ® Resort Paris is a magical destination where dreams can come true. All the family can meet and greet some of their favourite characters.

Disneyland ® Park

Disneyland ® Park offers a huge range of fabulous parades for kids of all ages.

Divided into 5 themed areas the park includes restaurants, shops and attractions from the exhilarating Space Mountain: Mission 2 to the wildest ride in the Wild West, Big Thunder Mountain. If you want to slow things down fly with Dumbo and Peter Pan in Fantasyland or gently cruise around the river of the far west on one of the elegant steam boats in Frontierland.

Meet all your favourite Disney characters. Get a photo on main street USA with some of your favourite Disney characters, then be taken "to infinity and beyond!" on Buzz Lightyear Lazer Blast (inspired by Disney-Pixar's *Toy Story 2*) in Discoveryland.

The Walt Disney Studios ®

Welcome to the Walt Disney Studios ® Park …

Where its lights! Camera! Magic!

Everywhere! All the time!

Step through the Studio gates and let your imagination soar. Time to immerse yourself in the never-ending, always fascinating world of movies, animation and television.

Four production zones within the park featuring rides, shows and entertainment with one single focus: entertainment for the whole family.

Disneyland Resort Hotels

Choosing to stay at the resort can truly turn a weekend break into a magic experience. Thanks to the fact that there are hotels to suit every budget and taste – there is something for everyone. Each choice comes with its own magical experience.

Within the seven onsite hotels, guests will find numerous restaurants ranging from buffet style food courts to formal table service. In addition, each hotel has its own bar and gift shop.

But whether you choose to stay in a wild west town or a rustic hunting lodge, a big apple sky scraper or a Mexican Pueblo, you can be assured of one thing … Disney's outstanding quality and famous love for the magical details that will make your trip a truly unforgettable one.

Call our Disneyland® Paris Hotline Now

call us free on
0808 178 4750

* TERMS & CONDITIONS APPLY. CALL FOR DETAILS.

3 Read the three extracts from the advert on the right. Then copy the table below, add two rows for extracts 2 and 3, and complete the table with words you think are most persuasive. Explain the effect of the words used. The first one has been done to show you what to do.

Extract	Persuasive words	Effects
1	huge, fabulous	It makes the Park seem really large and impressive.

4 Look at the section about 'The Walt Disney Studios'.
   • Write out a list that is used to make the Park sound more impressive.
   • Pick out three words or phrases that make the Walt Disney Studios seem really fantastic.

5 The paragraphs in the advert are quite short. Why is writing short paragraphs effective in an advert?

↻ Taking it further

You have been asked by Disneyland Paris to design a new advert for them. They want you to come up with a **slogan** and some persuasive ideas that will make people go on holiday to Disneyland Paris.

Disneyland Paris have given you 10 facts about the park. Include some of these in your advert:
- Two magical parks with more than 50 attractions
- 14 hotels to suit every taste
- Disney Village for shopping and dining
- Kids under 7 are free
- Space Mountain: Mission 2 (new space-ride)
- There is plenty of family adventure
- Meet and greet Disney's favourite stars
- There are lots of shows to see
- Get one day and one night free
- Lots of parties going on all the time.

Remember to use powerful and **persuasive language** which really grabs the attention of your reader, such as 'fantastic place' or 'awe-inspiring location'.

Key language devices used in advertising include:
- You – using the word 'you' makes the advertisement appear to be talking directly to the reader.
- **Lists of three** – by listing ideas in threes, the advertiser makes their product sound more convincing.
- Slogans – often adverts have a slogan, which is an easily remembered catch phrase or word. Good slogans will help you remember why a product is worth buying.

Remember to make your advert suitable for both parents and children. Make sure you have presented your work clearly and effectively.

Extract 1

'Disneyland Park offers a huge range of attractions and fabulous parades for kids of all ages.'

Extract 2

'… shops and attractions from the exhilarating Space Mountain to the wildest ride in the Wild West, Big Thunder Mountain.'

Extract 3

'… gently cruise around the river of the far west on one of the elegant steam boats in Frontierland.'

ⓘ Concept bank

Slogan: a slogan is a catchy phrase that summarises how great the park is or what the park is like. It needs to be a phrase which everyone will remember, for example: 'The Magic Kingdom'.

Persuasive language: emotive or engaging language that convinces you of something.

List of three: when a writer or speaker repeats an idea three times in slightly different ways.

⌗ Grammar link

Punctuation can also help add emphasis to a point. For instance, if you use exclamation marks it shouts out to the reader that this is a good idea – 'Come on this holiday! You will love it!' This technique is used in the Disney advert.

4.2 Argument texts – newspaper articles

> You will learn how newspaper articles can argue a specific point.
> You will then write an argumentative article of your own.

↻ For starters

1 Read these sentences:

> It is a lie.   I can prove it.   Just let me.

2 The three sentences are short and make their point efficiently. Why might a writer use three short sentences like this? What is the effect of these three sentences?

3 Write three short sentences of your own. Remember to create a strong dramatic impact.

↻ Task

1 Using the **S3QR** checklist read the following article.

> **S3QR** stands for: **S**kim it, ask what **3 Q**uestions it is answering, then **R**ead it carefully.

HEALTH GROUPS SEEK BAN ON TV ADVERTS FOR FATTY FOODS

The Irish Heart Foundation and the National Heart Alliance are calling for a ban on television advertisements for fatty foods
5 **before the 9pm watershed.**

The groups say the prohibition should be applied to any adverts for foods which are high in fat, sugar or salt.

10 Irish Heart Foundation's health promotion manager, Maureen Mulvihill, said such a move by the proposed new Broadcasting Authority of Ireland was vital to ensuring that young people watching
15 programmes outside of children's viewing hours are protected from sophisticated ad campaigns that promote unhealthy eating:

'A 6am to 9pm ban would protect the health of children, address the concerns of Irish parents and respond to the robust scientific evidence that 20 links commercial promotion of foods and beverages to poor diets in children,' she said.

'The recent review of regulations in the UK, where 25 ads to children for unhealthy foods were banned, showed that the law did not go far enough.

'Advertising to children was 30 reduced, but children still saw the same amount of ads, because advertising during children's programmes switched to adult viewing times, when more children watch soaps and other family entertainment programmes 35 than children's programmes, and there was an increase in TV channels.'

Working with a partner, answer these questions:

2   What does the writer of the article say about advertising food for children? Write *two* sentences summarising this. Try to make sure your sentences are not too long.

3   What do you think about the issues mentioned in the article? Do you agree with them? What areas, if any, do you disagree with? Try to explain why you think the way you do.

4   The writer uses these techniques in the article:
   • quotations
   • **facts**
   • **opinions**
   • **persuasive language**.
   On the right, there is an example of each technique. Identify which example matches each bullet point. As a clue, the fourth one has speech marks around it.

⟳ Taking it further

Write two paragraphs of an article for your school newspaper or magazine putting forward your views on whether advertising for children is a good idea.

You could discuss advertising for children in general or look at a specific area of advertising, such as:
• music or DVDs
• food or drink
• clothes
• beauty products
• computer games.

Use:
• quotations from other people
• facts
• opinions
• persuasive language.

To make sure you have a clear structure to your **argument text**, you need to have an effective opening. This does not need to be longer than two or three lines.

You could begin:

> Advertising for children can be seen on the television and in magazines everywhere you go. The more adverts you see, the more you feel you must buy some of the products.

You would need to carry on from here with the details of a product that you have seen advertised and what was good or bad about this.

Examples

1   The Irish Heart Foundation and the National Heart Alliance are calling for a ban on television advertisements for fatty foods before the 9pm watershed.

2   … such a move by the proposed new Broadcasting Authority of Ireland was vital to ensuring that young people watching programmes outside of children's viewing hours are protected from sophisticated ad campaigns that promote unhealthy eating.

3   The groups say the prohibition should be applied to any adverts …

4   'The recent review of regulations in the UK, where ads to children for unhealthy foods were banned, showed that the law did not go far enough.'

ⓘ Concept bank

Fact: a statement that can be checked and proved to be true or false.

Opinion: one person's thoughts or feelings about something – other people may not agree.

Persuasive language: emotive or engaging language that convinces you of something.

Argument text: presents different sides to a debate and comes to a conclusion.

4.3 Writing and performing speeches

You will learn how to write a persuasive speech.

⊃ For starters

In 1940, the Second World War had been going on for nearly a year. On 4 June 1940, the Prime Minister, Winston Churchill, gave a radio speech.

Read this extract from the speech. What was its purpose?

> We shall go on to the end, we shall fight in France,
> we shall fight on the seas and oceans,
> we shall fight with growing confidence and growing strength in the air, we shall defend
> our Island, whatever the cost may be,
> we shall fight on the beaches,   5
> we shall fight on the landing grounds,
> we shall fight in the fields and in the streets,
> we shall fight in the hills;
> we shall never surrender, and even if, which I do not for a moment believe, this Island or
> a large part of it were subjugated and starving, then our Empire beyond the seas, armed   10
> and guarded by the British Fleet, would carry on the struggle, until, in God's good time,
> the New World, with all its power and might, steps forth to the rescue and the liberation
> of the old.

⊃ Task

You are going to find the speech techniques that Churchill uses to tell the audience his message and then explain the effect of each example. Copy the table on page 41 and use it to record your answers to the following questions (one example has been done to help you).

1 Find examples of repetition in the speech. What are the effects of this repetition? Write your answers in the third column of your table.

2 Find lists of two or three ideas in the speech and explain their effects.

3 Churchill uses the pronoun 'we' to involve his audience. Look at how he uses this term of address and explain its effects.

↑ *Winston Churchill*

4 What questions might a listener want to ask Churchill as he delivers his speech? How has he planned for or anticipated these questions? Write your questions and his answers in your table under 'Examples' and explain their effects.

Feature	Examples	Effects
Repetition	We shall fight	This is repeated many times to emphasise that this is what the audience have to do to win the war. It sticks in their mind, as a result.
Lists		
Terms of address		
Anticipating questions		

5 What makes this speech effective as a piece of persuasion?

⊃ Taking it further

Write a speech of your own to deliver to the rest of your class. The title is: 'I do not like adverts because they mislead people. They are based totally on lies.'

You will need to plan what you are going to write. Think about points for and against the title. Plan ideas you will speak about in pairs – for and against. Remember that you are trying to persuade the audience that your point of view is right.

Try to include some of these key speech techniques:
- **lists of three**
- **rhetorical questions**
- voice or style of address
- anticipating questions
- effective openings and endings.

Remember when you deliver your speech:
- speak with a loud, clear voice
- do not rush
- look at your audience
- do not hide your face behind your notes
- keep still
- sound like you mean what you are saying.

⊡ Grammar link

Pronouns are often used in speeches to involve the audience. Pronouns are words such as: 'we', 'you', 'I', 'us'.

ⓘ Concept bank

Lists of three: when a writer or speaker repeats an idea three times in slightly different ways. Politicians often use lists of three in their speeches. For example: 'We must pick ourselves up, dust ourselves off, and begin again the work of remaking America' (from Barack Obama's inauguration speech as U.S. president in 2009).

Rhetorical questions: questions that are addressed to an audience but do not require an answer. The questions are used for dramatic effect and/or designed to make an audience think. For example: 'Would you jump off the edge of a cliff just because someone asked you to?'

4.4 Persuasive writing – making a sales pitch

You will learn how to write and deliver an effective sales pitch.

↻ For starters

If you invented a new product for children, what would it be?

1   Brainstorm ideas in a small group and come up with a few suggestions for a product. Then select one idea to develop further. It could be:
    *   a new music-playing device
    *   a new phone with an original feature
    *   a machine that does homework.
2   Make a list of all the good things about your product and a list of some of the bad points. Think of things such as size, colour and who is likely to buy it.
3   Draw a sketch of what it might look like.

↻ Task

Imagine you are going to appear on a programme called *Fab New Ideas*. You will put a new idea to a small panel of experts who then decide if your product is good enough to be developed and put into shops.

Prepare a two-minute sales **pitch** for the panel. In your sales pitch you will need to give some basic details:

*   your name and your company's name – something interesting and snappy that people will remember
*   what your product is called – something catchy so everyone will know what it is and remember it
*   what it does – think about what your product or invention can do for people in their daily lives
*   what it looks like – a rough drawing may help here
*   how much it will cost to produce – think about how much the materials will cost and how much time will be spent making it
*   how much people will pay for it – make the price something that will attract people to buy the product. If it is too expensive it will put people off. If it is too cheap people will think it is rubbish. Perhaps you need to research other similar products to see how much they cost and come up with a similar price.
*   how many you will sell in each of the first three years – you need to think through how many people are likely to buy your product in each of the first three years and why
*   why the panel should invest in your product – you need to be able to convince the panel to part with their money to help you develop and build your product. What can you say to convince them? Come up with something special about your product which will convince them.

ⓘ Concept bank

Pitch: a short speech where you try to persuade someone to buy a product. A pitch is often given to a group of people from businesses.

You will need to be persuasive to make sure that the panel is convinced by your idea. Think of the persuasive writing techniques that you have looked at so far in this unit and try to use some of them here.

Think of words and phrases that you can use to make your product seem more amazing. For example:

- fantastic
- brilliant
- superb
- completely unique
- excellent value
- extremely popular.

Include things in your pitch that will make you sound authoritative – as though you know what you are talking about. For example, try to include:

- **facts**
- examples
- specialist vocabulary
- some short, powerful sentences.

Make sure that you:

- are smart, polite and friendly
- are well-rehearsed
- use appropriate body language to show you are keen and trustworthy
- are very clear what your product does and why it is worth investing money in
- try to anticipate questions that may be asked by the panel.

⟳ Taking it further

In class, present your sales pitch to a small panel of students (as well as the rest of your class). The panel will listen to your pitch and ask you questions about your product before deciding whether to invest in it. Each member of the panel will then get a chance to say why they will or will not invest in your product.

Everyone in the class should have a chance to be on the panel and be able to present their own product.

ⓘ Concept bank

Fact: a statement that can be checked and proved to be true or false.

4.5 Letters of persuasion and argument

You will learn how letters can be persuasive as well as argue a case.
You will then write a persuasive and argumentative letter of your own.

⊃ For starters

Look at the poster on the right. It is designed to persuade parents to monitor what their children are eating.

In a small group, discuss your views on healthy eating:

- Is it important?
- Do you eat healthily?
- What problems might you have if you do not eat healthily?

⊃ Task

CODE ON THE ADVERTISING OF FOOD PRODUCTS TO CHILDREN

We recently spoke about this. I am now writing to OFCOM to consider proposals for strengthening the existing code on advertising food to children.

This reform is but one part of the developing programme to tackle childhood obesity, which is currently under close scrutiny by the Food Standards Agency, the Department of Health and the Health Select Committee.   5

Although I am well aware that there are many factors involved in the increase in levels of childhood obesity – and Government is committed to halting and reversing the decline in levels of physical activity in particular, not least through our work to boost PE and school sport and to encourage physical activity more generally – I take the issue of food advertising very seriously. I believe the current code of conduct governing the advertising of food and drink products to children to be inadequate and in need of review.   10

I know that you will want to take into account the conclusions of the FSA Report, the Department of Health's Food and Health Action Plan and the Health Select Committee's inquiry into obesity. I also know that industry is willing to work with us, and this is welcome because a package of solutions is required. I will be exploring further with the food and drink manufacturers how they can partner with Government to promote healthy eating and active lifestyles.

15

I also believe that the problem of childhood obesity highlights the importance of OFCOM's statutory duty to promote media literacy among children. In addition to understanding the need for a balanced diet and regular exercise, children and young people need to understand that companies advertising any product (not just food and drink) to them are doing so for commercial reasons and want them to spend more of their money on the products of those advertisers.

20

I look forward to hearing what plans you have to conduct research, review regulation and strengthen the code in this area, and to promote greater media literacy among children.

1   Using the **S3QR** checklist on the right, read the letter on page 44 and above from the Minister for the Olympics and for London, Tessa Jowell, to MP David Currie. An exam question might ask you to look at the letter and to examine how Jowell uses language to argue her case.

When you read the letter, think about what she is writing about. To help you, here is a bit of information:

  • OFCOM are responsible to the government and have to check that TV, radio and all other communication networks are providing reliable information to the public.

Working with a partner, discuss and make notes on the following:

2   Look carefully at the language used in the letter. What is the effect on the reader of these phrases and sentences?

  • '... I take the issue of food advertising very seriously.'
  • 'I believe ...'
  • 'I will be exploring further with the food and drink manufacturers how they can partner with Government to promote healthy eating and active lifestyles.'

3   In the second to last paragraph ('I also believe ...'), what does Tessa Jowell state must be done now? What must children be told?

4   How does she end the letter? (Can you spot the **list of three**?)

5   The final few words 'and to promote greater media literacy among children' turn the list of three into a list of four. Why has she chosen to end with these words?

S3QR stands for: **S**kim it, ask what **3 Q**uestions it is answering, then **R**ead it carefully.

ⓘ Concept bank

List of three: when a writer or speaker repeats an idea three times in slightly different ways.

Rhetorical questions: questions that are addressed to an audience but do not require an answer.

⊃ Taking it further

Write your own first two paragraphs of a letter to the Health Minister presenting your views on either the Healthy Eating Campaign or the Anti-Smoking Campaign. (You can find an anti-smoking poster on page 46.)

Remember to use persuasive writing techniques. You could use:

  • **rhetorical questions** such as 'What would you do if it was your child?'
  • a clear personal style of address such as '**We** can make a better future for **our** children.'

Both of these techniques clearly involve the reader and make them emotionally involved in the issues. This means they are more likely to do something about the problem.

⌻ Grammar link

When you are letter-writing, use of the appropriate register (see page 10) is very important. If you are writing a formal letter to someone who you do not know, you will normally end 'Yours faithfully'. If you are writing to someone who you have met, you will end 'Yours sincerely'.

4.6 Role-play and exam practice

You will learn how to role-play a character in a school debate and answer an exam-style question.

⟳ For starters

1 The advert on the right about stopping people smoking has been criticised by many people. They see it as too extreme and frightening. In pairs, discuss what you think of the advert and why.

2 Look in more detail at the advert. Why might people be offended by this and why might others think it is really good? Think about:
   • what it says
   • the presentation and pictures.

"I'm not scared of spiders.

I'm scared of my mum dying from smoking."

NHS

Over 2,000 people die every week in the UK from smoking related diseases. For help quitting, call 0800 169 0 169.

www.nhs.uk/smokefree

 SMOKEFREE

⟳ Task

1 Imagine the advert is put up in a secondary school:

> Some parents hear that the advert is being displayed in their child's secondary school. They see it then write a letter to the Headteacher, explaining why they object to it.
>
> The Headteacher tracks down the teacher responsible for placing the advert around the school – the Head of Health Education. She replies, defending the advert.
>
> The Headteacher also asks the school council to consider the advert. Two students reply. They have opposing views that they put into writing – one says it reminds him of a dying relative, the other says the advert is not hard-hitting enough.

2 You are going to take part in a group meeting to discuss the advert and whether you feel it should be allowed to stay up. There will be five people in each group. Each person will play one of these roles:
   • the Headteacher, who will be chairperson
   • a complaining parent
   • the Head of Health Education
   • the two students with opposing views.

3 Work with a partner who shares a similar view to you. Using the **APPLE** checklist on the right, prepare ideas for playing your role. You will need to put together a short speech on what the character you are playing thinks about the advert.

4 Remember to use the key techniques for writing **arguments** you have learnt in this unit. For example, you could include a **list of three** or repetition to get across your views.

5 Remember to use the correct **register** to try to involve the audience. Here you just need to speak directly to the audience as a group – for example, call them 'you':

   *'**Your** children will see this advertisement every day of the week. **You** will have to see it whenever **you** walk past.'*

   This is a powerful technique as it directly involves the audience and makes the subject seem to be very relevant to them.

⟳ Taking it further

Once you have planned and prepared what you are going to say, you will be given the chance to put forward your views during the meeting. You will also have a chance to discuss other people's views.

At the end a vote will be taken to decide whether the advert stays or goes. Your teacher will guide what is to happen in the debate.

APPLE checklist

Plan your speech so that it:
• suits the **A**udience
• achieves its **P**urpose
• has good **P**resentation
• uses the right **L**anguage
• has a powerful **E**ffect.

ⓘ Concept bank

Argument: a logical statement in support of a point, backed up with relevant facts and figures.

List of three: when a writer or speaker repeats an idea three times in slightly different ways.

Register: the way a text sounds to its readers or listeners. This could be formal, bossy, amusing, friendly, or cold … or many other registers.

Writing an argument text

Plan and write the answer to the exam-style question on the right.

Plan your **argument text** essay by thinking up TWO good reasons to ban children's advertising, and ONE reason why it should not be banned.

First, **write a short introductory paragraph** explaining why you are writing the letter.

Next, write two paragraphs in which you **argue your two good reasons** to ban children's advertising. Start each paragraph with a topic sentence making the point, and then support your point with evidence and a developed explanation.

Next, write a paragraph in which you **reject the counter-argument** that children's advertising should not be banned. Start by writing: 'Some people might say that…' and outline their point. But in the middle of your paragraph, write: 'However, …' and explain why it is a wrong idea.

Finish with a paragraph in which you **make a direct appeal** to the Minister to ban children's advertising. Start with the word: 'Therefore …' and use lots of **emotive language**.

Good writing techniques

Your writing should include:
- Clear **discourse markers**, both at the start of a paragraph ('Firstly, …' 'Secondly, …') and also within a paragraph ('Also, …' 'However, …').
- Some **complex sentences**, with a number of clauses, joined by connectives, especially 'because', 'which' and 'although'.
- **Short sentences** to give excitement and pace.
- A blunt **fragment**.
- All the **senses** (see, hear, smell, taste, touch).
- **Adjectives**.
- **Adverbs** (-ly words).
- **Specialist words**.
- The appropriate **person** ('I', 'You', 'we', 'they').

If appropriate, somewhere in your essay, use:
- A range of **punctuation**: . , ? ! : ; ( ) " "
- One **list** of details, separated by commas.
- **Direct speech**, "correctly punctuated".
- At least one **rhetorical question**.
- **Repetition** of a key phrase.
- A **list of three**.
- At least one **simile** ('like …'/ 'as … as …').
- A **colloquialism**.
- A **hyperbole**.

5 Tell Me About It – Explaining, Advising and Informing

Learning aim

In this unit you will learn how to explain, advise and inform so that you know what to do in the exams. You will see that speaking uses many of the same rules as writing. You will also use explaining, advising and informing skills in speaking and listening activities, including giving a presentation and role-play. The presentation and role-play will be marked and the marks will go towards your final GCSE grade.

- Have you ever given a talk to the class?
- What do you think are your strengths as a speaker?
- What areas of speaking do you think you need to improve?
- Have you ever heard a good talk in an assembly or a lesson?
- What do you think a good talk should include?

'Speak to communicate clearly and purposefully; structure and sustain talk, adapting it to different situations and audiences; use Standard English and a variety of techniques as appropriate.'

ⓘ Concept bank

Standard English: writing or speaking that is generally accepted as grammatically correct.

5.1 Speaking to communicate

You will learn that, when informing an audience, you need to think about the 5Ws and 1H: who, what, when, where, why and how.

⊃ For starters

Speaking and listening marks are worth 20 per cent of your overall grade. Getting top marks for your speaking and listening work could mean a difference of two or three grades!

Think about your past speaking and listening activities. Use the questions on the left to help you. Note down your ideas and then share them with a partner. Can you give each other advice on how to be a better speaker?

⊃ Task

Later you will give a short presentation to inform your class about a topic you feel confident about. To help you, you need to understand what the GCSE specification says (see left):

The objective has four parts. Look at what each of these parts means:
- speak to communicate clearly and purposefully
- structure and sustain talk
- adapt to different situations and audiences
- use **Standard English** and a variety of techniques as appropriate.

Speak to communicate clearly and purposefully

This means that you need to get your information across, make yourself heard and speak quickly enough so that your audience does not get bored, but not so quickly that they cannot follow you. You must also know the reason why you are speaking.

↑ *Speak clearly and purposefully so your audience does not get bored.*

1   Imagine you have been asked to speak to some new students in a few days' time. You have not been told any of the 5Ws and 1H. You have no idea:

   • **who** the students are (age)
   • **what** the talk is about
   • **when**, exactly, you need to give the talk
   • **where** you will talk
   • **why** you are talking to these students
   • **how** you are supposed to give your talk.

   Write down between three and five problems that you would have when planning this talk. Would your talk be 'clear' and 'purposeful'? Why or why not?

Structure and sustain talk

'Structure' means that you need to order your ideas in a logical and linked way so that they are not muddled up and so that they flow.

'Sustain' means that you must keep your talk going. You need to have enough ideas to keep your audience interested. You also need to be able to develop your ideas with reasons and examples.

2   Read this student's plan on the right to inform someone how to make a mug of coffee. Rewrite it in the correct order as a series of sentences, adding more detail and explanation.

> Pour boiled water onto coffee in mug.
>
> Stir in sugar to taste.
>
> Boil water in kettle.
>
> Add milk to taste.
>
> Drink.
>
> Place one spoon of coffee in mug.
>
> Measure a mug of water into kettle.

Adapt to different situations and audiences

This means that you need to change the way you speak depending upon whether the situation is formal or informal, and whether your audience is young or old, male or female. This is important because it makes your talk suitable for your listeners and appropriate for the situation.

3   Read the examples on the right where someone is providing information for another person. Work with a partner to decide:

   • what was bought
   • when it was bought
   • where it was bought from.

   Decide if the example is 'communicating clearly and purposefully'. In what situation do you think each one would be the best? (Think about the audience each one would be suitable for.)

> Well, it was like Tuesday but it could have been like Monday. No it was Tuesday cos I was with Shania and I like got it from like Tesco.

> I bought the CD from the shop last Tuesday.

> I beg to inform you that I purchased the digitally reproduced audio performance from the supermarket shortly after the commencement of last week.

Use Standard English and a variety of techniques

'Use Standard English' means that you need to speak in a way that is understood anywhere in the world (by people who know English).

This means not using slang but using English that follows established, standard rules. For example, 'I done it!' does not follow the rules of grammar, but 'I did it!' does.

When you have to listen to boring information, what helps you to concentrate on what the speaker is saying? A 'variety of techniques' means using different ways to keep your audience interested.

- **Who** is the leaflet aimed at?
- **What** information are they given?
- **When** might someone be given this leaflet?
- **Where** might the leaflet be available from?
- **Why** would a person need this leaflet?
- **How** is the leaflet presented so that it helps to give information?

4 Look at the leaflet below giving information on drug driving. Write down exactly what information is provided. See if you can answer the 5W and 1H questions on the right:

COCAINE

Cocaine leads to a sense of over confidence and this is reflected in their driving style. Users typically perform higher risk, more aggressive manoeuvres at greater speeds, which is obviously dangerous.

The specific effects of driving on cocaine are:

- Aggressive manoeuvres
- Speeding
- Poor control of the vehicle
- Erratic driving
- Over-confident, high risk behaviour

The following effects are likely to occur once someone has stopped taking the drug and are related to the fatigue that results from cocaine use:

- Inattentive driving
- Distraction and drowsiness
- Falling asleep at the wheel

ECSTASY

Although it's not a drug that makes people violent, it is extremely dangerous to drive on ecstasy because it results in:

- Distorted vision
- Heightened sounds
- Increased fatigue and tiredness
- Affected perception and judgement of risks

ECSTASY (continued)

- A more aggressive attitude
- Day-after effects similar to cocaine, leading to distraction, drowsiness and inattentive driving

USING MORE THAN ONE DRUG

People often take more than one drug or mix drugs with alcohol. For example – a stimulant like cocaine to 'sharpen up' after having alcohol or cannabis. In fact, combining drugs can have a dramatic and unpredictable effect on the user's state and driving.

WHAT ABOUT LEGAL DRUGS?

Medicine is obtained either on prescription or over the counter because people need to take it for their health. Medicines should always be taken properly. Advice about this is provided on the packaging and in the patient information leaflet supplied and packed in with the medicine. Advice can also be obtained from a doctor who has prescribed the medicine or pharmacist who dispenses it.

If you want more information on drug driving, please visit **www.dft.gov.uk/think/drugdrive**

For confidential drugs information and advice, please visit **www.talktofrank.com**

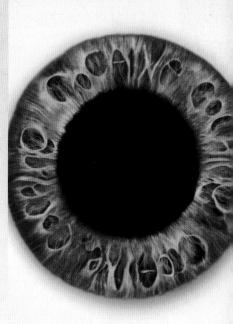

DRUG DRIVING.
YOUR EYES WILL GIVE YOU AWAY.

5 Write a set of instructions to inform a friend how to do something. Choose either how to put on a coat or go to the school office. Read your instructions to a friend and ask them to try them out. Did they work? If not, why not? Did your audience need more information? Did they have too much information?

⟳ Taking it further

So, what have you learnt in this section? Think about the tips and information about good speaking you have been given. Write down two or three sentences explaining what has been the most useful tip or piece of information for you. How do you think it will help you to become a better speaker?

5.2 Presenting information

You will learn at least three things to do and three things to avoid doing when preparing visual aids for a formal information speech.

⊃ For starters

Look at the step-by-step instructions below informing an audience how to measure their shoe size. What makes this informative text successful? What needs improving?

Sometimes, informing and explaining can be very similar.

Many information presentations need images or sound – **visual aids** – to help the audience follow what is being said.

ⓘ Concept bank

Visual aid: an object, poster, image, film clip or prop that will help you to present information in a visual way so that others can **see** what you are talking about.

All you will need to get your proper foot measurement at home is: • A piece of paper larger than your foot • A pencil and a ruler or measuring tape	
Sit with your foot firmly on the floor, and your leg bent slightly forward so that your shin is slightly in front of your ankle. Trace the outline of your foot. Measure your foot without shoes, but with socks like those you'll be wearing with the shoes you are buying. Hold the pencil upright and not at an angle. Make sure the pencil is resting snugly against your foot as you draw around it.	
Use your pencil to draw straight lines touching the outermost points at the top, bottom, and both sides of the outline.	
Use your ruler or measuring tape to measure the length from the bottom line to the top line that you drew in step three. Be sure to hold the measuring tape straight, and find the closest mark that you can (for inches, use the closest 16th mark) – don't round up or down.	
Many people will need a narrow or wide shoe. This step will help you to find the width of your foot. Measure the width of your foot by using your measuring tape or ruler to measure from the line on one side of your tracing, to the line on the other side. Again, be certain to find the closest mark that you can (for inches, use the closest 16th mark). Write this number down.	
Repeat these steps for your other foot, and use the larger of the two. After you have your numbers written down, take away $\frac{3}{16}$ of an inch from the numbers. These final numbers are your actual foot measurements.	

⟳ Task

Barry Hines' book *A Kestrel for a Knave* (1968) tells the story of a day in the life of Billy Casper, a disadvantaged pupil from a poor family, who keeps a kestrel as a pet.

1 Read the extract below where Billy tells his class how to train a kestrel to fly and return to its keeper. Then answer these questions:
   • What facts does he tell us?
   • How clearly has he got his information across?

> Jesses are little leather straps that you fasten round its legs as soon as you get it. She wears these all t'time, and you get hold of 'em when she sits on your glove …
>
> Then you get your swivel, like a swivel on a dog lead, press both jesses together, and thread 'em through t'top ring of it. T'jesses have little slits in 'em near t'bottom, like buttonholes in braces, and when you've got t'jesses through t'top ring o' t'swivel, you open these slits with your finger, and push t'bottom ring through, just like fastening a button.

Look at the version on the right of Billy's information as a PowerPoint presentation.

2 What is wrong with this presentation? How would you make it better so that it gives clear information for an audience of students aged 15 or 16?
3 Working with a partner or small group, look back at what you have learnt in this section and suggest three things that a visual aid must **not** do.
4 Now, thinking about what you have learnt and perhaps some visual aids you remember seeing, think of three good things a visual aid **should** do.
5 Make a list of your 'Top Ten Rules' for a good PowerPoint presentation.

⟳ Taking it further

Create a storyboard for a PowerPoint presentation for your class on a subject of your choice. You might inform them about a hobby or keeping an animal. Perhaps you play an instrument, have a Saturday job or are in a sports team.

First, think of five or six aspects of your topic that you would wish to tell the class about. Then, storyboard the five or six illustrations for your PowerPoint, using your 'Top Ten Rules' of a good presentation.

⬇ *Billy's PowerPoint slides*

5.3 Presenting explanations

You will learn that a good explanation speech must include a variety of facts, reasons, adjectives and adverbs. You will practise how to use them for effect.

↻ For starters

To be successful in role-play, you need to understand the difference between **facts** and **explanation**.

1 Read the newspaper article on the right. Then:
- write down two facts
- write down one explanation – saying why something happened or describing its effect.

2 Read this information about road traffic accidents:

- In 2007, 2946 people were killed on Britain's roads.

- In 2007, a third of road accident deaths were of young people and children under the age of 25.

- One in six teenagers knocked down suffers from Post Traumatic Stress disorder.

- One in five of a group of 70 adults involved in a road accident were unable to do their job eight months later.

- Road accidents cost the country £16,000 million a year.

3 Now read (below) what the charity Brake has to say about the effects of traffic accidents:

DEATHS on our roads

Deaths and serious injuries on roads are violent and sudden, ripping apart families and devastating communities. They result in serious mental conditions, such as Post Traumatic Stress Disorder and depression as well as devastating grief and social consequences, such as loss of work.

Brake's comment is not a brilliant explanation text because it does not include any facts. With a partner, try to improve the comment by rewriting it and adding a couple of facts from the newspaper article in question 1 and the information box in question 2. Try to use some of these phrases:

- this is because
- this means that
- as a result
- this is proved by
- this evidence suggests
- the consequence is that

The number of people killed in road accidents involving alcohol rose last year, from 410 in 2007 to 430 in 2008.   5

The number of drink-drive fatal accidents – where at least one person was killed – also rose, from 370 to 380.

MPs accused the   10
Government of relying too much on speed cameras for road safety, but a spokesman defended its record. 'Thirty years of   15
Government campaigns have succeeded in making drink-driving socially unacceptable and reducing the number of people   20
killed in drink-drive accidents by almost three quarters since 1979.'

ⓘ Concept bank

Fact: a statement that can be checked and proved to be true or false.

Explanation: saying why something happened or describing its effects. Texts that explain often contain facts and figures, like information texts, but they can also give personal opinions and be biased.

⟲ Task

1 You are going to take part in a role-play debate about the proposed building of a new sports centre in a small town. Read the information extract below. The extract was written by the building constructors who want to build the centre. In pairs, find the factual information and any aspects that provide explanation. Then read the newspaper article on the right that also contains information and explanation for use in your role-play. You will need these points to develop your role-play later.

> The site is close to the Eastgate Court sheltered accommodation for the elderly and some two miles from both the primary and secondary schools. It backs onto the Spinney Woods nature reserve and is next to a mixed housing development of local authority and private housing for some 16,000 people.
>
> The proposed development will provide a range of facilities including a play area, swimming pool, sports field, bowling alley and a cafeteria with Internet access.
>
> Building is estimated to take 14 months to complete. During this time, access to two main local roads will be restricted.
>
> It is anticipated that the Crowson Sports Centre will improve a run-down area and provide a facility for all ages to use.

After three years of struggling, the Crowson Court Sports Centre has finally got the go-ahead. Public debates meant   5 that the £2.75 million project was delayed as builders fought to calm fears over damage to the environment and danger   10 to children through increased traffic. Project manager Steve Hill said, 'This is a thumbs up for common sense because   15 the local community will have a place that improves the quality of life for everyone.'

2 You will be given a role to play in a public meeting about whether the proposed sports centre should go ahead. The roles are:
  • the developers
  • local schools
  • residents of the local houses
  • elderly people living in the sheltered accommodation
  • the local nature conservation society
  • teenagers.
Talk about how each type of person (role) might feel about the new sports centre.

3 Make sure that your group is ready for the public meeting:
  • prepare a list of questions to ask the developers
  • prepare a set of views for your group about the development and explanations for your views
  • think about the explanations that others might put forward for their views and be prepared to fight them.

4 Play your role in the public meeting.

⟲ Taking it further

Think about your performance in the role-play. Look back on the notes you made at the beginning of this section about your last speaking and listening assessment. Have you managed to improve? If so, how? If not, what do you need to do next time?

⟐ Grammar link

Adjectives (words that describe a noun) can be used in an explanation text to help explain the effect something has.

Verbs (words that say what something does) can also be used in an explanation text to help explain the effect something has.

5.4 Linking speaking and listening with writing

You will learn the links between speaking and listening and writing. You will learn some features of how to write to advise, ready for the exams.

⊃ For starters

Think back to when you had to choose your options in Year 9. Write down where you could go to get advice about your choices.

Advice can come in many different text types, including spoken ones. It might come in a leaflet, letter, article or a conversation.

⊃ Task

1 Still thinking about the options you faced at the end of Year 9, write three sentences giving useful and sensible advice to a Year 9 student about choosing their options.

2 Working with a partner, listen to each other's sentence and check if you have included the 5Ws and 1H: **w**ho, **w**hat, **w**hen, **w**here, **w**hy and **h**ow. Now rewrite your sentences adding any missing aspects. One way to improve your work is to say it 'aloud' in your head. Ask yourself if what you are writing sounds right for your purpose and audience.

3 Many magazines and newspapers have advice columns. Identify the who, what, where, when, why and how features (5Ws and 1H) of this response to a letter from a mum worried about her son's drinking. Can you find a modal verb too?

🔗 Grammar link

Modal verbs, such as 'could', 'should', 'ought to', 'might' or 'may', are useful when giving advice.

DRINKING becomes a problem

First let me say what a lucky person your son is to have you so concerned about him. If you can find an appropriate time, you should talk to your son and tell him how worried you are. Drinking becomes a problem when it starts to change how well we cope with life and affects our relationships. As alcohol can be very dangerous to health, you do need to get help. There are many places where you can get advice about alcohol. If you log on to the Internet www.nhs.uk has some helpful advice. You could also ring Frank (0800 77 66 00) and talk through your problems with a trained person.

4 Read these letters to an agony uncle and aunt:

Dear Bill,

There is a girl I really like at school but she is two years older than me. Do you think I should ask her out? How can I get to talk to her?

Dear Jane,

I have to do a Saturday job and work three evenings a week to help out with money at home, but I'm always in trouble at school for not doing my coursework on time. What should I do?

You are now going to explore the link between speaking and listening and writing:

5 Discuss with a partner what advice you would give for each problem in the letters.

6 Then, using role-play, try to act out an advice session.

7 Now, using headings 'Who', 'What', 'Where', 'When', 'Why', 'How' (5Ws and 1H), make notes for the responses to the letters. What would you write in your replies?

↻ Taking it further

1 Choosing one of the scenarios above, write a response as though you were the newspaper's agony aunt:

- Start with a sentence or two reassuring the worried person.
- Write one or two sentences about the problem in general terms.
- Move on to some specific advice for the worried person – remember to use conditional verbs such as 'might' and 'could', and to include developed explanations.
- Finish by suggesting places they might go to get extra help.

2 Build your own library of leaflets and agony aunt or agony uncle examples from magazines or online. The more you read, the more you will understand the text type.

5.5 Writing to advise

You will now learn key advice words to use when writing to advise. You will know when to start a new paragraph.

⊃ For starters

Read these two sentences:
- Do your coursework on time.
- You should do your coursework on time because you may have less stress in trying to balance a workload and you might have more time to review your writing and get a higher grade.

The first sentence instructs and the second one advises. What are the differences between them? Find the **connectives** and **explanations** in the writing to advise.

⊃ Task

When you are giving advice, you need to use modal verbs (see Grammar link on the right) that suggest that the reader should do something.

1 Write a sentence using modal verbs giving advice to someone who is falling behind with their school work.

2 Extend and explain your sentence by adding a clause using one of the connectives 'because', 'which' or 'although'.

3 Now write similar sentences for each of the following situations:
- someone going rock climbing (to keep them safe)
- someone who has fallen out with their boyfriend or girlfriend
- someone who wants to do something nice for Mother's or Father's Day.

4 Swap your work with a partner and check each other's sentences carefully. Have you used modal verbs and connectives? Have you included capital letters and full stops? Are all the spellings correct? Have you used other types of punctuation such as a semicolon?

5 Read the notes on the right a student has made for writing a letter of advice to a friend who has recently moved to another part of the country and is finding it hard to make new friends.

Write a letter using a separate paragraph for each of these pieces of advice and give clear reasons for them. Think carefully about how you will link the paragraphs and the order they should be in. Remember to use the right language for your target and audience – this is a friend so be quite personal.

ⓘ Concept bank

Connectives: linking words such as 'because', 'which' or 'although'.

Explanation: saying why something happened or describing its effect.

🔗 Grammar link

Modal verbs, such as 'could', 'should', 'ought to', 'might' or 'may', are useful when giving advice.

🔗 Grammar link

A clause is a part of a sentence. A clause may give extra information.

Connectives are linking words such as 'because', 'which' or 'although'.

A semicolon is a piece of punctuation that looks like this ; . It can join two short, simple sentences together when they are about the same topic.

A paragraph is a section of your writing. A new paragraph starts on a new line.

You begin a new paragraph for a change of:

S **S**peech
P **P**erson
L **L**ocation
A **A**ction
T **T**ime

Tell parents

Join school club

Talk to teachers (other students might be better)

Go to local youth club

Bullying?

⊃ Taking it further

1 Look at the leaflet below. As you discuss it as a class, make a note of all the features that make this an effective leaflet to advise people living in Kent how to protect themselves from flooding.

2 Now turn your letter of advice to the friend who has moved away into a more impersonal advice leaflet using the techniques you learnt about from the Kent flooding leaflet.

BEFORE the Floods

△ Know what the flood warning codes mean

△ On receiving a flood warning, inform your neighbours

△ Plan to allow time to protect your valuables and important documents.

△ Find out whether your Local Council supplies sandbags

△ Consider it may be dark before the flooding arrives - so keep a torch handy

△ Know how to turn off gas and electricity

△ If evacuated, try to tell friends and relatives where you are going

△ Take medication with you along with any food for special dietary needs (such as baby foods)

△ Co-operate with any requests to evacuate your premises

△ If you are evacuated, domestic pets will be cared for by the RSPCA while you are at the rest centre

DURING the Floods

△ Do not return to your property until you have been informed that it is safe

△ Be aware that flooding may not have reached its peak, or may be predicted to return

△ When driving in a flooded area, obey 'Road Closed' signs

△ If driving in a flooded area, drive slowly to avoid making waves which may put rescue workers in danger

△ Respond to the instructions from Police Officers - they have your safety in mind

△ Avoid unnecessary contact with water, it maybe contaminated

△ Pets which are normally kept in tanks or cages should, wherever possible, be left where they are or moved upstairs

AFTER the Floods

△ Gas and electricity should only be restored after consultation with an approved contractor

△ Throw away food that has come into contact with contaminated water - even sealed or tinned food

△ Take photographs or video footage of all flood damage to your property and personal possessions

△ Wear protective clothing when handling debris it may have come into contact with contaminated water

△ Good ventilation is essential to dry your property - remember to lock and secure your property when unoccupied

△ Obtain several quotations before any repairs are undertaken. Consider using locally known and recommended companies

Flooding

Floodline 0845 988 1188　　　　Be prepared for flooding.

Try to include some or all of the following features:
- Advice organised into lists of suggestions and statements
- Formal, impersonal **register**
- Facts and specialist words to make it sound authoritative
- Direct address – 'you'
- Verbs of command and instruction
- Short, powerful sentences
- Prominent helpline phone number (the Childline number is 0800 1111) or other place to get help (for example, the school bullying counsellor)
- A good slogan.

Design your leaflet appropriately for its audience.

ⓘ Concept bank

Register: the way a text sounds to its readers or listeners. This could be formal or informal, bossy, amusing, friendly or cold … or many other registers.

5.6 Writing advice – exam practice

> You will learn how to plan a piece of advice writing, organising ideas in a clear, separate way.

⊃ For starters

Look at the list of techniques (on the right) on how to advise which you have learned in this unit. (You might also wish to look back at the 'Ten features of an advice text' on page 11.)

Discuss these techniques with a friend, making sure you know what they are, how to use them, and what effect they have.

⊃ Task

1 Choose one of the exam questions to do from the *Taking it further* section (below). Use the **APPLE** checklist (on the right) to help you think about how you might approach the question.
   Write down all the ideas for reassurance and advice you can think of to include in your essay; you will need about five different points. For each point you think of, include a reason why they need to do that; this will be useful when you come to explain your points.

Then:

2 First, write a short introductory paragraph explaining why you are writing.
3 Then, organise your points into the best order to present them to your reader and write them up as a series of paragraphs. Start each paragraph with a topic sentence making the point, and then support your point with evidence and a developed explanation.
4 Finish with a paragraph suggesting where they could go for further help and recommending the advice you have given.

⊃ Taking it further

Exam practice

Time allowed: 25 minutes

Choose one of the following:
1 Write a letter to a friend giving them advice about stopping smoking.
2 Write a help sheet advising Year 9 students how to organise a school disco.
3 Write an article for a school magazine advising Year 7 students on how to survive their first day in secondary school. (16 marks)

Writing advice techniques

- Appropriate register, including modal or instructional verbs
- Direct address
- Clear explanations, including connectives, facts and specialist words
- 5Ws and 1H
- Reassurance
- Specific suggestions or instructions
- Where to find further help

Plan your essay so that it:

- suits the **A**udience
- achieves its **P**urpose
- has good **P**resentation
- uses the right **L**anguage
- has a powerful **E**ffect.

! Examiner's tip

Use the 'Good writing techniques' listed on page 48.

5.7 Writing explanations – exam practice

> You will learn how to write an answer to an exam-style question about writing to explain.

Writing explanation techniques

- Facts and specialist words
- Saying why something happened
- Describing the effects of an event
- Connectives (especially 'because', 'which' and 'although')

⟳ For starters

Discuss the list of techniques (on the right) on writing to explain with a friend, making sure you know what they are, how to use them, and what effect they have.

⟳ Task

1 Look at how this student has planned an answer to a question on how to make the most of your time at school. What is good about this plan?

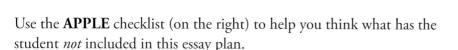

Writing to explain so quite formal

Audience – school so 11–16-year-olds

Explain how to make the most of your time at school

Make the most – paragraph for each:

Lessons and exams

Sports

Clubs, trips, etc.

Friends

The future

Use the **APPLE** checklist (on the right) to help you think what has the student *not* included in this essay plan.

2 Choose one of the exam questions to do from the *Taking it further* section (below) and plan your essay using the **APPLE** checklist.

3 Write down all the reasons you can think of to include in your essay; you will need about five different points.

4 Write up your points as a series of paragraphs. Start each paragraph with a topic sentence making the point, and then support your point with evidence and a developed explanation, using facts and connectives.

Plan your essay so that it:

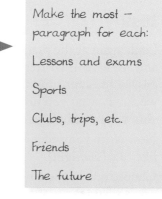

- suits the **A**udience
- achieves its **P**urpose
- has good **P**resentation
- uses the right **L**anguage
- has a powerful **E**ffect.

⟳ Taking it further

Exam practice

Time allowed: 25 minutes

Choose one of the following:

1 Explain why you enjoy a particular sport.
2 Explain why keeping pets is good for children. (16 marks)

! Examiner's tip

Use the 'Good writing techniques' listed on page 48.

5.8 Looking back, looking forward

You will learn exactly what you do well and what you need to do better when you write to inform, explain or advise.

↻ For starters

Think back over the work you have done in this unit. Be prepared to tell the class one thing you can now do better than before and say how you know. It might be that you can paragraph non-fiction writing better because you know how to use a topic sentence. It might be that you know what you need to do when you write in an exam as you can identify audience and purpose in questions. It might be that you know what makes a successful presentation and can tell others what they should do in their presentations.

↻ Task

1 Look again at the mark schemes you have worked with in this unit and see what is written next to the marks you got for your latest answer in exam conditions. Look at your writing with a partner and work out what you need to do to get into the next mark band when you write to advise, explain or inform in the future.

2 Now write yourself a reminder checklist. You might do something like this (see right):

3 Choose one of the written tasks you have done and rewrite at least two paragraphs to make them even better. Some of the things you might do to improve them are:
   • have a clear topic sentence at the beginning
   • use different sentence lengths
   • make vocabulary more, or less, formal to fit the task and audience.

You may wish to use the list of 'Good writing techniques' on page 48 to help you.

Things to remember:

• use a topic sentence at the start of each paragraph

• check full stops and capital letters

• keep thinking about the audience and purpose for each answer.

↻ Taking it further

Make sure you keep collecting examples of different types of texts that inform, explain and advise.

Plan different answers using the titles and ideas in this unit. Practise writing the answers in exam conditions. Give yourself about 15 minutes to plan and 25 minutes to write.

Practice makes perfect!

6.1 'The Charge of the Light Brigade'

This section introduces you to a poem from the Conflict section of your Anthology. You will think about some of the ideas in the poem and learn about how the poet has written it. You will start using a checklist which will help you to read any poem.

In this section you will need a copy of 'The Charge of the Light Brigade' by Tennyson from your Anthology.

'The Charge of the Light Brigade' was written in 1854, in response to the Battle of Balaclava, during the Crimean War, which was fought between England and Russia. Because of a mix-up in orders, the Light Brigade followed a command to ride to the end of a valley and attack the enemy, even though they were outnumbered and outgunned.

⊃ For starters

A way of remembering how to write about poems is simply to think of the checklist **WRITER**:

W **What** is happening in the poem? **Who** is speaking?
R Rhyme, rhythm and structure
I Imagery
T Tone
E Effects
R Response

To practise using the checklist, you need a copy of the poem and six highlighters, or a set of six coloured pencils.

⊃ Task

Use a different coloured pencil to do the highlighting in each of the sections below.

What?

The poem is about an unsuccessful charge towards the enemy guns by soldiers on horseback armed only with sabres. The order to charge was a mistake, but the men obeyed the order without question.

1 Find and highlight the two lines in **stanza** 2 which tell you this.

After charging to the end of the valley and attacking the Russian guns, the Light Brigade turned around and rode back.

2 Find and highlight the line in stanza 4 which tells you this.

3 Did all six hundred return? How do you know? Highlight the lines in stanza 4 and stanza 5 which tell you this.

Who?

Tennyson wrote this poem to celebrate the bravery of the Light Brigade, despite their defeat. He was a well-known public figure and published the poem in a newspaper.

4 What did he want the newspaper readers to do in response to the poem? Highlight the two lines in stanza 6 which tell you this.

Rhyme

5 Highlight all the words in the poem which rhyme with 'hundred'. (Clue: there are seven – two appear twice, and one is a **half rhyme**.) Why might these words be important?

6 'Shell', 'well' and 'Hell' rhyme in stanza 3. Highlight them. What does this tell you about the bravery of the soldiers? Highlight where the words are repeated in stanza 5. This time another rhyming word is added. Highlight it. What was happening to the soldiers and their horses now?

7 'Reply', 'why' and 'die' rhyme in stanza 2. Highlight them. What does this tell you about what the soldiers could and could not do at this point?

8 'Bare', 'air' and 'there' rhyme in stanza 4. Highlight them. What does this tell you about what the soldiers were doing with their sabres? In the same stanza, as the soldiers rode through 'smoke', they 'broke' through the enemy lines and gave them a sabre 'stroke'. How do these rhyming words tell you how well the soldiers were attacking the enemy?

There are lots of technical terms you can use to describe **rhythm**, the 'beat' of a poem, but the best thing you can do is to read it aloud, or listen to someone else read it aloud. Think about how fast or slow, calm or exciting, serious or fun, it sounds.

9 Think about how the sound of horses galloping creates a drumming sound. Stanzas 1, 3, 4 and 5 echo this sound as the soldiers gallop into and then out of the valley.

ⓘ Concept bank

Stanza: a group of lines arranged together in a poem, sometimes called a verse.

Half rhyme: where the rhyme is suggested but is not obvious.

Rhythm: the 'beat' of a poem.

10 Look at the beginning of stanza 2. Do the first two lines sound like horses galloping? Why not? Who is speaking?

11 What about the next two lines? When does the galloping rhythm get going again?

12 Look at stanza 6. Why does the galloping rhythm stop here?

The following questions are about structure.

13 The stanzas are different lengths – count the lines in each. Why might this be?

14 There is a great deal of repetition in the poem. Find an example and think about why repetition is used.

Imagery

You can use the words **metaphor** and **simile** if you like, but if you think you might forget which is which, just talk about images or word pictures.

15 'The valley of Death' – can a valley literally be made of death? What might this mean?

16 In medieval times people imagined that the entrance to hell was rather like a huge dog's mouth – the picture on the right shows an example. What is Tennyson seeing as 'the jaws of Death' and 'the mouth of Hell'?

Tone

17 What does Tennyson think about the actions of the Light Brigade? Highlight the two questions he asks in the poem. Highlight the five exclamations (!) he uses. This will help you answer.

18 'Someone had blunder'd' – who might Tennyson mean?

19 'All the world wonder'd' – the poet uses these words twice. Do you think they mean the same both times? (Hint: 'wonder' can mean to think about something, to worry. It can also mean to be in awe of something, to be impressed.)

Effects

This is where you explain how the poetic techniques which you have found add to the effect of the poem. For example:

> The strong rhythm creates the effect of the cavalry galloping bravely into the valley and then returning. The change in the rhythm when the officer orders the charge creates an exciting and dramatic pause – we wonder if the men will obey. The rhythm changes at the end when Tennyson wonders when the brigade's glory will fade and asks the reader to 'honour' them. This makes us pause and think about his message.

ⓘ Concept bank

Metaphors: compare one thing with another more directly. Example: 'the jaws of Death'.

Similes: compare one thing with another using 'like' or 'as'.

20 Now you try. Match the correct endings to the beginnings of the sentences:

1 The repetition of the words 'six hundred' makes the reader realise that …

2 The words 'flash'd', 'sabring', 'charging' and 'plunged' create the effect that …

3 The words 'reel'd', 'shatter'd' and 'sunder'd' suggest that …

4 The image of the entrance to the valley being like 'the mouth of Hell' creates the effect that …

5 The image of the entrance to the valley being like the 'jaws of Death' makes the reader realise that …

A … what lies ahead will be like hell, a place of torment and pain.

B … the number of soldiers who set out on the charge was not the same number as returned.

C … the British soldiers are charging towards the enemy, attacking them with their sabres and breaking through the enemy line.

D … almost certain death lies ahead and there is no turning back, just as you can not escape when you are in the grip of powerful jaws.

E … the Russian soldiers are shocked and injured in the attack, breaking their ranks apart.

↻ Taking it further

You are now going to look at the last part of the **WRITER** checklist.

Response

English Literature is one of the few exams you will take where you will be asked what you think!

What is your own, personal response to this poem?

• What did it make you think about?

• How did it make you feel?

• How relevant is it to you today?

• How might different people respond to it?

Now write a paragraph of your own.

Here is an example:

At first when I read this poem I did not realise it would be so interesting to me as it is about a battle long ago. The bravery of the soldiers, following an order to charge towards guns, comes across very strongly. Some people might think they were foolish to obey without thinking. However, I agree with Tennyson that even though they were defeated, they were heroes. Today's soldiers also need to obey commands without question and I now realise what bravery this takes.

➔ *Augustus Butler's engraving of the charge of the Light Brigade*

6.2 Comparing 'Flag' with 'The Charge of the Light Brigade'

You will learn about a more modern poem from the Conflict cluster, using the **WRITER** checklist. You will then compare it with 'The Charge of the Light Brigade'.

In this section, you will need a copy of 'The Charge of the Light Brigade' by Tennyson and 'Flag' by John Agard from your Anthology.

⟳ For starters

1 Here are the flags of six countries. Can you identify them?
2 What are flags for? Why do they mean so much to people?
3 You might have seen news stories on TV where people were filmed burning the flags of other countries. Why were they doing this?

⟳ Task

You are going to use the **WRITER** checklist to talk about the poem 'Flag' and to **compare** it with 'The Charge of the Light Brigade'.

Who?

1 Read 'Flag' aloud in pairs, with one person reading the first line in each **stanza**, the other person reading the next two.
2 Now try reading it in different ways:
   • one person reads all the questions, five people read one answer each
   • five people read a question each, one person reads all the answers
   • five people read one stanza each
   • any other way you can think of.
3 How many people might be speaking in the poem?

In these questions you start to compare the two poems.

4 Tennyson asks two questions in his poem. Is there an answer?
5 Agard asks five questions in his poem. What do you think about the answers?
6 What do the questions in each poem make the reader think about?

What?

7 Where do you think you would see the flags described in Agard's poem?
8 Highlight 'just a piece of cloth' wherever you see it. Highlight 'flag'. What do you think John Agard is saying about flags?

Poetry – Contemporary and Heritage

> ### ⓘ Concept bank
>
> **Compare:** to examine people or things for similarities and differences.
>
> **Stanza:** a group of lines arranged together in a poem, sometimes called a verse.

Rhyme, rhythm and structure

9 Find the rhyme in stanzas 1 and 2 of 'Flag'. Which lines rhyme? Highlight the rhyming words.

10 How is the rhyme different in the last stanza?

11 Is there any rhyme in stanza 3?

12 Clap out the beats of each line – you will find there are 4 beats, then 3, then 4. What does this do to the second line of each stanza?

13 What sentence is repeated in the second line of each stanza? How does it change in the last one? Which word stays the same? What do you think John Agard is trying to make us realise about flags?

14 Both poems contain repetition of important words. Both poems use rhyme and rhythm. Can you see any differences, though?

Imagery

Talk to a partner about these questions.

15 How can a nation be brought 'to its knees'? Can this be actually true? What does the image mean?

16 How can 'the guts of men grow bold'?

17 How can a 'piece of cloth' outlive a person?

18 A conscience is something we all have inside of us. Can it really be blinded? What might the poet mean at line 15 of 'Flag'?

19 Both poems use shocking images to make the reader think. Choose an image from either poem which shocked you or made you think.

Tone

20 What is John Agard's attitude to flags? Look at how he repeats the words 'just' and 'cloth'. What does Agard think happens when people take loyalty to a flag and country seriously?

21 Does John Agard admire soldiers in the same way as Tennyson?

Effects

Look at 'flutter**ing**', 'unfurl**ing**', 'ris**ing**' and 'fly**ing**'. The *-ing* endings suggest that this is happening **now**, in the present tense.

22 'The Charge of the Light Brigade' is about a historical event, and is therefore mostly in the past tense. It changes at the end when Tennyson is telling the reader what to do now. Agard ends his poem with an instruction too: 'Just ask for a flag, my friend.' Do you think he means the word 'friend'?

⟳ Taking it further

Response

1 What is your response to 'Flag'? Write a paragraph about your response to 'Flag'. Think about the questions on the right.

2 Look back at your paragraph responding to 'The Charge of the Light Brigade'. Then write a paragraph where you compare your responses to the two poems. Which did you prefer, and why?

Response questions
- What did it make you think about?
- How did it make you feel?
- How relevant is it to you today?
- How might different people respond to it?

6.3 Comparing 'Bayonet Charge' with 'The Charge of the Light Brigade'

> You will learn about another poem from the Conflict cluster, using the **WRITER** checklist to develop your ideas. You will then compare it with 'The Charge of the Light Brigade'.

In this section you will need a copy of 'The Charge of the Light Brigade' by Tennyson and 'Bayonet Charge' by Ted Hughes from your Anthology.

↻ For starters

Talk to your partner about what these statements might mean:
- My country – right or wrong.
- For Queen and Country.

↻ Task

1 Look at the image on the left. What is your first impression of the soldier? What might he be thinking?

2 Look at the image on the right. Imagine that the soldier is caught up in this battle. What might he be thinking now?

Who? What?

Ted Hughes was born in Yorkshire in 1930. His poems are often about nature, but he was also interested in the First World War, in which his father and his uncle had fought. His father was one of only 17 survivors of a whole regiment of Lancashire Fusiliers killed at Gallipoli.

3 On your copy of 'Bayonet Charge', highlight all the words which are to do with war or soldiers. Have you any ideas about when and where this event might have taken place? Does Ted Hughes give you any clues? Compare this with 'The Charge of the Light Brigade', which is about a particular battle on a particular day.

4 Now highlight all the words in 'Bayonet Charge' which are to do with nature. How is the fighting changing the landscape?

Rhyme, rhythm and structure

5 How many stanzas are in the poem? How many sentences? Highlight the beginnings and ends of the sentences. What is happening in each sentence?

6 Highlight the dashes in the first stanza. Highlight the *-ing* words in the first and second stanzas. Copy this sentence and choose two of the words on the right to fill the gaps:

Taken together, the sentence lengths, dashes and *-ing* words suggest that the soldier's movement is .... and ....?

7 Find and highlight the question mark where the action seems to stop for a moment. Why do you think time is 'standing still' here?

Imagery

Hughes uses **similes** and **metaphors** to show the soldier's fear.

8 Line 6: 'He lugged a rifle numb as a smashed arm'. How is the soldier carrying his rifle? Why is this a suitable simile?

9 Line 8: 'Sweating like molten iron from the centre of his chest'. How is the soldier feeling?

10 Line 23: 'His terror's touchy dynamite'. Why might the soldier's fear be 'touchy' and like 'dynamite'?

Tone

Look back at the images on page 69.

11 'The patriotic tear that had brimmed in his eye'. How had the soldier in 'Bayonet Charge' felt when he first joined up? How does he feel now?

12 'King, honour, ...'. What inspired the soldier to join the army?

13 'King, honour, human dignity, etcetera / Dropped like luxuries ...'. Does the soldier still feel like this?

14 Find the line in 'The Charge of the Light Brigade' which emphasises the unquestioning obedience of the soldiers. Could it apply to the soldier in this poem? If not, why not?

Effects

15 Highlight words or phrases which suggest the noises and sights of battle. Which do you think is the most effective?

16 Three colours are used in 'Bayonet Charge'. Find them. Which colours are associated with nature and which with battle?

17 What happens to the hedge, the ploughed field and the hare during the battle?

18 The battle is 'unnatural' and terrifying. Which words or phrases create this effect the best, in your opinion?

slow	relaxed
careful	fast
jerky	calm

ⓘ Concept bank

Similes: compare one thing with another using 'like' or 'as'.

Metaphors: compare one thing with another more directly. Example: 'the jaws of Death'.

⊃ Taking it further

Response

1 What is your response to 'Bayonet Charge'? Write a paragraph about your response. Think about the questions below.

2 Look back at your paragraph responding to 'The Charge of the Light Brigade' or your paragraph about 'Flag'. Write a paragraph comparing 'Bayonet Charge' with either 'The Charge of the Light Brigade' or 'Flag'.

Response questions

- What did it make you think about?
- How did it make you feel?
- How relevant is it to you today?
- How might different people respond to it?

6.4 'You have picked me out …'

You will look at a poem about a real event where ordinary people were caught up in acts of terrorism. You will use the **WRITER** checklist, and images of the day, to understand the poem.

In this section you will need a copy of 'You have picked me out …' by Simon Armitage from your Anthology. This is a section of a longer poem called 'Out of the Blue' written five years after 9/11 – the destruction of the Twin Towers in New York on 11 September 2001.

⊃ For starters

1 In pairs, look at the three images from 9/11. Choose one and write a title or caption for it. Share your choice with another pair.

2 In fours, do the same with another image.

⊃ Task

What? Who?

1 If you did not know already what the poem is about, what evidence could you find that it is about someone trapped in a burning building? Highlight the words or phrases.

2 Simon Armitage is writing as if he is one of the victims of 9/11, using the **first person** – 'me' and 'I'. What happens to him during the poem? Look at what seems to be happening in each stanza.

3 Who is the 'you' he is talking to, do you think?

Rhyme, rhythm and structure

4 How many *-ing* words can you find in the poem? Highlight them. Which are repeated? Just like in 'Bayonet Charge', these words give the impression that everything is happening now, at this moment.

5 Most stanzas begin with a short sentence followed by a longer one. Read aloud just the beginning sentences to your partner – do they tell the story? What details are added by the longer sentences? Why do you think the sentences get shorter towards the end?

🔗 Grammar link

Poets often use the first person – 'me' and 'I' or 'us' and 'we'.

6 There are four questions in the poem – are they all directed to the same person?

7 There is rhyme in the poem but it does not follow a regular pattern. Which pair of rhyming words do you think is the most effective?

Imagery

8 The man is waving from the window of a tower and wonders if he looks quite ordinary from a distance. What does he suggest in stanza 3 that it might look like he is doing? How do these activities compare with what he is **actually** doing?

9 'Wind-milling, wheeling, spiralling, falling' – if you dropped sheets of paper from a high window, or saw leaves fall from a tree, they might look like this. What is being described here, though?

10 In line 15 the trapped man says 'the white of surrender is not yet flying'. Waving a white flag is the traditional way of surrendering or giving up in a battle, so what do you think he means by this? What is he about to do?

Tone

The tone of the poem is very personal and we share the **persona**'s emotions.

11 Find and highlight examples which show where he is:
- hopeful
- scared
- determined
- giving up.

Effects

12 Highlight some examples of **alliteration** (when two or more words have the same first letters) as in '**b**uilding **b**urning'. Which example sounds the best, do you think?

13 Where can you find lots of S sounds? This is called **sibilance**. Where can you find lots of L sounds – not just at the beginnings of words?

14 What short sentence in stanza 5 makes it clear how high up the man is? What other words or images in the poem add to this effect?

Response

15 What is your own, personal response to this poem? Write a paragraph about your response. Think about the questions on the right.

⟳ Taking it further

1 Think about the images of the Twin Towers which you started with. Could you add a line or a phrase from the poem as a caption to any of them?

2 Find or design an image of 9/11 to illustrate the poem. Write three sentences explaining why you chose the image. Present your image to the rest of the group.

ⓘ Concept bank

Persona: where poets write as if they are characters, not themselves. We should be careful of always thinking that the 'I' in a poem is the poet.

Alliteration: repeating the first letters of words, as in '**P**eter **P**iper **p**icked a **p**eck of **p**ickled **p**epper'.

Sibilance: repeating **S** sounds, in the middle as well as the beginning of words.

Response questions

- What did it make you think about?
- How did it make you feel?
- How relevant is it to you today?
- How might different people respond to it?

6.5 Comparing 'Cameo Appearance' with 'You have picked me out ...'

> You will learn about another contemporary poem from the Conflict cluster. You will use the **WRITER** checklist to help you understand it and to compare it with 'You have picked me out ...'.

In this section you will need a copy of 'You have picked me out ...' by Simon Armitage and 'Cameo Appearance' by Charles Simic from your Anthology.

⊃ For starters

Do any of your older relatives tell you stories about being involved in important events or meeting someone famous? Do they ever show you any proof, like a photo or newspaper article? Do you, in fact, believe them? Share your stories in pairs, then fours, then with the whole class.

⊃ Task

What? Who?

Charles Simic was born in Hungary but now lives in the USA. 'Cameo Appearance' may be about his experiences when he was young and living in a Communist country during civil war.

1 What is the experience the speaker is talking about? Who is he talking to? Highlight the words which tell you this.
2 What evidence does he have to convince his audience that he was there? Highlight the words which tell you this.
3 'I had a small, nonspeaking part / In a bloody epic.' The speaker in 'You have picked me out ...' could say this too. Explain why.
4 Both speakers are talking to loved ones. Find a quote which supports this in 'You have picked me out ...' and write it next to the highlighted quote in 'Cameo Appearance'.

Rhyme, rhythm and structure

5 Just as in 'You have picked me out ...', there is not a regular rhyme scheme in 'Cameo Appearance'. In the last stanza there are three pairs of rhyming words – not always at the ends of lines. Can you find them?
6 Copy and complete this sentence:

The poem is structured in ...... stanzas, the first and fourth are ...... lines long and the middle two are ...... lines long. The middle two stanzas are linked by a sentence which runs on.

Imagery

7 Find the image in the first stanza which tells us that the leader is loud and attention-seeking. **Hint:** it is a simile.

8 The speaker is talking to his children. Find and highlight words or phrases in the poem which make you think of children and families.

9 'You have picked me out …' talks about waving a white flag. What is the image of surrender in 'Cameo Appearance'?

10 In both poems the people are not soldiers and are not in control of what is happening to them. Which of these descriptions fits them best: victims, casualties, bystanders or civilians?

Tone

11 Choose an adjective from the box (top right) for each statement:
  • The speaker's attitude to the leader is …
  • The speaker's attitude to the filmmakers is …
  • The speaker's attitude to his children is …

12 Now find a quote from the poem which supports your decision.

Effects

13 Just as in 'You have picked me out …', there are words and phrases in 'Cameo Appearance' to do with death and destruction. Find and highlight three which you think are effective.

14 Like 'You have picked me out …', 'Cameo Appearance' is about being seen or noticed. This time the speeches and crowds are filmed, but not the bombing which followed. Find and highlight all the words in the poem to do with filming and recording.

Response

15 What is your own, personal response to 'Cameo Appearance'? What did it make you think about? How did it make you feel? How relevant is it to you today? How might different people respond to it? Write a paragraph about your response.

⊃ Taking it further

1 Plan and write answers to the exam questions below.

2 Note – if you are using the **WRITER** checklist – that question a is about **What** the poem says (i.e. the 'W' of **WRITER**), and question b is about **how** they say it (i.e. the 'RITE' of **WRITER**)

3 Finish question b with a conclusion comparing your response to the two poems.

loving	critical
mocking	sarcastic
proud	impatient
bitter	

⊄ Grammar link

Discourse markers – including words such as 'however' and 'so' – let the reader know where the argument in a text is going.

Discourse markers of similarity include:
• **Similarly**…
• **Equally**…
• **In the same way**…

Discourse markers of difference include:
• **By contrast**…
• **On the other hand**…
• **However**…

They are very useful in an exam essay comparing two poems.

! Examiner's tip

To compare how the two poems deal with their subject, take each of the four points of comparison (RITE) in turn and:

1 For the first poem:
  • say what it does
  • give an example
  • explain the effect.

2 … put a discourse marker of similarity or difference …

3 Repeat for the second poem.

Exam practice ⚙

Time allowed: 45 minutes

Answer both parts (a) and (b):
a What attitudes to conflict are shown in 'You have picked me out …'
b Compare the ways that attitudes to conflict are shown in this poem and one other poem from the Conflict cluster. (36 marks)

(i) **Concept bank**

Stanza: a group of lines arranged together in a poem, sometimes called a verse.

I am very bothered when I think
of the bad things I have done
 in my life.
Not least that time in the
 chemistry lab
when I held a pair of scissors
 by the blades
and played the handles
in the naked lilac flame of the
 Bunsen burner;
then called your name, and
 handed them over.

O the unrivalled stench of
 branded skin
as you slipped your thumb and
 middle finger in,
then couldn't shake off the two
 burning rings. Marked,
the doctor said, for eternity.

7.1 One writer – Simon Armitage

> You will read and think about some poems by Simon Armitage and practise using the **WRITER** checklist. You can use this checklist for writing a response to any poem.

⊃ For starters

A good way to remember how to write about a poem is to use the **WRITER** checklist:

W **What** is happening in the poem?
 Who is speaking?
R Rhyme, rhythm and structure
I Imagery
T Tone
E Effects
R Response.

1 Read this first **stanza** (top left) of the poem by Simon Armitage.
2 **What** trick does the speaker play? (Do not try this yourself!)
3 **Who** is the speaker? Is it the poet? Or someone else? How long ago do you think this 'bad thing' happened?

⊃ Task

You can usually get a good idea of what a poem is about by just reading it carefully. The poet wants you to understand the poem.

1 How 'bothered' do you think the speaker really is?
2 Reading the second stanza (bottom left), the results of the 'trick'

become clear. The speaker's victim has been scarred ('marked') for life. But what do the words 'rings' and 'eternity' make you think of?

The third stanza (below right) gives more information.

3 Read a student's response below to the poem, answering:
  • What do you think the speaker feels about the incident?
  • How does the poet present the speaker's feelings?
  She is using the **WRITER** checklist. Where is she using each letter?

The speaker makes his feelings clear in the first line. He is 'very bothered' and he classes the incident in the chemistry lab as one of the 'bad things' he has done in his life. He is remembering a time at school when he heated up a pair of scissors in a Bunsen burner flame and then gave them to a girl he liked. She was scarred for life. 5

The poem does not have a clear rhythm, it just sounds like someone talking. There is not a strict rhyme scheme, though 'skin' and 'in' rhyme, maybe because this is an important moment, when the girl is actually hurt. In the next line 'rings' is a half rhyme, which tells us some more about the marks on her 'skin' when she put her fingers 'in'. The poem is structured in three stanzas. The first one tells us what the speaker did. The second one tells us the results of his behaviour. The third stanza tells us what the boy might have meant by it. 10 15

The images in the poem are horrible but also romantic. A 'naked flame' sounds dangerous but this one is 'lilac', which is a soft, romantic colour. The girl's skin is 'branded' and there is a 'stench' as her skin burns, but 'rings' and 'eternity' are words which remind me of marriage. 20

The tone of the poem is mixed too. He says he is sorry, but then in line 8 he seems to enjoy the smell of burning skin! In the last stanza he seems to be trying to explain to the girl what he was trying to do when he hurt her, but then he also says, 'Don't believe me...'. I don't really know what he thinks! 25

Overall the effect of the poem is confused. He has done something really horrible at the age of 13 and seems to be trying to apologise for it. I am not sure I would accept the apology if I was the girl, though I do think very immature boys sometimes try to get girls' attention by doing daft things. 30

Don't believe me, please, if I say
that was just my butterfingered
   way, at thirteen,
of asking you if you would
   marry me.

ⓘ Concept bank

Half rhyme: where the rhyme is suggested but is not obvious.

➲ Taking it further

1 In pairs, choose one of these Simon Armitage poems from your Anthology: 'The Clown Punk', 'A Vision', 'Give' or 'The Manhunt'.

2 Read it carefully. Who is speaking and what is the poem about?

3 Present your ideas to other pairs who have chosen your poem. Do you all agree? You may not – the question 'What is the meaning of this poem?' does not always have a 'right' or 'wrong' answer.

7.2 Forming opinions on poetry

You will form an opinion about a Simon Armitage poem. You will also practise using the **WRITER** checklist.

For starters

A local business has offered free concert tickets to a group of students who can show that they deserve a treat.

1 What reasons would you give to try to win a ticket? Talk to your partner about it.
2 Then join with another two pairs. Who do you think came up with the best reasons?

Task

1 Form five groups and each take one of these Simon Armitage poems from your Anthology:
   - 'The Clown Punk'
   - 'Give'
   - 'A Vision'
   - 'The Manhunt'
   - 'Harmonium'.

2 Read your poem together in your group.
3 In your group, use the **WRITER** checklist to organise your ideas about the poem. One person should be responsible for writing them down, but everyone should give suggestions.
4 Now talk about parts of the poem you enjoyed or found difficult or found easy.
5 Is this a good poem for GCSE students to study? Why or why not?

Your task is now to persuade the rest of the class that your poem **is** a good one for GCSE students to study, and that it should stay in the Anthology.

6 Read your poem to the other groups and present your reasons for keeping it in the Anthology.
7 After all the groups have presented their poem, the class votes on which poem to keep. Each student has one vote. You do not have to vote for the poem you presented, if another group has done a good job of convincing you about their poem. The poem with the fewest votes will be 'thrown out' of the Anthology.

Taking it further

Choose one of the four poems presented by other groups. Use the **WRITER** checklist to make notes on this chosen poem.

7.3 Poetry stories

You will read two poems which tell a story and will use another checklist (**DISC**) to help you write about them.

⟳ For starters

1 Did you have an imaginary friend when you were young? Do you know anyone who did? Why do small children imagine friends? Share your ideas with a partner.

2 Can you remember a time when you hurt yourself as a small child? What did you learn from the experience? How do you think your parents or carers felt? Share your stories in groups.

⟳ Task

Read the poem 'Brendon Gallacher' by Jackie Kay:

He was seven and I was six, my Brendon
    Gallacher.
He was Irish and I was Scottish, my Brendon
    Gallacher.
His father was in prison; he was a cat burglar.   5
My father was a **communist party**
    full-time worker.
He had six brothers and I had one, my Brendon
    Gallacher.

He would hold my hand and take me by the river   10
where we'd talk all about his family being poor.
He'd get his mum out of Glasgow when he got older.
A **wee holida** some place nice. Some place far.
I'd tell my mum all about my Brendon Gallacher

how his mum drank and and his daddy was a   15
    cat burglar.
And she'd say, 'Why not have him round to dinner?'
No, no, I'd say, he's got big holes in his trousers.
I like meeting him by the **burn** in the open air.
Then one day after we'd been friends for two years,   20

One day when it was pouring and I was indoors,
My mum says to me, 'I was talking to Mrs Moir
who lives next door to your Brendon Gallacher.
Didn't you say his address was 24 Novar?
She says there are no Gallachers at 24 Novar.   25

There never have been any Gallachers next door.'
And he died then, my Brendon Gallacher,
flat out on my bedroom floor, his spiky hair,
his impish grin, his funny, flapping ear.
Oh Brendon. Oh my Brendon Gallacher.   30

Communist party: a political party which works for equal rights for ordinary people.

Wee holida: little holiday.

Cat burglar: person who steals from houses by climbing into an upper storey.

Burn: stream.

Another checklist which you can use to write about poems is **DISC** (right). Use the **DISC** checklist to talk with your partner about the following questions.

Diction

1 What do you think is the speaker's accent?
2 Are there any words in the poem which are not **Standard English**?
3 Is the speaker talking to us formally or informally?

Imagery

4 Look at the description of Brendon in the last stanza. What details of his appearance are given? Can you imagine what he looks like?
5 Did he really 'die'?

Sound

6 Read the last word of each line aloud. What do you notice about how they sound?
7 There is some **alliteration** (repeating of first letters of words) in the last stanza – can you find it? What effect does it have?

Structure

8 How many **stanzas** are there? How many lines in each?
9 What three words are repeated throughout the poem? Why do you think this is?

Comparison

You will come to this when you have read a second poem.

Jackie Kay tells a story about having an imaginary friend. In this next poem, Vernon Scannell tells a story about his son having an accident:

D Diction – the language used in the poem

I Imagery – the word pictures or images in the poem

S **Sound** and **structure** – the way the poem sounds and the way a poem is organised

C Comparison – comparing poems

ⓘ Concept bank

Standard English: writing or speaking that is generally accepted as grammatically correct.

Alliteration: repeating the first letters of words, as in 'Peter Piper picked a peck of pickled pepper'.

Stanza: a group of lines arranged together in a poem, sometimes called a verse.

My son aged three fell in the nettle bed.
'Bed' seemed a curious name for those green spears,
That **regiment** of spite behind the shed:
It was no place for rest. With sobs and tears
The boy came seeking comfort and I saw   5
White blisters beaded on his tender skin.
We soothed him till his pain was not so raw.
At last he offered us a watery grin,
And then I took my **billhook**, **honed** the blade
And went outside and slashed in fury with it   10
Till not a nettle in that fierce parade
Stood upright any more. And then I lit
A funeral **pyre** to burn the fallen dead,
But in two weeks the busy sun and rain
Had called up tall **recruits** behind the shed: 15
My son would often feel sharp wounds again.

Regiment: a large unit or group of soldiers.

Billhook: a short curved blade used to cut back weeds in gardening or farming.

Honed: sharpened.

Pyre: a pile of material on which to burn a dead body.

Recruits: people who have just joined the army.

Read the poem 'Nettles' by Vernon Scannell on page 79.

Use the **DISC** checklist (right) to talk to your partner about the following questions.

Diction

10 Is the speaker talking to us formally or informally?

11 What are his feelings as he tells the story? How do you know?

Imagery

12 Find the words in the poem which are to do with soldiers or war. Why do you think the nettles are described in this way?

Sound

13 Read the last word of each line aloud. What do you notice about how these words sound?

14 There is some **alliteration** in line 6 – can you find it? What effect does it have?

Structure

15 How many **stanzas** are there?

16 Does the poem have a regular rhythm? Read it aloud. What is the effect?

Comparison

17 The speakers in the poems are different. How?

18 The poems are different in their use of imagery. How?

19 Both poems use alliteration. Which do you prefer and why?

20 The poems are structured differently. One poem has a strict rhyme scheme, one does not. What do you think of the difference?

↻ Taking it further

1 Using all the ideas you have talked about for both poems, design a poster which shows the **DISC** reading you have done of one of the poems. You may draw or use computer-generated images to illustrate the poem but you should also show examples of diction, imagery, sound and structure, using quotations from the poem.

2 Once you have finished, you could join up with someone who did the other poem for their poster and produce a linking comparison poster.

The posters can be displayed to help others revise the poems.

D Diction – the language used in the poem

I Imagery – the word pictures or images in the poem

S **Sound** and **structure** – the way the poem sounds and the way a poem is organised

C Comparison – comparing poems

ⓘ Concept bank

Alliteration: repeating the first letters of words, as in 'Peter Piper picked a peck of pickled pepper'.

Stanza: a group of lines arranged together in a poem, sometimes called a verse.

7.4 Writing a response to an unseen poem

You will learn how to use the **WRITER** checklist to write your response to an unseen poem. You will look at a detailed example showing how this checklist can be used and then you will practise using the **WRITER** checklist on a second poem.

⊃ For starters

Beat the clock!

1 Think about the last poem you studied in class.
2 In 60 seconds, tell your partner everything you can remember about it.
3 Now your partner should tell you anything you missed out – again in 60 seconds.
4 What sorts of things did you remember?
   • Interesting images?
   • The story?
   • The rhyme?
5 What did your partner remember?

Different people are affected by poems in different ways. This is why the final **R** of **WRITER** is so important. It is your **response** that the examiner is interested in.

⊃ Task

1 Read or listen to the poem 'The Falling Leaves' by Margaret Postgate Cole:

> Today, as I rode by,
> I saw the brown leaves dropping from their tree
> In a still afternoon,
> When no wind whirled them whistling to the sky,
> But thickly, silently,   5
> They fell, like snowflakes wiping out the noon;
> And wandered slowly thence
> For thinking of a gallant multitude
> Which now all withering lay,
> Slain by no wind of age or pestilence,   10
> But in their beauty strewed
> Like snowflakes falling on the Flemish clay.

2   Look at the table below and on the next page. It shows how to use the **WRITER** checklist to write about this poem. The **WRITER** questions column lists questions to ask about the poem. The Responses column shows answers to the questions – examples of what you could write about this poem.

W **What** is happening in the poem?
    Who is speaking?
R Rhyme, rhythm and structure
I Imagery
T Tone
E Effects
R Response

	WRITER questions	Responses to 'The Falling Leaves'
W **Who is speaking?**	• First person (I) or not? • Is it the poet speaking or a **persona** created by the poet? • Could it be anyone speaking? • Is there a 'you' spoken to in the poem?	• Written in the first person. • It could be the poet herself speaking. • The poem is not addressed to anyone in particular. The person speaking is sharing her thoughts.
W **What is happening?**	• What happens in the poem? • When do the events take place? • What has happened previously? • What will happen next?	• The speaker sees leaves falling from the trees as she is out riding one autumn afternoon. • She thinks about the 'gallant multitude' who lie dead on 'Flemish clay' – the First World War dead. • Perhaps she wants us to think about them too.
R **Rhyme**	• Is there a regular rhyme scheme? • Can you find rhyme anywhere else? • Is there any reason you can think of for the words being rhymed?	• Words at the end of lines rhyme following this regular pattern: ABCABCDEFDEF. • The meaning of words which rhyme is emphasised – 'lay' and 'clay', 'multitude' and 'strewed' suggests bodies on the battlefield.
R **Rhythm**	• Read the poem to yourself, noticing the number of strong beats in each line. Are they all the same? • Does the rhythm make you read the poem quickly or slowly, or a mixture?	• Line 1 has 3 strong beats, line 2 has 5. This pattern is followed in the rest of the poem. • The shorter lines make us hesitate and think a bit more about what is being described. The longer lines are about the movement of the leaves or snowflakes.

	WRITER questions	Responses to 'The Falling Leaves'
R **... and Structure**	• How many stanzas are there? • Do they each deal with something different? • How many sentences are there? • Do any of them run over stanzas? • Are short sentences used for effect?	• One stanza of 12 lines, structured by a rhyme scheme. • There is just one sentence, showing that the speaker is describing one short event. • There is a turning point after the semicolon in line 6, when the speaker thinks about the soldiers as she wanders away from the tree.
I **Imagery**	• What word pictures or images does the poem suggest to you? • Are there any similes – comparisons using 'like' or 'as'? • Are there any metaphors – comparisons which say something is something else?	• The falling leaves suggest the falling of soldiers in battle. • 'Like snowflakes' is used twice, the first time about the leaves, the second time about the soldiers. • 'Withering' and 'strewed' suggest the soldiers are flowers dying.
T **Tone**	• What mood does the poem create in the reader? • What is the attitude of the speaker or poet? Serious, angry, sad, regretful, amused, bored, cynical, objective, passionate … Choose your own word!	• The still autumn afternoon creates a calm feeling but by the end the tone is regretful, sad. • The speaker is thoughtful, admiring the 'gallant' soldiers' 'beauty' and regretting that they have been 'slain'.
E **Effects**	• Are there any sound effects such as alliteration – repeating the first letters of words – or onomatopoeia – words which sound like the sound described? • Which are the most important poetic effects you have noticed?	• 'No wind whirled them whistling' is alliteration and onomatopoeia, suggesting the sound of wind blowing leaves – which is <u>not</u> happening here, so the stillness is emphasised even more. • The sheer numbers of the soldiers are suggested by snowflakes and leaves, which are impossible to count.
R **Response**	• How did you respond to this poem? What did it make you think about or feel? • How do you think the poet wanted you to respond? • Was the poet successful?	• The poem made me think about the waste of war, especially in the First World War, when thousands of young men were killed in France and Belgium. • The poet wants us to remember them, how brave and handsome they were. • The poem does not really talk about the reality of war. It is a bit general for me.

Poetry – Unseen

➲ Taking it further

Using this analysis of 'The Falling Leaves' as a model, select another poem from the Anthology (for example, 'Out of School' by Hal Summers).

Use the **WRITER** checklist to analyse the poem, answering all the questions in the '**WRITER** questions' column of the table on these pages.

7.5 Exam practice for poetry – unseen

In this unit you have been learning to write a response to unseen poems. In this section, you will practise these skills by answering an exam-style question.

⊃ For starters

Remind yourself of the **WRITER** checklist you have been using to write about unseen poetry.

⊃ Task

Use the **WRITER** checklist and the suggested questions on pages 82–83 to make notes on 'A Good Poem' by Roger McGough:

> I like a good poem
> one with lots of fighting
> in it. Blood, and the
> clanging of armour. Poems   5
>
> against Scotland are good,
> and poems that defeat
> the French with crossbows.
> I don't like poems that
>
> aren't about anything.   10
> Sonnets are wet and
> a waste of time.
> Also poems that don't
>
> know how to rhyme.
> If I was a poem   15
> I'd play football and
> get picked for England.

⊃ Taking it further

Exam practice

Time allowed: 30 minutes

Answer both parts (a) and (b):

a What is the speaker's attitude to poetry?
b How does Roger McGough show us this attitude? (18 marks)

! Examiner's tip

Note, if you are using the **WRITER** checklist, that:

- question a is about **What** the poem says (i.e. the 'W' part of **WRITER**)
- question b is about **how** they say it (i.e. the 'RITE' part of **WRITER**).

8

Creating a Personal Voice

Learning aim

This unit will help you prepare for the Creative Writing Controlled Assessment Task. You will learn how to write in an interesting way about people, places and events from your life.

8.1 Introducing personal writing

> You will learn how to write interesting sentences to describe a person. You will write a chatty text about yourself.

⊃ For starters

1 People have always enjoyed writing and talking about themselves! In the past, people often used diaries and letters to tell others about themselves and their experiences. What methods do we use today to tell other people about ourselves? Discuss your ideas with a partner.

2 Why are social networking sites and reality TV programmes so popular today?

⊃ Task

1 Find out, and write down, three facts about your partner.

2 Turn these three facts into a paragraph. Add detail and description to introduce your partner in an interesting way. Use the examples about Natalie below to help you.

See how:
Natalie is 14.
She lives in Bournemouth.
She lives with her parents and two sisters.

becomes:
Natalie is a friendly 14-year-old girl who lives in the beautiful seaside town of Bournemouth with her parents and two younger sisters, Lucy and Claire.

Adjectives = **friendly**, **beautiful**

Precise detail = **girl**, **seaside town**, **younger**

3 Now add two more sentences to your paragraph. Aim to add two or three more pieces of information about your partner.

⊃ Taking it further

In your Controlled Assessment Task, you should show that you are able to write 'clearly, effectively and imaginatively' and that you are able to 'engage the reader'. The following activities will help you to build these skills.

1 Read this blog entry from an up-and-coming popstar.

Hi Guys,

I've spent what feels like the past 24 hours on the set of my new (and first!) music video. It's the video for my single 'Out of This World' which will be released in about a month's time. The director's idea was to make it a futuristic, space-age love story so we were all dressed in super-shiny silver suits. But, rather than feeling like a sexy astronaut, I just felt like I should have been a contestant on '**Hole in the Wall**'! Sad, eh? To make it even worse, we were filming in the middle of a snow storm! Very bizarre … Do they even have snow on the moon?! It was such a long day but now I'm just really excited to see the final, finished product. Everyone I worked with was so experienced and professional, I just know they'll make it look fantastic; it'll be amazing when I see it on MTV, I just can't believe how far I've come in such a short space of time. Listen out for the song next month and keep those eyes peeled for my shiny suit on the music channels – you really can't miss it!

Catch ya later!

'**Hole in the Wall**': a television game show where they dress in silver suits

2 Find an example of each of these devices in the blog:
- humour
- **colloquialisms**
- **adjectives**.

3 Write five sentences about something you have done recently:
- **Sentence 1:** introduce what you have been doing.
- **Sentence 2:** explain what you wore – can you make a funny joke about this?
- **Sentence 3:** write about what the weather was like and how it affected your day.
- **Sentence 4:** sum up how you felt about what you did – for example, did you enjoy it or hate it?
- **Sentence 5:** explain why you felt this way about it.

4 Rewrite your five sentences. Add colloquialisms, humour and adjectives to present yourself in an interesting way.

ⓘ Concept bank

Colloquialisms: informal words or phrases, including slang. Example: 'Hi Guys'.

Adjective: a word which describes a noun (a thing, object or person). Example: '**silver** suits'.

⬡ Grammar link

Using punctuation is important. Commas will help you add more detail and keep your writing well structured.

8.2 Writing about people

You will learn three language devices which will help you write interesting passages about people. You will write descriptively about a person who has been important to you, using **similes**, **metaphors** and **emotive language**.

⊃ For starters

We all have people in our lives who have helped us become who we are today. Who are the people that have had the most positive impact on your life so far?

Choose three people and discuss with a partner why each one is important or memorable to you. Are there any specific memories or events connected to each person?

Use the **S3QR** checklist on the right to read the extract below, taken from Roald Dahl's autobiography *Boy*. Here, Dahl writes about Captain Hardcastle, a teacher from his boarding school.

> ### ⓘ Concept bank
>
> **Similes:** compare one thing with another using 'as' or 'like'. Example: He ran as fast as lightning.
>
> **Metaphors:** compare one thing with another more directly. Example: Her eyes were sparkling diamonds.
>
> **Emotive language:** words or phrases which describe the writer's emotions and/or make the reader feel a certain way.

S3QR stands for: **S**kim it, ask what **3 Q**uestions it is answering, then **R**ead it carefully.

This man was slim and wiry and he played football. On the football field he wore white running shorts and white gymshoes and short white socks. His legs were as hard and thin as ram's legs and the skin around his calves was almost exactly the colour of mutton fat. [5] The hair on his head was not ginger. It was a brilliant dark vermilion, like a ripe orange, and it was plastered back with immense quantities of brilliantine in the same fashion as the Headmaster's. The parting in his hair was [10] a white line straight down the middle of the scalp, so straight it could only have been made with a ruler. On either side of the parting you could see the comb tracks running back through [15] the greasy orange hair like little tramlines. Captain Hardcastle sported a moustache that was the same colour as his hair, and oh what a moustache it was! A truly terrifying sight, a thick orange hedge that sprouted and flourished [20] between his nose and his upper lip and ran clear across his face from the middle of one cheek to the middle of the other. But this was not one of those nailbrush moustaches, all short and clipped and bristly. Nor was it long and droopy [25] in the walrus style. Instead, it was curled most splendidly upwards all the way along as though it had had a permanent wave put into it or possibly curling tongs heated in the mornings over a tiny flame of methylated spirits. The only [30] other way he could have achieved this curling effect, we boys decided, was by prolonged upward brushing with a hard toothbrush in front of the looking-glass every morning …

Captain Hardcastle was never still. His orange [35] head twitched and jerked perpetually from side to side in the most alarming fashion, and each twitch was accompanied by a little grunt that came out of the nostrils.

| Find a simile. What impression of Captain Hardcastle does it create? | Find a metaphor. What impression does it create? | Find some emotive language. What impression does it create? |

⟳ Task

1 Answer the questions in the boxes underneath the extract on page 87. Think carefully about the different devices Dahl has used to describe the teacher.

2 Give the Roald Dahl passage a mark out of 10 for how good it is at describing Captain Hardcastle. Then explain why you gave the mark you did.

⟳ Taking it further

In your Controlled Assessment Task, you may be asked to write descriptively about a person who is important to you. The following tasks will help you practise the planning and drafting that you will need to do for this.

1 Think back to the special people from your life that you were talking about earlier in this section. Choose one person you would now like to write about.

2 Write down at least five details about this person. You could write down notes on:

- **their appearance** – for example, their height, hair colour or the clothes they wear
- **their personality** – for example, are they funny, clever or kind?
- **their skills or hobbies** – for example, a great darts player, a good cook.

3 Turn these details into five simple sentences.

4 Add a simile, metaphor or emotive language to each sentence for description.

See how:
Uncle Frank is really tall.

Becomes:
Terrifying Uncle Frank **is a giant**; he towers over me **like a block of flats**.
Emotive = **terrifying**   Metaphor = **is a giant**
Simile = **like a block of flats**

5 Turn your five descriptive sentences into a paragraph of writing introducing your person.

⟐ Grammar link

Remember, commas can be used to punctuate lists, which are really useful when you are writing detailed character descriptions.

8.3 Writing about place

You will learn two language devices which will help you to write interesting passages describing places. You will write about a place you know, using opinions and personal pronouns.

⊃ For starters

We all have special places – they might be our home town, which we know really well, or a holiday destination we have visited only once.

1 What places are special or important to you and why?
2 What memorable places have you visited? What made them memorable?
3 Where have you really enjoyed visiting or really hated visiting?
4 Discuss your thoughts with your partner.

Use the **S3QR** checklist on the right to read the extract below about Bill Bryson's experience of visiting Liverpool.

I took a train to Liverpool. They were having a festival of litter when I arrived. Citizens had taken time off from their busy activities to add crisp packets, empty cigarette boxes, and carrier-bags to the otherwise bland and neglected landscape. They fluttered gaily in the bushes and brought colour and texture to   5
pavements and gutters. And to think that elsewhere we stick these objects in rubbish bags …

Here's a piece of advice for you. Don't go on the **Mersey** ferry unless you are prepared to have the famous song by **Gerry and the Pacemakers** running through your head for about eleven days   10
afterwards. They play it when you board the ferry and they play it when you get off and for quite a lot of time in between. I went on it the following morning thinking a bit of a sitdown and a cruise on the water would be just the way to ease myself out of a killer hangover, but in fact the inescapable sound of 'Ferry 'cross the   15
Mersey' only worsened my cranial plight. Apart from that, it must be said that the Mersey ferry is an agreeable, if decidedly breezy, way of passing a morning. It's a bit like the Sydney Harbour cruise, but without Sydney …

Now don't get me wrong. I'm exceedingly fond of Liverpool. It's   20
probably my favourite English city. But it does rather feel like a place with more past than future. Leaning on a deck rail gazing out on miles of motionless waterfront, it was impossible to believe that until quite recently – and for two hundred proud and prosperous years before that – Liverpool's ten miles of docks and shipyards provided employment for   25
100,000 people, directly or indirectly.

S3QR stands for: **S**kim it, ask what **3 Q**uestions it is answering, then **R**ead it carefully.

What does Bryson think about Liverpool? Identify three phrases which show his different views.

Does the writing make you want to visit Liverpool? Find three phrases and explain how they make you feel about this place.

What techniques does Bryson use to keep the reader interested as they are reading?

Mersey: a river in Liverpool. You can travel on the river Mersey on a ferry.

Gerry and the Pacemakers: a 1960s rock-and-roll group from Liverpool. They sang a song about the ferry across the river Mersey.

⊃ Task

Travel writing allows people to share their experiences of different places, people and cultures with others. Travel writing describes places with lots of detail so that the reader can imagine being there. Travel writers use different techniques to keep the reader interested in their writing.

1 Discuss with a partner your ideas and answers to the questions in the boxes beside the extract on page 89.

2 Answer in detail these questions about Bryson's technique:
   - What **personal pronouns** does Bryson use? What effect is created?
   - What examples of colloquial language (**colloquialisms**) can you find? What effect do they have?
   - Can you find a **fact** and an **opinion**? What is the effect of using both in a piece of travel writing?

⊃ Taking it further

The following activities will take you through the planning and drafting that you will need to do for a piece of writing. It is really important to do this for your Controlled Assessment Task.

1 Choose a place you know well or that means a lot to you.

2 Make notes on the specific details about that place:
   - What is the weather like?
   - What buildings or scenery can you see?
   - Is it busy, with lots of people? Or quiet and peaceful?
   - What smells fill the air?
   - What different noises can you hear? Think carefully about even the quietest ones.
   - How do you feel in this place – excited, happy, scared? Try to say why.

3 Use your notes to write at least six simple sentences about your place.

4 Now, write a paragraph or two introducing this place in 100–200 words. Add detail and description to your sentences, using the checklist for travel writing on this page to help you.

ⓘ Concept bank

Personal pronouns: words which indicate the person/people being spoken about: 'I', 'me', 'my' – first person pronouns; 'you', 'your' – second person pronouns; 'they', 'their' – third person pronouns.

Colloquialisms: informal words or phrases, including slang. Example: 'Hi Guys'.

Fact: a statement that can be checked and proved to be true or false.

Opinion: one person's thoughts or feelings about something – other people may not agree.

Checklist for travel writing:

✓ simile

✓ metaphor

✓ emotive language

✓ personal pronouns

✓ fact

✓ opinion

✓ humour.

⊡ Grammar link

Using a range of sentence types and sentence structures can help prevent your writing from becoming boring or repetitive. Follow a long sentence by a short one to add impact and keep the reader interested.

← When choosing a place, you could select somewhere you have been on holiday or for a day trip.

8.4 Writing about events

You will organise your memories about something into a piece of writing. You will use three language devices to add interest to your writing.

⊃ For starters

What happy events from your life stand out in your memory? Have any situations helped to shape you into the person you are today? Have there been any special occasions you have shared with friends or family?

Spend a few minutes sharing your thoughts with a partner.

There are many important events in our lives which help us become the people we are.

⊃ Task

A major event which we have all been through is the first day at secondary school!

1   Begin by writing down all the things you remember about this day, using the questions below to prompt you. Do not worry – your ideas do not need to be in any particular order. You will look at organising your writing later.

Who did you share the day with?

What did you hear?

What did you see?

Did you meet anyone new?

What were you thinking about?

How did you feel?

How did you look?

What smells and tastes did you come across?

2   Use a flowchart to organise your memories about the day into the order that they happened. Complete a flowchart with five to six stages.
3   For each stage on the flowchart, add at least three specific details. If you cannot remember everything, just make it up!

⊃ **Taking it further**

You have now had lots of practice at planning a piece of writing in preparation for your Controlled Assessment Task. You are now going to focus on writing up the notes in your plan with lots of detail. The following activities will help you to add strong description using a range of the devices you have looked at in this unit.

1 Look at the following passage. Here a student remembers the moment that she first walked through the school doors.

> Nervously, I reached for the cold, grey handle. My palms felt clammy. Pulling the heavy door open allowed a loud, threatening wave of sound to wash over me. Looking around, I could see boys and girls scurrying in all directions like ants trying to escape from the foot   5
> of an enormous elephant! They all seemed to know someone else, or at least where they were going; I felt completely alone. Suddenly, I was jolted forward by a boy who towered over me like a giant.
>
> 'Shove it, squirt!' he yelled aggressively at me.   10
>
> 'Aw, leave her, she's only a little year 7 – you were like that once,' his girlfriend teased. Then, laughing manically, they disappeared into the sea of faces in front of me.

2 Think about the five senses: sight, sound, touch, taste and smell. Which of the senses have been used in this piece of writing? Give an example from the text for each sense you find.

3 Find an example of some of the language devices we have looked at in this unit. Use the checklist for personal writing below to help you.

> **Checklist for personal writing:**
> ✓ adjectives
> ✓ similes
> ✓ metaphors
> ✓ emotive language
> ✓ personal pronouns.

4 Choose one of the boxes from your flowchart about one of your memories from the first day at secondary school.

5 Write a paragraph or two about this memory using three devices from the checklist for personal writing.

Challenge! Add a short section of direct speech to introduce a person.

ⓘ **Concept bank**

Adjective: a word which describes a noun (a thing, object or person).

Similes: compare one thing with another using 'as' or 'like'.

Metaphors: compare one thing with another more directly.

Emotive language: words or phrases which describe the writer's emotions and/or make the reader feel a certain way.

Personal pronouns: words which indicate the person/people being spoken about. Examples: 'I', 'you', 'they'.

⊂⊃ **Grammar link**

When using speech punctuation, always remember to begin a new line for a new speaker.

Creating Characters, Mood and Atmosphere

Learning aim

In this unit you will prepare for the Controlled Assessment Tasks by looking at a variety of skills you will need to write creatively and descriptively. You will learn to create the right mood and atmosphere in your writing, create effective characters, and to use language techniques effectively when writing creatively.

9.1 Effective description – adjectives

> You will learn how to use specific words and ideas to build up mood and atmosphere in your writing.

⟳ For starters

When you are creating a mood or atmosphere in your writing you are building up a specific feeling: for instance, you may want your writing to appear sad, happy or to be full of tension.

In pairs, read the following two extracts. What mood or atmosphere do you think is created in each one? Which words or phrases create this atmosphere?

> The wood was deep and dark. All around me were trees, oppressive and threatening, bearing down on me like bullies. Suddenly, a bird flew out of the branches above my head, shrieking in the deadly silence, cutting through it like a knife.

> The water was warm and inviting, a well earned bath at the end of a hard day. I swam amongst the gentle waves, relaxed and at peace with the world. The sun smiled down on my face, kissing my forehead and making the droplets of water glisten in its golden rays.

⊃ Task

1   You need to make your creative writing for your Controlled Assessment interesting for your readers. You will need to use the right sorts of words and phrases to help build the right mood or atmosphere.

Read the following extracts. Put them in order of which one you think is the most convincing to the least convincing. Why did you put them in the order you chose?

A

It was a cold, dark night and I could hear the owls shrieking in the distance. The moon had vanished behind a large, black cloud.

B

They were on my tail, but I had to keep moving. I ran through the streets, past the fish and chip shop and turned down a narrow alleyway. Suddenly it was much darker and I couldn't see as clearly. I could hear my heart pounding in my chest and it felt as if it would explode at any moment.

C

The summer breeze blew gently over the field, brushing the grass, almost caressing it like a mother's hand.

D

The traffic roared in every direction. It seemed almost impossible to cross this busy road.

E

I could hear the hissing sound all around me. I looked down and could see hundreds of snakes writhing around my feet, slipping over my shoes and leaving a slimy feeling over my feet.

2   The way in which a writer uses **adjectives** is very important in creating an appropriate mood and atmosphere.
   *   Can you find any effective adjectives in the extracts above?
   *   When creating mood and atmosphere in your own writing, use effective adjectives in your work. Look at this sentence:

> The *tall* man walked down the *long* street.

   *   There are two adjectives, 'tall' and 'long', but these are rather dull examples. Make them more interesting like this:

> The *elongated, creepy* man walked down the *never-ending* street.

   *   What are the adjectives this time?
   *   Make the following sentences more interesting with better adjectives:
       The small girl had lost her plastic doll.
       The large boat sailed across the rough sea.
       I could hear the loud music across my big room.
   *   Now come up with two more examples of your own.

ⓘ Concept bank

Adjective: a word which describes a noun (a thing, object or person). Examples are 'brilliant', 'massive', 'awesome'.

Taking it further

Write a paragraph of about 50 words creating a clear mood and atmosphere. You can choose to continue any one of the effective examples in this section or to write something of your own. If you select one of the examples in the book, remember to continue the story from that point and to build the mood and atmosphere in an appropriate manner. Think about:

- what mood has been created so far
- what words you might use to build this mood.

Grammar link

Use appropriate and interesting adjectives in your writing. Think more about creating the mood and atmosphere and less about developing a story.

9.2 Creating mood and atmosphere

You will explore atmospheric description and apply it to your own writing.

For starters

When writers create a mood or atmosphere, they often have a picture in their mind of a specific scene or event. Look at the two photographs below. What mood and atmosphere do these pictures create for you?

List ten words for each photograph. Share your ideas with the rest of your class.

⊃ Task

Frankenstein is a well-known horror story about a man who creates
his own creature from the body parts of the dead and then brings it to
life. The extract here is the moment when the monster comes to life
for the first time and the reaction of Frankenstein to the monster that
he has created. The writer, Mary Shelley, has deliberately created an
unpleasant mood and an atmosphere of horror throughout this passage:

It was on a dreary night of November that I beheld the
accomplishment of my toils. With an anxiety that amounted
almost to agony, I collected the instruments of life around me,
that I might infuse a spark of being into the lifeless thing that lay
at my feet. It was already one in the morning; the rain pattered   5
dismally against the panes, and my candle was nearly burnt out,
when, by the glimmer of the half-extinguished light, I saw the dull
yellow eye of the creature open; it breathed hard, and a **convulsive**
motion agitate its limbs.

How can I describe my emotions at this catastrophe, or how   10
delineate the wretch whom with such infinite pains and care I
had endeavoured to form. His limbs were in proportion, and I
had selected his features as beautiful. Beautiful! – Great God!
His yellow skin scarcely covered the work of muscles and arteries
beneath; his hair was of a **lustrous** black, and flowing; his teeth   15
of a pearly whiteness; but these **luxuriances** only formed a more
horrid contrast with his watery eyes, that seemed almost of the
same colour as the dun white sockets in which they were set, his
shrivelled complexion and straight black lips.

> **Convulsive:** sudden, jerky movement.
> **Delineate:** describe.
> **Lustrous:** bright, shiny.
> **Luxuriances:** rare and delightful qualities.

ⓘ Concept bank

Pathetic fallacy: where
the weather or surrounding
landscape reflects the mood of
the scene.

What is important about when the moment is set: 'on a dreary night
of November'? Why not in June or July or a clear, sunny day? This
is an example of **pathetic fallacy** where the author has matched the
nature of the weather to the mood of the scene in the book.

1   Shelley uses many negative words throughout the passage to show
    how horrifying the scene is, for example: 'anxiety', 'agony' and
    'breathless horror'. What other negative words and phrases are used
    in the passage to build this up? Make a list of these and explain
    what effect these words have on building up the horrifying nature of
    the scene.

Writers often use pathetic fallacy. Here is an example from Chapter 2 of *Jane Eyre* by Charlotte Brontë on the right.

2   The gloomy atmosphere of wind and rain and the cloudy skies reflect Jane's dark mood and sadness at living in Gateshead Hall where no one seems to love or care for her. What other words and phrases from the first paragraph add to the pathetic fallacy created?

Writers often use **similes** or **metaphors** in their work to help create the mood and atmosphere. For example, Frankenstein describes himself as an evil being to show how he feels responsible for creating the monster and for all the terrible things the monster has done: 'I wandered like an evil spirit' (simile). Shelley compares the monster's teeth to a pearl as they are so white: 'his teeth of a pearly whiteness' (metaphor). It makes the teeth seem almost unreal or unnatural, which reflects the fact that the monster is unnatural.

3   The sentences in the table below are either similes or metaphors. Identify which they are and then explain the effect of them. The first example is given to help you.

> Daylight began to forsake the red-room; it was past four o'clock, and the beclouded afternoon was tending to drear twilight. I heard the rain still beating continuously on the staircase window, and the wind howling in the grove behind the hall …

Example	Simile or metaphor	Explanation of effect
'his teeth of a pearly whiteness'	Metaphor	The writer compares the monster's teeth to a pearl as they are so white. It makes the teeth seem almost unreal or unnatural, which reflects the fact that the monster is unnatural.
'He stood there looking at me like the devil.'		
'The mountains lay before me as if they were a masterpiece painted by the greatest painter alive.'		
'For some time I sat upon the rock that overlooks the sea of ice.'		

⊃ Taking it further

You have decided to enter a short story competition for your local newspaper. You have been given the following guidelines:

- Write a short story that creates a mood or atmosphere. You do not have to create horror or unpleasantness; it could be a happy mood.
- You will need to think about what the plot will be; who the characters are; where it is set – you will need to describe this place in detail.
- Think of as many words as you can to describe your location and try to make them interesting.
- Try to use examples of similes, metaphors and pathetic fallacy.
- Make sure there is a good balance between description and dialogue.

ⓘ Concept bank

Similes: compare one thing with another using 'as' or 'like'.

Metaphors: compare one thing with another more directly.

9.3 Creating characters

> You will explore how a writer uses words to create a character and apply this technique to your own writing.

⊃ For starters

Read the two extracts below. Each is a description of a character in a novel.

> Big Joe doesn't have to go to school and I don't think that's fair at all. He's much older than me. He's even older than Charlie and he's never been to school. He stays at home with Mother, and sits up in his tree singing *Oranges and Lemons* and laughing. Big Joe is always happy, always laughing. I wish I could be happy like him. I wish I could be at home like him. I don't want to go with Charlie. I don't want to go to school.
>
> (A description of Big Joe from Michael Morpurgo's *Private Peaceful*, page 8)

> Gran hadn't changed much; her face looked just the same as I remembered it. The skin was soft and withered, bent into a thousand tiny creases that clung gently to the bone underneath. Like a dried apricot, but with a puff of thick white hair standing out in a cloud around it.
>
> (A description of Gran from Stephenie Meyer's *New Moon*, page 3)

In pairs, discuss which is the most effective character description and why. Think about:
- what we are told about each character
- what adjectives (describing words) are used to describe the characters.

Which do you think is better? Be prepared to explain your reasons why to the rest of your class.

⊃ Task

Read the extract on page 99 from *Great Expectations* by Charles Dickens which was written in 1860. A young boy called Pip has met a prisoner on the run in a graveyard of a local church.

'Hold your noise!' cried a terrible voice, as a man started up from among the graves at the side of the church porch. 'Keep still, you little devil, or I'll cut your throat!'

A fearful man, all in coarse grey, with a   5
great iron on his leg. A man with no hat, and with broken shoes, and with an old rag tied round his head. A man who had been soaked in water, and smothered in mud, and lamed by stones, and cut by flints, and stung   10
by nettles, and torn by briars; who limped and shivered, and glared and growled; and whose teeth chattered in his head as he seized me by the chin.

'O! Don't cut my throat sir,' I pleaded in   15
terror. 'Pray don't do it, sir.'

'Tell us your name!' said the man. 'Quick!'

'Pip, sir.'

'Once more,' said the man, staring at me.
'Give it mouth!'   20

'Pip. Pip, sir.'

Sentence length can be important when creating the mood and atmosphere in a piece of writing. Long, flowing sentences can make a scene much more gentle and sweeping, whilst short sentences can make a passage much more tense.

1   Notice how Dickens uses a lot of short, sharp sentences throughout the passage.
    Pick out three examples of a short sentence in this passage and write them out. 'Quick!' is a sentence on its own. Why do you think Dickens has used a one-word sentence here? How does this help build up the tension of the scene?

2   Read again the dialogue between the two characters, Pip and the prisoner (Magwitch). Copy the table below and fill in all the information you can gain about each character from the extract. One example is given to help you.

Pip	Magwitch (man)
	Terrible voice

3   What a character says helps the reader to find out a lot more about them. List two things that Pip says which tells us about his character. And what does the way Magwitch speaks tell us about him?

⊃ Taking it further

Create a piece of writing which involves two characters. You will need to make sure there is a mood of tension between them. Use some of the examples in this unit to help you with your description. Build up in your mind's eye a description of the characters first:

- What do they look like?
- How are they standing?
- What do their faces look like?
- What are they wearing?
- What do they say?
- How do they say it?

Think about:

- how you will *describe* each character
- how you will use *dialogue* to build up each character and create the tension
- how you will use *short* sentences to help create tension.

You could begin:

They stood across the road from each other, watching the other's every move.

Remember to have a good balance of description and direct speech.
Dickens uses direct speech when Pip and Magwitch talk to each other.

ᗶ Grammar link

When writing direct speech:	For example:
• Always have speech marks around the words that are *spoken*.	• "This is how to do it," he said.
• All punctuation that goes with that line of speech should go inside the speech marks.	
• If you interrupt the speech with some narration, such as Mike answered, you need to put commas at the end of the first part of the speech and after the narration. The second part of the speech should begin with a small letter as it is still the same sentence.	• "I know," Mike answered, "and it gets you extra marks!"
• Note that if the narration comes after the speech, a comma is placed inside the speech marks with the speech; if the narration comes before the speech, the comma stays outside the speech with the narration.	• Peter replied, "But it is quite complicated."

9.4 Developing description and characters

You will look at how to create more descriptive and effective character writing.

⊃ For starters

When writing, writers often use their senses to help create the scene. The five senses are sight, sound, taste, touch and smell. In pairs, discuss which sense each of the following examples uses.

A The ball hit her hard on the head and immediately she felt a dull throbbing of pain where the impact had been.

B He was guided by the welcoming scent of fish and chips, as if nothing else mattered in the world any more.

C The scene in front of them was magnificent. There were trees made of chocolate, marzipan bushes and flowers of every colour you could imagine.

D The curry was far too strong for him. As he put the first piece of chicken in his mouth he felt as if his whole head would explode as the surge of spices and herbs hammered at his every fibre.

E The tremendous thud, thud, thud of the bass seemed to get louder every night and it was not long before Mr Johnson went round next door to complain about the ridiculous music playing into the night.

⊃ Task

At the very beginning of Barry Hines' *A Kestrel for a Knave*, he introduces the central character, Billy Casper, through description of what he does and where he lives rather than by what he says:

There were no curtains up. The window was a hard-edged block the colour of the night sky. Inside the bedroom the darkness was of gritty texture. The wardrobe and bed were blurred shapes in the darkness. Silence.   5

Billy moved over, towards the outside of the bed. Jud moved with him, leaving one half of the bed empty. He snorted and rubbed his nose. Billy whimpered. They settled. Wind whipped the window and swept along the wall   10 outside.

Billy turned over. Jud followed him and cough-coughed into his neck. Billy pulled the blankets up round his ears and wiped his neck with them.

Most of the bed was now empty, and the   15 unoccupied space quickly cooled. Silence. Then the alarm rang. The noise brought Billy upright, feeling for it in the darkness, eyes tight shut. Jud groaned and hutched back across the cold sheet. He reached down the   20 side of the bed and knocked the clock over, grabbed for it, and knocked it farther away.

In the first paragraph the atmosphere of where Billy lives is created very clearly by Hines. This gives us some key information about Billy's life and is an important part of his character development. We are told a lot about where he lives.

9

1 Look in detail at the five sentences used in the first paragraph:
   - There were no curtains up.
   - The window was a hard-edged block the colour of the night sky.
   - Inside the bedroom the darkness was of gritty texture.
   - The wardrobe and bed were blurred shapes in the darkness.
   - Silence.

   What do all these sentences tell us about where Billy lives?

2 Now read the rest of the extract. Look at how his movement is described. Copy the table below and write into it the words from the passage which describe Billy as: vulnerable; uncomfortable; resentful; alarmed. The first one is given to help you.

Vulnerable	Uncomfortable	Resentful	Alarmed
'Billy whimpered'			

3 To help make the atmosphere clearer, writers often use the senses in their writing. Write a list of any of the senses (sight, sound, taste, touch and smell) used in the passage.

↻ Taking it further

1 You are now going to build up an interesting character of your own. You will need to make some important decisions about your character. The pictures below of interesting-looking people may help to give you some ideas.

On a blank piece of paper make some notes about your character. Try to be as detailed as possible. The more information you can come up with about your character, the more you will be able to develop your own writing later on. For example, instead of just writing 'tall' for appearance, you could write 'tall, skinny, but neat and tidy with a clear complexion'.

2 Now write a paragraph describing a character for the first time in a story. Think how you will describe this person to your reader to make it interesting for them. Use the ideas from the planning activities above to help you.

10 Re-creations

Learning aim

In this unit you will prepare for the Controlled Assessment Task called 'Re-creations'. You will transform one text into another. This unit will help you understand the choices you make about **form** and **style**.

ⓘ Concept bank

Form: the way in which subject matter is presented; the shape of the text on the page.

Style: the choices about words and sentences that a writer or speaker makes, such as the level of formality of a text.

10.1 Playing with texts

> You will look at the ways in which one text can be transformed into another.

⊃ For starters

Here is an illustration of the nursery rhyme 'Humpty Dumpty'.

How closely does the picture match how you imagined Humpty Dumpty to look?

This nursery rhyme never tells us one important piece of information. What *actually* happened to Humpty Dumpty? How did he fall off the wall and die? There are four possible answers:

- He fell off by accident.
- Someone pushed him.
- He just died of natural causes.
- He jumped off deliberately.

Choose one of these four options. Make up a story about Humpty Dumpty that ends with this choice. Remember the basic ingredients of any story (the 5Ws and 1H – see page 50) and make sure you can answer each as it fits your story: Who? What? When? Where? Why? How?

➲ Task

You will now transform the nursery rhyme version into a new text.
Here are four different forms in which the Humpty Dumpty story can
be recreated and the opening of each.

A

LOCAL MAN DIES IN TRAGIC ACCIDENT

Tamptown residents could only stand in shock at
11.30 pm last Tuesday evening as they watched
the King's cavalry men fail to resuscitate popular
local baker Mr Humpty Dumpty following a fall
from his garden wall. It is believed he was
seeking to aid a bird with a broken wing ...

B

Here at *Estelle* we're all fond of celeb gossip and juicy
scandals and no man has provided more shocking news
than rapper 'Humpty Dumpty', real name Shaun Wesley.
From his shock engagement to socialite Paris Ritz to his
alleged secret baldness, Humpty Dumpty's death from a
heart attack yesterday has stunned the world. The heart
attack happened during a performance from the top of
Tamptown wall …

C

```
'Help!'  A bloodcurdling scream pierced
the still night air, jolting the sleeping
residents of Tamptown from their
untroubled slumber.  Mrs Gloria Peacock
stumbled from her once-elegant townhouse,
wearing a crumpled silk dressing gown
and gazed out fearfully into the thick,
heavy darkness.  Silence.  Nothing.  Eyes
adjusted to the ink-black night, she could
make out a ...
```

D

Dear Mother,

I thought I would write to let you know how I
am getting along on holiday. Remember how you
were saying I should try and come out of my shell
a bit? Well, you will be glad to know I have been
trying out Extreme Sports this week! Tomorrow I
am BASE jumping, which is leaping off a high wall
with a parachute … It should be fun …

1 For each opening (A–D) say what type of text it is and why you
   think this. Think about the information in each opening. Think
   about how it is written. What words and phrases make it sound like
   a particular style of writing?

2 Each of these openings presents Humpty Dumpty's 'great fall' and
   the reason for it in a particular way. Choose one of the openings
   and continue writing it from the point where it stops. Try to add at
   least another 100 words or more. As you write, think about:
   • the kind of content to include for this form
   • the type of language you should use to match the opening.

3 Look back at the original nursery rhyme and at what you have
   turned it into. List six ways in which your version is different from
   the original. Which version do you think people will prefer? Why?

➲ Taking it further

Think of another nursery rhyme that you could turn into another text.

1 Which nursery rhyme will you choose?
2 What form will you transform it into?
3 Write the first 100 words exactly and stop – even if you haven't
   finished!

10.2 Honour the charge they made

You will see how a famous poem is actually a recreation of another text. You will look at how the poet transformed the original by changing its form and style to create a new text.

➲ For starters

Look closely at this picture of a famous military attack, the charge of the Light Brigade. It is of a charge made by British cavalrymen against their Russian enemy at the battle of Balaclava on 25 October 1854.

Describe what the picture shows you.

➲ Task

On 14 November 1854, the journalist William Howard Russell published his article 'The Cavalry Action at Balaclava 25 October' in *The Times* newspaper.

At ten past eleven our Light Cavalry Brigade rushed to the front ... As they passed toward the front the Russians opened on them with guns from the right, with volleys of **muskets** and rifles. They swept proudly past, glittering in the morning sun in all the pride and splendour of war. We could hardly believe the evidence of our senses. Surely that handful of men were not going to charge an army in position? Alas! It was but too true ... They advanced in two lines, quickening the pace as they closed towards the enemy. A more fearful spectacle was never witnessed than by those who, without the power to help, saw their heroic countrymen rushing to the arms of sudden death.

At the distance of 1200 yards the whole line of the enemy belched forth, from thirty iron mouths, a flood of smoke and flame through which hissed the deadly cannon balls. They never halted or checked their speed an instant. With a cheer which was many a noble fellow's death cry, they flew into the smoke of the batteries ... They were exposed to fire from the **batteries** on the hills on both sides, as well as to a direct fire of muskets.

Through the clouds of smoke we could see their sabres flashing as they rode up to the guns and dashed between them, cutting down the gunners as they stood. The blaze of their steel, an officer standing near me said, "was like the turn of a shoal of mackerel." We saw them riding through the guns, as I have said; to our delight, we saw them returning, after breaking through a column of Russian infantry and scattering them, when the fire of the guns on the hill swept them down. Wounded men and dismounted troopers flying towards us told the sad tale. At the very moment when they were about to retreat, a regiment of Russian lancers attacked their flank. Colonel Shewell, of the 8th Hussars, saw the danger and rode his men straight at them, cutting his way through with fearful loss.

At twenty-five to twelve not a British soldier, except the dead and dying, was left in front of these bloody Russian guns. Our loss in killed, wounded, and missing at two o'clock today, was as follows: Went into action 607 strong. Returned from action 198. Loss 409.

Muskets: a type of gun
Batteries: a row of cannons

Russell's article was a powerful piece of journalism about a horrific event. However, the charge on the Light Brigade would hardly be known about today but for one other event – the publishing by Alfred Lord Tennyson a few weeks later of his poem, 'The Charge of the Light Brigade'. Tennyson, inspired by the news report, had taken it and transformed it into a text of his own:

Half a league half a league,
Half a league onward,
All in the valley of Death
Rode the six hundred.
'Forward, the Light Brigade!   5
Charge for the guns' he said:
Into the valley of Death
Rode the six hundred.

'Forward, the Light Brigade!'
Was there a man dismay'd?   10
Not tho' the soldier knew
Someone had blunder'd:
Theirs not to make reply,
Theirs not to reason why,
Theirs but to do and die: 15
Into the valley of Death
Rode the six hundred.

Cannon to right of them,
Cannon to left of them,
Cannon in front of them   20
Volley'd and thunder'd;
Storm'd at with shot and shell,
Boldly they rode and well,
Into the jaws of Death,
Into the mouth of Hell   25
Rode the six hundred.

Flash'd all their sabres bare,
Flash'd as they turn'd in air
Sabring the gunners there,
Charging an army while   30
All the world wonder'd:
Plunged in the battery-smoke
Right thro' the line they broke;
Cossack and Russian
Reel'd from the sabre-stroke,   35
Shatter'd and sunder'd.
Then they rode back, but not
Not the six hundred.

Cannon to right of them,
Cannon to left of them,   40
Cannon behind them
Volley'd and thunder'd;
Storm'd at with shot and shell,
While horse and hero fell,
They that had fought so well   45
Came thro' the jaws of Death,
Back from the mouth of Hell,
All that was left of them,
Left of six hundred.

When can their glory fade?   50
O the wild charge they made!
All the world wonder'd.
Honour the charge they made,
Honour the Light Brigade,
Noble six hundred.   55

Re-creations

Russell presents the charge in the form of a newspaper article. Tennyson presents the charge in the form of a poem. He has turned prose into poetry. You are now going to look at some of the changes and think about the effect of those changes.

1. Which version gives us the most *information* about the event? You might work with a partner to produce a tally of each one, taking turns to read and count the pieces of information.
2. Which version presents the event in the most *detail*?

Look again at the paragraph in the newspaper that begins, 'Through the clouds of smoke …' and ends, '… with fearful loss.'

Now look at the verse that begins, 'Flash'd all their sabres bare …'.

3. Which version uses the most description?
4. Which version uses the most **figurative language**?
5. Which version uses the most **emotive language**?
6. Tennyson uses **rhythm** and rhyme in the poem. Why does Tennyson use sound in this way?
7. Tennyson repeats words and phrases in the poem. Find two examples of repetition of words and phrases. Explain why he repeats these words and phrases.
8. The poem and the newspaper article use language in different ways. Which version do you prefer? Explain why.
9. Why do you think these two versions of the same event are so different?

⊃ Taking it further

Taking your answers to tasks 1–9, work with a partner to organise your ideas under four topic questions:
- What do you think each writer was trying to achieve in his text?
- What does the news article tells us that the poem does not?
- Does the poem include anything that is not in the news article?
- Do you prefer Russell or Tennyson's way of writing? Why?

Use these ideas to write four paragraphs to answer the question:

Which presentation of events do you find most effective – the news article or the poem? Why?

(i) Concept bank

Figurative language: descriptions in which one thing is compared with another to create interesting or powerful images. Examples include similes, metaphors and personification.

Emotive language: words or phrases which describe the writer's emotions and/or make the reader feel a certain way.

Rhythm: the 'beat' of a poem.

Re-creations

10.3 Out of the valley of Death …

You will produce your own short piece of writing, recreating Tennyson's poem 'The Charge of the Light Brigade'. You will think about how the words you use have an impact on the reader.

⮎ For starters

Which of these four phrases that Tennyson uses to describe the charge of the Light Brigade would be the best title for this painting?

- The valley of Death
- The mouth of Hell
- Storm'd at with shot and shell
- Flash'd all their sabres bare

Explain your answer.

⬆ *This painting of the charge of the Light Brigade was painted by Richard Caton Woodville in 1897. Woodville was an expert war illustrator who had served in the army.*

⮎ Task

Scene One: 25 October 1854

Look at the cavalryman on the white horse at the centre of this painting. Imagine yourself as him in the scene in the painting. You are he – Captain Hobbs of the Light Brigade – in the middle of battle, with cannons all around you. Death is never more than a sabre's length away. As you answer the following questions, remember you are the cavalryman, so use the first person – 'I'. You survive the charge when many of your friends do not …

1 Describe the Russian cavalryman you see to your left – give lots of detail. What are you thinking at this point?

2 Describe what you can smell. (Think of all the things around you that would create a terrible stink).

3 There are all sorts of noises around you. Describe four of them.

4 You see Thomas, your dear friend, standing over his badly-injured horse. What do you think when you see him?

5 You are seconds away from capturing the Russian cannons. Look how close you are to the guns! At this point you might be feeling several emotions at the same time. Describe them.

6 Suddenly, there is a huge explosion. As you fall from your horse, describe what is going on around you and what you can see and hear.

… and then black-out. Nothing. Darkness.

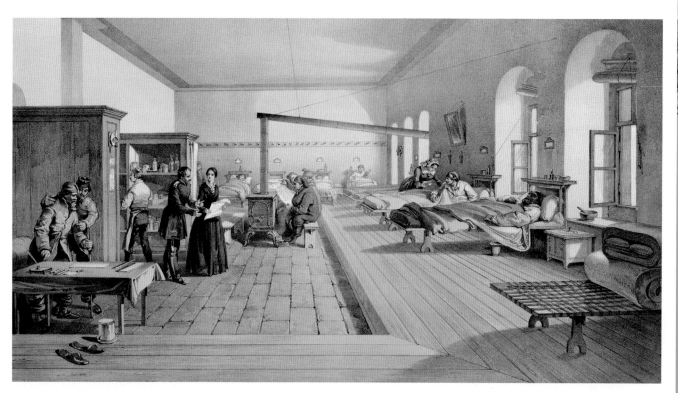

↑ This lithograph from April 1856 shows Florence Nightingale (left, in the black dress) talking with an army officer at the Barracks Hospital in Scutari. It is a drawing from life by W Simpson, an artist who travelled through the Crimea making drawings of the war.

Scene Two: 21 November 1854

You wake up, and raise your bandaged head to see the scene above. You have been in a coma for many days, but you have survived! A man in the bed next to you whispers between groans, 'We are at Scutari Hospital … she is an angel … Nurse Nightingale …'

7 Look at the picture above. This is what you can see from your bed. Your eyes scan from left to right, moving slowly. As you see things, describe what you see in as much detail as you can.

8 Make a list of what you can smell, and of what you can hear.

Nurse Florence Nightingale sees you are awake. Coming to your bed-side, she says, 'Good afternoon, Captain Hobbs. We have been tending to your wounds the past weeks.'

9 What are your feelings about this place? About being wounded? About Miss Nightingale and the nurses?

Scene Three: 22 November 1854

Night time. Scutari military hospital in Turkey. Across the Black Sea and 350 miles away from the Crimea and that valley, the place of such horror. It is around 3.30 am. Something has woken you – perhaps the screams of a young man to your left, but more likely a nightmare. Your mind races wildly over the events and emotions of your recent experiences.

10 Looking back over the events, what do you think are your main thoughts and reflections upon what has happened? Has the experience changed your opinion about war? About yourself? About your future and what you want out of life?

You pick up your pen to write …

⊃ Taking it further

You are now going to write up EITHER Captain Hobbs' diary OR Captain Hobbs' letter to his fiancée, Emily, whom he last saw in London, many months ago.

Which of the two options, diary or letter, are you going to write?

Before you start writing, look back at Russell's description of the charge on page 105, and remind yourself of Tennyson's poetic interpretation on page 106. Then use the **APPLE** checklist (right) to help you think about how you might approach the question.

Consider also these questions before you start to plan your writing:

Plan your writing so that it:

- suits the **A**udience
- achieves its **P**urpose
- has good **P**resentation
- uses the right **L**anguage
- has a powerful **E**ffect.

The diary:

- What facts will you mention in your diary? How will you talk about your feelings? Remember, in a diary you will write more openly and honestly – you are writing to yourself.
- Write in the first person ('I', 'my').
- Write your diary as three entries, for each of the different scenes; put the date and place at the start of each entry.
- For each entry, start with a single-sentence summary of the day's events or how you felt (e.g. 'A dreadful, bloody day …').
- Don't just say what happened. Include how you felt, and also your PERSONAL REFLECTIONS on events.

The letter:

- What facts will you mention in your letter to Emily? This is a letter to your loved one back in England – you will wish to spare her the most gruesome details, and you may not be honest about your real feelings.
- Write in the first person ('I', 'my'), but also address comments to Emily as 'you'.
- Write your letter in three paragraphs, describing in turn each of the three scenes. Start each with a clear topic sentence making it obvious what you are going to talk about. Don't just say what happened; include how you felt.
- Finish with a final paragraph where you share your PERSONAL REFLECTIONS on events.

If you need help starting you could begin with the suggestions below:

25 October 1854

And so I have lived, but it is with difficulty that I look back four weeks, to that terrible day when we charged the Russian guns in the valley of death.

The first thing I remember is …

Dearest Emily

My thoughts are forever with you, and it is with deepest love that I write to tell you what has happened to me in the last few weeks.

My story starts …

Write the first 100–150 words, then read your essay out loud to a friend. Does it 'work'? Did it gain their interest?

Ask them to give you feedback on these points:

- Did it describe events using exciting words?
- Did it have a style appropriate for a diary (or a letter to a fiancée)?
- Did it include feelings and reflection as well as description?

Now, finish the writing you have started. Revise your first draft and add a further 200 or so words.

! Essay tip

Use the 'Good writing techniques' listed on page 48.

11

Linking Words and Images

Learning aim

In this unit you will learn about the features of a typical review, and the skills and understanding you need to write a good review for a 'Moving Images' Creative Writing Controlled Assessment Task.

11.1 What is a review?

You will learn what a review is.

(i) Concept bank

Review: a critical report and evaluation of a film, book, play, performance or concert, often found in newspapers, in magazines or on the Internet.

⊃ For starters

Spend a short time telling a partner about a film you know well, then swap so they tell you about theirs. You've just given a film 'review'!

⊃ Task

Read this review from the Heart 106.2 website about the film release *Public Enemies.*

Public Enemies

Johnny Depp turns in the performance of his career in this superb gangster drama.

Who's in it? Johnny Depp, Christian Bale, Marion Cotillard

What's it about? The Feds try to take down notorious American gangsters John Dillinger, Baby Face Nelson and Pretty Boy Floyd in the 1930s.

What type of film? Drama

Is it any good? Wow! After watching Johnny Depp camp it up as Willy Wonka and Jack Sparrow I almost forgot what an acting powerhouse he is doing a straight role. Without a doubt this is a career best performance from him and don't be surprised if there are acting nods for him come next February. Marion Cotillard is pitch perfect as his love interest while Christian Bale FINALLY stops doing that Batman Voice for 90 minutes and pulls a stunning performance out of the bag. The supporting cast are also spot on and thanks to the direction of Michael 'Heat' Mann this is as stunning visually as it is emotionally involving ... which is, very. The script is not over-egged or too earnest, and all the lines come across as real rather than cliché-riddled monologues which can be the case with gangster movies. Whilst there is a lot of gun action and violent set pieces in this, it's really a piece that is really all about the characters and it is hands down the best gangster movie of the last decade ... at least. One of this year's few must see movies.

Marks out of 10? 9

The review of *Public Enemies* is probably very different from the film review you have just shared with your friend!

1 The review is structured around *five* key questions. What are they?
2 Why is the section 'What's it about?' so short?
3 The section 'Is it any good?' is the longest and most important. Find *five* aspects of the film that it bases its judgement on.

↺ Taking it further

Uncut film review: *Up*

DIRECTED by Pete Docter

STARRING THE VOICES OF Ed Asner, Christopher Plummer, Jordan Nagai, Bob Peterson

(May contain **spoilers**!)

The 3D extravaganza *Up* is... a bittersweet contemplation of ageing and mortality.

You could read it that way – or alternatively see this brisk fantasy as a surreal, sweet-natured comedy about a cranky old man, a flying house and some talking dogs.

Ed Asner provides the voice of elderly balloon seller Carl, who once shared a dream   5
of airborne escape with his late wife. Hitching his balloons to his house, Carl flies off with a bedazzled young Wilderness Explorer (Jordan Nagai) to a lost domain, where they encounter a villainous air ace (Christopher Plummer) and a winningly goofy 13-foot-bird named Kevin.

The humour gets weirder as it goes on and it's among the lightest of Pixar's films,   10
but the first 20 minutes offer the saddest, most poignant sequence seen in an animation film since Bambi's mother died.

JONATHAN ROMNEY

This review of the film *Up* has a different **form** from the review of *Public Enemies* (it is not organised under five key questions), but Romney still asks four of the five same key questions.

1 Which question does he not ask?
2 Find the sentences in the review which answer the other four questions.
3 The Heart 106.2 review of *Public Enemies* looked at five criteria to answer the key question: 'Is it a good film?':
   • **script** and **dialogue**   • action
   • acting performance   • emotional impact
   • visual impact and special effects.

Which of these criteria does Romney use to evaluate *Up*? Identify the parts of the review where he addresses each criterion.

4 Think again about the film you described to a friend (on page 111). Tell your friend again how good it was, but this time use the five criteria above to organise your ideas.

Linking Words and Images

11.2 Writing for an audience

You will see how different reviews are written in very different styles to suit the interests of the people who read them.

⊃ For starters

Read Review A and decide who you think it is aimed at: males or females? Adults or children? Newcomers or *Transformers* fans?

Review A

Transformers – Revenge of the Fallen

1 What's it about? You won't be surprised to learn this is a follow-up to the summer blockbuster *Transformers*. Think huge clunking robots that transform with max noise into all manner of objects and you'll not be far wrong! Sam Witwicky – the 16 year old from the original – again finds himself involved in huge set piece battles, screen-filling action sequences and ear-piercing sound effects. We're talking serious decibels here! More would be to spoil the plot …

2 Who's in it? Sam is played by Shia LaBeouf, with the lovely Megan Fox playing girlfriend Mikaela. The main characters are the Transformers themselves with Decepticons and Autobots hogging most of the frames. Optimus Prime returns, there's the big baddie, The Fallen, and fans will warm to new 'Formers Mudflap and Skiddy. Heavy metal heaven!

3 What else is it like? Good old mainstream sfx-, cgi-dominated summer-season blockies is what we're talking here. Action. Explosions and fighting. Jaw-dropping speed and frantic camera work. Animation in its screen origins, we're not looking at subtlety of characterisation or brain-busting plotting. This is as in yer face as it gets. Batman crossed with a car-wreck.

4 Why should I bother? Because it is an amazing film that you will want to watch over and over again until your eyes can't take the action any longer. The special effects are breathtaking and the pace is relentless. Wow!!! And Ow!!! At the same time!

5 Why should I stay home and play on my console? Maybe because the cameras are too close to the people, the slow-motion can get repetitive after a while, the plot is a bit pants, the film is overall confusing and when you watch it first time at the cinema you will be wondering what's happening because everything is so fast or really slow. But, but … you'll still love it!

6 Cinema or DVD? This is cinema at its loudest, most frantic, most screen-busting. The sound effects, the light and magic, and that slo mo when it most matters. Huge explosions will be just plain wimpy at home compared to the multiplex megascreen and isn't that why you're there!

Bums on seats score 7/10.

Linking Words and Images

1 Review A on page 113 is aimed at young people (mainly boys), who like *Transformers*. Working on your own, find *one* sentence aimed at this audience. How is the sentence attractive to this audience?

2 How does the review's **form** make it suitable for young people?

3 Find *one* phrase or sentence which shows that the reviewer enjoyed the film.

4 The review was not wholly positive. Find the section which makes negative comments.

ⓘ Concept bank

Form: the way in which the subject matter is presented; the shape of the text on the page.

Style: the choices about words and sentences that a writer or speaker makes. The choices result from such aspects as word choice, tone, and grammar.

↻ Task

Now look at this very negative review of the film *Transformers – Revenge of the Fallen*, written in a very different **style**:

Review B

Transformers – *Revenge of the Fallen*

Michael Bay, that prince of unsubtlety, rejecter of nuance and repudiator of light-and-shade, has returned with another of his mega-decibel action headbangers. I found it at once loud and boring, like watching paint dry while getting hit over the head with a frying pan. And at two and a half hours, it really is very 5 long. Once again, we are in the world of the Transformers, and again the star is Shia LaBeouf: allegedly a Tom Hanks for the future.

This movie franchise is based on a branded toy manufactured by Hasbro: basically, cars that 10 can transform themselves, with much whirring and clanking, into vast, ungainly and incredibly dull robots. The good ones are the Autobots 15 and they are on our side; the bad ones are the Decepticons, defeated in the first movie, but now intent once more on crushing Earth. For about 20 two-thirds of this mind-frazzlingly dull film, we are led to believe that the 'fallen' of the title refers to this resurgent army. But then 25 we find out it kind of means something else, and the storyline completely transforms itself into something even more boring than it was originally. 30

Because this film really is quite staggeringly uninteresting, the loud explosions – so densely packed as to resemble a 150-minute drum roll – are 35 the only things keeping you awake. While the Transformers were clanking noisily around, my mind wandered and I found myself thinking about Hazel 40 Blears, swine flu and whether Waitrose was going to take over all the empty Woolworths buildings.

The cherry on this cake of 45 direness is the performance of Megan Fox, playing LaBeouf's sultry girlfriend – a performer so poutingly wooden she makes Jordan look like Liv Ullmann. 50 You'll get better acting and superior entertainment at a monster truck rally.

1 Find words or phrases which show that Review B is aimed at an audience which is older and more sophisticated than Review A.

2 Study the text. Which of the five criteria for evaluating the key question: 'Is it a good film?' (script and dialogue; acting performance; visual and special effects; action; emotional impact) does the reviewer consider when making his judgement of how good the film is?

3   Review writers use a number of writing techniques to create a style which will interest and suit their readers. Working as a whole class, compare Review A with Review B to find examples of the points listed in the table.

Review A:		Review B:
• has a form …		• has a form …
• uses words …		• uses words …
• uses short sentences …	whereas	• uses complex sentences …
• uses informal language and **colloquialisms** …		• uses more formal language …
• uses the second person …		• uses the third person …
• is aimed at young people.		• is aimed at sophisticated adults.

⊃ Taking it further

A good opening to your review is essential.

1   In this unit, you have studied four different reviews (see pages 111–114). Read the first sentence of each one. Which do you think would grab the attention of:
   •   a teenager?
   •   a sophisticated adult?
   •   an experienced movie-goer?
   Which do you think is the best?

A good opening to a review will:
•   mention the title of the film (so the reader knows what film is being reviewed)
•   make a provocative statement (to grab the reader's attention)
•   ask a **rhetorical question** (to make the reader want to read on).

Here is one student's opening to her review of the film *Matilda* for a school magazine:

> Matilda is the most amazing, cute, sweet-natured, perfectly-cast, emotionally-satisfying film of all time! And tell me if you have never wanted to terrify that tyrant-teacher by pelting them with fruit?

2   Copying the style of this student's review, write the opening to a review of the film you described at the start of this unit (on page 111).

3   Using different writing styles, write two-sentence openings for reviews aimed at:
   •   teenage boys
   •   sophisticated adults
   •   experienced movie-goers.

⊡ Grammar link

A review written using the first person singular 'I' is personal and reflective; the first person plural 'we' is friendly and persuasive; the second person 'you' is direct and can be confrontational; and the third person 'it' and 'they' are formal and fair.

ⓘ Concept bank

Colloquialisms: informal words or phrases, including slang.

Rhetorical questions: questions that are addressed to an audience but do not require an answer.

11.3 Writing a review

You will prepare for writing the main body of your review.

⭕ Grammar link

An adjective is a word which describes a noun (a thing, object or person). Examples are 'brilliant', 'massive', 'awesome'.

⊃ For starters

1 Look at the table below. One column contains a collection of extracts from reviews of *Harry Potter and the Half-Blood Prince*, while the other column is a list of the sources they came from. For each extract, look at the content, form and style, and explain why it is suited to the people who read it.

Review extracts	Sources
BEST CHARACTER: Dumbledore is the new Obi-Wan Kenobi – inscrutable. **FAMILY RATING:** One mild swear word, one death, several snogs. **BUM NUMBNESS:** Time flies like an owl. **OVERALL RATING:** Five hats.	***The Sun*** A daily tabloid newspaper published in the United Kingdom with the highest circulation within the UK. It is famous for its clever use of words and its page three girls. It is supposed to have a reading age of nine.
`Dark, thrilling, and occasionally quite funny, Harry Potter and the Half-Blood Prince is also visually stunning and emotionally satisfying..`	**Rotten Tomatoes** An Internet forum that collects reviews from a variety of sources (newspapers, online, magazines) and averages them into a single rating.
It's probably a bit too thin on the action but as a well-crafted film it works well. *For the first time a Potter film goes beyond the magic and gives us all something to think about.*	**CBBC *Newsround* film reviews website** A website based on the BBC children's news programme which is aimed at thinking children.
HP7 Part One arrives, ETA November, 2010. We're marking time before the final battle between Good and Evil, with the promised darkness sitting somewhat clumsily with teen romance and humour.	**Empire magazine** The biggest selling film magazine in Britain, aimed at movie-goers who are interested in films.
But on the evidence of The Half-Blood Prince there is a real chance that Potter, like The Lord of the Rings before it, will be a fantasy franchise that ends in a bang, not a whimper.	***The Times*** A daily national broadsheet newspaper aimed at sophisticated adults and business people.

2 Film reviews use exciting nouns and adjectives to grab the readers' attention and to convey strong opinions. Looking back at the reviews on page 111–116, make a list of words and phrases which you think might be 'good ones to pinch' for your own review.

⟳ Task

The final step is to examine a review from the website *e-shed*, which publishes reviews for 'young people who love film'.

1 Twilight Cert: PG

Run time: 122 min
Cast: Kristen Stewart, Robert Pattinson, Billy Burke, Peter Facinelli
Director: Catherine Hardwicke

2 Based on the first in a series of novels by Stephanie Meyer, Catherine Hardwicke's *Twilight* tells the story of Bella Swan (Kristen Stewart), a broody teen who is forced to swap her life in sunny Phoenix to live with her father (Billy Burke) in dreary Forks, a small town with a mere population of 3120. On Bella's first day of school she meets handsome and mysterious loner, Edward Cullens (Robert Pattison).

3 When Edward saves Bella from being flattened by a speeding truck (with his bare hands), Bella makes it her mission to learn more about his mysterious strength. It does not take her long to discover that in fact, Edward is a vampire. On Bella's discovery, Edward explains that he and the rest of the Cullens family are in fact 'vegetarians' (by 'vegetarians', Edward explains, they eat animals, not people), but his desire for her is so strong, that he is not sure if he can stop himself from biting her.

4 The film as a whole does cause some controversy for me as a viewer – as a thriller/'vampire movie' it does not really work and this is mainly due to the representation of the Twilight vampires and lack of action. Unlike any other vampire movie ever written, these vampires can walk in the sunlight (traditionally, they should combust into flames), and there is not a sharp tooth in sight; eye colour is the only thing that changes when they are about to feed or fight.

5 Of course it is essential to remember that this is a film based on a novel, therefore the characters must be depicted as they are in the series, but hardcore vampire fans will probably feel disappointed.

6 However, not all is lost thanks to Forks local vampire villain, James: what he lacks in vampire props, he makes up for in sadism (as seen in the one and only fight sequence at the end of the film). The main problem is the action that does make it into the film is just not good enough – some dodgy wirework is about all we are offered and you expect more.

7 As a romance, however, the film works well. Edward and Bella's love story is charming and you can't help but be drawn into it. Stewart and Pattison have an undeniable chemistry and Pattison in particular does a brilliant job of portraying the broody and angst-ridden Edward. Many of the film's other characters, however, just feel unnecessary. In particular, Bella's friends are nothing more than irritating. The Cullens are more enjoyable as the local vampire family, but still there are not really any stand-out performances from any of the supporting cast.

8 Having not read the books, I expected this to be a vampire thriller movie, and that was my problem. As a thriller, it does not deliver, but as a love story, it ticks all the boxes. However, there is nothing really new here – like many films before it and many films to come, it is a story of forbidden love, a story that has been repeatedly retold since Shakespeare's *Romeo and Juliet*. All that said, the two leads do an excellent job of portraying the lust, angst, desire and heartache that would be present in a relationship like this and this is where most of the appeal of the film lies. It does have its exciting moments and will undoubtedly appeal and be worshipped by its target audience of teenage girls. In a nutshell: a pleasant but flawed watch. **6/10**

1 Read the review using the S3QR checklist (see right). Then go through it, making a brief note of the 'message' of each paragraph.

2 Discuss with a friend:
   - how well the reviewer opens the review
   - how well the reviewer has addressed the *five* key questions about a film (Who's in it? What's it about? What type of film is it? Is it any good ? Marks out of 10?)
   - how well the reviewer has commented on the content of the film without spoiling it for the reader (paragraphs 2 and 3)
   - how well the reviewer has used the five criteria for evaluation (script and dialogue, acting performance, visual and special effects, action, emotional impact) in paragraphs 4 to 8.

   Overall, how good a review is it? Could you do better?

> **Taking it further**

Write a film review of 500–700 words.

1 First, plan your review.
   - Decide who your target readership is – age and gender, specialist or general, sophisticated or ordinary.
   - Choose a suitable film to review – choose one you know well.
   - Decide how you will organise the form of your review – either with questions or headings, or as an essay of linked paragraphs.
   - Choose a suitable style for your audience – are you going to be formal and fair? Colloquial and enthusiastic? Negative and nasty?

2 Then write your review.
   - Start with an exciting opening, with a provocative statement and a rhetorical question, to grab the interest of your readers.
   - Use words which are appropriate to the style and audience.
   - Use some specialist nouns and adjectives from your review vocabulary list.
   - Show that you know other good writing techniques – try to include, for example: **modal verbs**, a mixture of complex sentences and short sentences for effect, a range of punctuation, **similes** and **metaphors**, a **list of three** and at least one **hyperbole**.
   - When you evaluate your film, do not forget to use the five criteria for evaluation: script and dialogue, acting performance, visual and special effects, action, emotional impact.
   - Finish with a summary paragraph and give the film a score in a creative way.

S3QR stands for: **S**kim it, ask what **3 Q**uestions it is answering, then **R**ead it carefully.

ⓘ Concept bank

Modal verbs: suggest that the reader does something. Examples: 'could', 'would', 'should', 'might'.

Similes: compare one thing with another using 'as' or 'like'.

Metaphors: compare one thing with another more directly.

Lists of three: when a writer or speaker repeats an idea three times in slightly different ways.

Hyperbole: exaggeration. Example: 'It would be just the greatest thing on earth if you could think of one'.

⌾ Grammar link

A complex sentence is a sentence which has a number of parts (or 'clauses'), joined by connectives such as 'because', 'which' and 'although'.

Unit 12 — Themes and Ideas – Family Relationships

Learning aim

In this unit you will look at three poems by William Wordsworth. Each poem shows a different aspect of love within a family. You will analyse the language and structure in each one. You will notice similarities and differences, and you will learn about the background to each poem. You will be aware of the key things you need to comment on when analysing a poem.

12.1 'We Are Seven'

You will learn to read and understand a poem which explores a child's view of family relationships. You will consider the way that an adult tries to understand a child's point of view. In this section you will need a copy of 'We are Seven' by Wordsworth.

William Wordsworth was born in 1770 and died in 1850. He lived most of his life in the Lake District where he appreciated the beauty of his surroundings. In his poems, he expresses ideas in a way that people can understand. He often writes about innocence, love and beauty.

⟳ For starters

1 Your first task is to build up a bank of words associated with the theme of family relationships. On your own, write down words (or phrases) that you associate with this theme. Now share your ideas with a partner.

2 Now share your ideas with at least three other people. You should aim for at least 10 different words or phrases.

3 Finally, share and discuss these ideas with the rest of your class, and in doing so, build up a useful bank of words that you will add to during the course of this unit.

4 Look at the pictures on the left. What words or phrases might you use to describe these families? Add these to your word bank.

12

Themes and Ideas – Family Relationships

➲ Task

1 When you write about poems, there are key words that you will need to use. Match each of these key words with the correct definition on the right. The first one has been done for you.

2 Read the poem 'We Are Seven' and underline any words that you are unfamiliar with. In pairs, try to work out the meanings from the rest of the sentence. These definitions should help you:

Rustic: relating to the countryside (in this poem it may mean simple or unsophisticated).

Porringer: a bowl or cup (in this poem it means a soup or gruel that the child has for supper).

3 Now look closely at the first stanza of the poem:

> A simple child
> That lightly draws its breath,
> And feels its life in every limb,
> What should it know of death?

Repetition	How the rhymed line endings are arranged
Stanza	The way that lines or stanzas are organised
Simile	A group of lines or unit within a longer poem
Structure	A word or phrase that sparks off the senses, especially visually
Imagery	Key words, phrases, ideas and sentence patterns are repeated to create an effect
Rhyming pattern	A comparison of two things usually using the words 'like' or 'as'

- Notice the words, 'simple', 'life' and 'death'. What do these words suggest to you? Write down your ideas.
- How does the writer emphasise the word 'death'?
- Does the word 'death' surprise the reader?
- Read stanzas 2 and 3. What is our first impression of the little girl? Pick out two or three words or phrases that help to create that impression?
- How does the narrator of the poem behave towards the little girl?
- Read stanzas 4 to 9. What do we learn about the little girl's family?

4 Look at the words in the box below. Choose the three words that you think best describe the little girl and her attitude to her family.

> distant   grieving   united   loving   emotional
> loyal   hopeful   innocent   close

5 For each of the three words chosen, find a quotation to back up your point. Then explain your idea more fully. Look at the example below:

Word	Point	Evidence	Explanation
'close'	The little girl seems *close* to her family. She insists that they are united, even though her brother and sister are dead.	This is shown in the line: 'Seven are we …'	Wordsworth uses simple, child-like language to show the child's simple attitude to the family. He repeats the idea to show how determined the girl is that death has not separated her family.

120

6 Wordsworth conveys the information about the little girl's family through her conversation with the narrator. What does she tell him? How does she speak to him? How does this affect him?

There are a lot of powerful **images** in stanzas 10–15. For example, the girl having her supper by the graves in the dusk.

7 Find two or three more examples of powerful images.

8 Choose one of these images to draw. Underneath your drawing, write the line (or lines) that create this image. With a partner, explain why you have chosen this image and the line (or lines) that support it. You may want to say more about your picture.

9 Look at the extract on the right (top) about the girl sewing and knitting by the graves. Notice how Wordsworth uses the following ways to create this powerful image:

- Simple words build up a clear image.
- Repetition of 'my', 'I' and 'there', shows how the experience is personal to the little girl and how important the place is to her.
- The rhyming pattern is simple and child-like.

10 Now look at the final stanza of the poem on the right (bottom). The writer shows his frustration at the little girl's refusal to accept that her brother and sister are dead. How does he show this? To help you answer this question, look at the words he uses, and compare the structure of this stanza with the other stanzas in the poem.

○ **Taking it further**

Write two paragraphs to answer the question:

> How does Wordsworth present the relationship between the girl and her brother and sister in 'We Are Seven'?

In the first paragraph, describe the relationship Wordsworth writes about in the poem. In the second, explain the poetic techniques he uses to present that relationship very powerfully.

ⓘ Concept bank

Image: using words in a way which creates a picture in the mind's eye of the reader.

My stockings there I often knit,
My 'kerchief there I hem;
And there upon the ground I sit,
And sing a song to them.

"But they are dead; those two are dead!
Their spirits are in heaven!"
'Twas throwing words away; for still
The little Maid would have her will,
And said, '*Nay, we are seven!*'

12.2 'The Mad Mother'

> You will develop your understanding of the themes of family relationships. You will learn how the writer creates a strong character in this poem. In this section you will need a copy of 'The Mad Mother' by Wordsworth.

↻ For starters

'We Are Seven' shows family love from the point of view of a child. 'The Mad Mother' shows the love of a mother for her child.

1 Look at the pictures above. Write one or two sentences for each picture describing the relationship between the mother and her children. Share these ideas with a partner.

2 In pairs, discuss what you think makes a good mother.

↻ Task

Read the first two stanzas of 'The Mad Mother' on the right.

1 Use these words to fill in the blanks in the copy of the first stanza below.

> talked and sung   coal-black   wild   alone   stain

What impressions do these stanzas give:
- of the mother's appearance
- of the mother's behaviour
- of the mother's state of mind?

Explain your answers.

2 Look at the rhyming pattern of these stanzas. Work with a partner to work out the pattern of rhyme. Some people believe that Wordsworth chose the poem's relentless rhythm and rhyme to simulate the madness of the mother, as if she were talking to herself in a distracted, rocking way.

1 Her eyes are … her head is bare,
The sun has burnt her … hair,
Her eye-brows have a rusty …
And she came far from over the main.
She has a baby on her arm,
Or else she were …;
And underneath the hay-stack warm,
And on the green-wood stone,
She … the woods among;
And it was in the English tongue.

2 'Sweet babe! they say that I am mad,
But nay, my heart is far too glad;
And I am happy when I sing
Full many a sad and doleful thing:
Then, lovely baby, do not fear!
I pray thee have no fear of me,
But, safe as in a cradle, here
My lovely baby! thou shalt be,
To thee I know too much I owe;
I cannot work thee any woe.'

Now read the rest of the poem. In stanza 3 the writer develops the character of the mother and shows her state of mind.

3 From the first three lines of stanza 3 (right), pick out three words that describe the mother's torment. For each word, explain what effect it has on the reader; for example, 'fire' suggests something destructive and difficult to control.

4 At which point in stanza 3 does her mood change? Why?

5 Looking at stanza 5 (right), which statement best describes the mother's feelings?
- the baby protects her from harm
- she feels desperate
- she feels anxious and afraid
- she knows the baby needs her
- she is brave and defiant
- she knows no fear when actually she should.

Explain your answer, supporting it with a quote from the stanza.

6 Why do you think Wordsworth makes so many references to nature in this poem?

7 Read the final stanza (right). In pairs, spend two or three minutes discussing these questions:
- Does Wordsworth finish the poem on a positive or negative note?
- What questions do you still want to ask at the end of the poem?

⊃ Taking it further

1 In the last four stanzas of the poem we find out a few things about the baby's father. Working with a partner, discuss:
- Where does the father live?
- What kind of work does he do?
- Does he love the mother?
- Does he love the child?
- Does he know the child exists?
- What do you imagine the father is like?
- Do we believe what the mother says about the father of her child?

2 Use your answers to plan a role-play where one person takes the role of the father and the other takes the role of an interviewer. The aim of the interview is to let the father have his say and comment on the wife's behaviour. Be prepared to show your work to the rest of the class.

3 A fire was once within my brain;
And in my head a dull, dull pain;
And fiendish faces one, two, three,
Hung at my breasts, and pulled at me.
But then there came a sight of joy;
It came at once to do me good;
I waked, and saw my little boy,
My little boy of flesh and blood;
Oh joy for me that sight to see!
For he was here, and only he.

5 Oh! love me, love me, little boy!
Thou art thy mother's only joy;
And do not dread the waves below,
When o'er the sea-rock's edge we go;
The high crag cannot work me harm,
Nor leaping torrents when they howl;
The babe I carry on my arm,
He saves for me my precious soul;
Then happy lie, for blest am I;
Without me my sweet babe would die.

10 Oh! smile on me, my little lamb!
For I thy own dear mother am.
My love for thee has well been tried:
I've sought thy father far and wide.
I know the poisons of the shade,
I know the earth-nuts fit for food;
Then, pretty dear, be not afraid;
We'll find thy father in the wood.
Now laugh and be gay, to the woods away!
And there, my babe; we'll live for aye.

12.3 'Anecdote for Fathers'

You will understand how the theme of family relationships is presented in this poem. You will learn how to support your ideas with evidence from the text. In this section you will need a copy of 'Anecdote for Fathers' by Wordsworth.

ⓘ **Concept bank**

Anecdote: a short personal story used to make or illustrate a point.

⊃ For starters

1 In pairs, discuss how a child's relationship with their father might be different from their relationship with their mother. Write down the main differences (and perhaps the similarities). Be prepared to share your ideas with others in your group.

2 Read the poem 'Anecdote for Fathers'. What do you think the poem might be about, based on the title and your first reading of the poem? (When you write about a poem, the title is often a good place to start.) At this stage, this may seem to be a difficult question – if you write down some initial thoughts, you can return to it and expand on these ideas at the end of the unit.

3 Look closely at the opening stanza:

> I have a boy of five years old;
> His face is <u>fair</u> and <u>fresh</u> to see;
> <u>His limbs are cast in beauty's mould</u>,
> <u>And dearly he loves me</u>.

- What impression do we have of the boy?
- How does the father feel about his son?
- How does the writer show this?

Look at the underlined words to help you answer these questions.

⊃ Task

1 Read stanzas 3 to 6 below:
- How might you describe the father's mood and feelings in this section of the poem?
- What image of the father do you have?
- How do the words used to describe nature help you to understand the father's feelings?

Look at the underlined words to help you answer these questions.

3 My thoughts on former pleasures ran;
  I thought of Kilve's <u>delightful</u> shore,
  Our <u>pleasant</u> home when <u>spring</u> began,
  A long, long year before.

4 A day it was when <u>I could bear</u>   5
  <u>Some fond regrets</u> to entertain;
  With <u>so much happiness</u> to spare,
  I could not feel a pain.

5 The <u>green earth</u> echoed to the feet
  Of <u>lambs</u> that bounded through the glade,   10
  From <u>shade to sunshine</u>, and as fleet
  From <u>sunshine back to shade</u>.

6 <u>Birds warbled</u> round me – <u>and each trace</u>
  <u>Of inward sadness had its charm</u>;
  Kilve, thought I, was a favoured place,   15
  And so is Liswyn farm.

2 Look at the rhyming pattern. Suggest reasons why Wordsworth has chosen a very simple rhyming pattern for this poem.

3 The poem is based on a question that the father asks the child and the response that the child gives. Working with a partner, discuss the questions below and fill in a table like the one here to summarise your reading of the poem. (Use evidence from the poem to support your comments.)

What question does the father ask the child? How does he ask this question?	
What initial answer does the child give?	
How does the father react to this answer? How does the writer show this?	
In stanza 14, the child explains his answer. Why do you think he gives this explanation?	

4 Now look at the final stanza below. How does the father feel? How does Wordsworth show this? Pick out a quotation to support your answer.

> O dearest, dearest boy! my heart
> For better lore would seldom yearn,
> Could I but teach the hundredth part
> Of what from thee I learn.

5 Thinking about the poem as a whole, discuss these questions:
* Is the child being good or bad?
* If you were a father, what might you learn from this incident?
* Have you ever lied to protect someone's feelings?

⟲ Taking it further

Write two paragraphs to answer the question:

How does Wordsworth present the relationship between the father and his son in 'Anecdote for Fathers'?

In the first paragraph, describe the relationship Wordsworth writes about in the poem. In the second, explain the writing techniques he uses to present that relationship.

12.4 Review of the three poems

You will reflect on the importance of the fact that these poems were written at the end of the 18th century. You will consider some of the ways that you can compare these poems.

⊃ For starters

1 At the time that Wordsworth wrote these poems, about 50 per cent of children did not live beyond the age of five – today that figure is nearer 0.7 per cent. Look back at all three poems and for each write one comment that explains how this information affects our reading of these poems.

2 Looking at your initial bank of words about families and family relationships, do these three poems fit in with your ideas? If so, how? If not, how are they different?

⊃ Task

1 Now that you have looked at all three poems on your own, write down at least three similarities between them: for example, all three poems focus on relationships within a family.

2 Are there any important differences between the poems? Add these to your list. Read through your ideas and check that you have included at least one comment on each of these five areas: themes, characters, relationships, language and rhyming pattern.

⊃ Taking it further

1 Choose TWO of the three poems you have studied in this section. Write an essay to answer the question:

> How does Wordsworth present family relationships in two poems you have studied?

Write about your first poem, commenting on the relationship Wordsworth described, and the poetic techniques he used to describe it.

2 Put a discourse marker – either 'Similarly' or 'By Contrast' – and write about your second poem, commenting on the relationship Wordsworth described, and the techniques he used to describe it.

3 Finish with a paragraph comparing the similarities and differences between the two poems.

⊂⊃ Grammar link

Discourse markers – including words such as 'however' and 'so' – let the reader know where the argument in a text is going.

Discourse markers of similarity include:

- **Similarly**…
- **Equally**…
- **In the same way**…

Discourse markers of difference include:
- **By contrast**…
- **On the other hand**…
- **However**…

They are very useful in an exam essay comparing two poems.

! Essay tip

When you have written your first section, read it to a friend or group of friends. Ask for feedback on these points:

- Have you explained your ideas thoroughly?
- Have you supported your points with facts and quotes?

Presenting People

13.1 Creating a first impression

> You will look at how a writer uses physical description to suggest character. You will analyse the character of Curley in *Of Mice and Men*.

⟳ For starters

Look at this 1930 painting 'Snack Bar' by the artist Edward Burra. Look at the two characters. Give them appropriate names.

Choose one character and write about them in three paragraphs:

1 Discuss with a partner what your character looks like. Agree on three words to describe your character.
2 Describe what they are doing in a way which is appropriate to the kind of character you are trying to create.
3 What is your character saying? Make up a dialogue between the woman and the waiter. Make sure that what they are saying is appropriate to their character.

Read your paragraphs out loud to a friend or small group of friends. Did your description gain their interest?

Ask them to give you feedback on these points:

* Did you describe the character in a consistent way?
* Did you include personality and emotions as well as just facts?

In this way, when authors create a character, they use **Description**, **Dialogue** and **Deeds** to create a written image of the person.

ⓘ Concept bank

Description: what the character is like physically.

Dialogue: what the character says.

Deeds: what the character does.

⟳ Task

Of Mice and Men, written by the American author John Steinbeck
in 1937, tells the story of George and his mentally impaired friend,
Lennie. George tries to look after Lennie, but Lennie is a liability; he
doesn't know his own strength and kills most things he touches.

The story starts as the two men start a new job. But the farm where
they have gone to work is a place of high tension. The boss's son,
Curley – said to be a good boxer – is agitated because he has just
married a 'purty' young wife … whom he does not trust.

The passage below is the first time that the reader meets Curley.
George has told Lennie to be quiet and let him do all the talking.

↑ *Curley and his wife. Looking at Curley, how
well does he fit the mental image of Curley
which Steinbeck's words create in your mind's
eye?*

> At that moment a young man came into the **bunk house**;
> a thin young man with a brown face, with brown eyes and
> a head of tightly curled hair. He wore a work glove on his
> left hand, and, like the boss, he wore high-heeled boots …
>
> His eyes passed over the new men and he stopped. He   5
> glanced coldly at George and then at Lennie. His arms
> gradually bent at the elbows and his hands closed into fists.
> He stiffened and went into a slight crouch. His glance was
> at once calculating and **pugnacious**. Lennie squirmed
> under the close look and shifted his feet nervously. Curley   10
> stepped **gingerly** close to him.
>
> 'You the new guys the old man was waitin' for?'
>
> 'We just come in,' said George.
>
> 'Let the big guy talk.'
>
> Lennie twisted with embarrassment.   15
>
> George said, 'S'pose he don't want to talk?'
>
> Curley lashed his body around. 'By Christ, he's gotta talk
> when he's spoke to.'

Bunk house: barn where the farm
workers slept.

Pugnacious: out for a fight.

Gingerly: quickly, sharply.

1 Using the details in the passage, draw a rough sketch of how Curley
   is standing and label the details of Curley's appearance. What kind
   of person does Steinbeck's description make Curley out to be?

2 List what Curley *does*. What kind of person does he seem to be?

3 What can we learn about Curley from what he *says*?

⟳ Taking it further

Write an essay about how Steinbeck presents Curley at this point in
the novel. Start with a short paragraph summarising what Curley is
like. Then write three paragraphs – using evidence and quotations to
support your ideas – about Curley's **D**escription, his **D**eeds and
the **D**ialogue.

13.2 Changing perceptions

You will look at how a character develops over the course of a text. You will look closely at the character of Curley's wife.

○ For starters

They say that it takes two minutes to form a first impression about someone, and six months to change it. Share a time when you made a quick judgement of someone you met, but gradually realised that your first impressions were wrong.

○ Task

The only female character in *Of Mice and Men* is the unnamed woman who is Curley's wife. At the start of the novel, we see her almost entirely through the eyes of the men on the ranch.

1 Here are some of the words the men use to describe Curley's wife:

> tart   got the eye   tramp   poison   jail-bait

For each, write an explanation of what you think it means.

2 Talk with a partner about what *reasons* the men might have had to speak about Curley's new wife in this negative way. And can you suggest reasons why George was so keen to persuade Lennie to stay away from her?

3 Eventually, the reader meets Curley's wife:

> She had full, rouged lips and wide-spaced eyes, heavily made up. Her fingernails were red. Her hair hung in little rolled clusters, like sausages. She wore a cotton dress and red mules, on the insteps of which were little bouquets of red ostrich feathers. 'I'm lookin' for Curley,' she said. Her voice had a nasal, brittle quality …
>
> She put her hands behind her back and leaned against the door frame so that her body was thrown forward.
>
> 'You're the new fellas that just come, ain't ya?'

Analyse how Steinbeck presents Curley's wife in this passage, by looking at his **D**escription of her, at what he has her **D**o, and at the **D**ialogue (what he has her say).

4 Practise saying out loud what Curley's wife says. How did you say it? Why? – think about the assumptions you were making about her when you put on the voice you used.

♦ *Nancy Allen Lundy plays Curley's wife in an operatic production in 2003. Which illustration better fits the mental image of Curley's wife which Steinbeck's words create in your mind's eye – this portrayal, or the image on page 128?*

Only in the second half of the book does the reader hear about Curley's wife *in her own words*. The first time is when the men – including Curley – have all gone out to a brothel, leaving behind Crooks (a black stable hand), Candy (an old man with one hand), and Lennie.

> 'They left all the weak ones here,' she said finally. 'Think I don't know where they all went? Even Curley …'
>
> The girl flared up. 'Sure I gotta husban'. You all seen him. Swell guy, ain't he? Spends all his time sayin' what he's gonna do to guys he don't like, and he don't like nobody. 5 Think I'm gonna stay in that two-by-four house and listen how Curley's gonna lead with his left twice, and then bring in the ol' right cross …
>
> 'Whatta ya think I am, a kid? I tell ya I could of went with the shows. Not jus' one, neither. An' a guy tol' me he could 10 put me in pitchers …' She was breathless with indignation. 'Sat'iday night. Ever'body out doin' som'pin'. Ever'body! An' what am I doin'? Standin' here talking to a bunch of **bindle-stiffs** – an' likin' it because they ain't nobody else.

Bindle-stiffs: poor travelling workers

Curley's wife is racist and nasty. But – if you look carefully at what Steinbeck makes her say in this passage – almost every sentence gives us a new insight into her life, and makes us feel sorry for her.

5 Copying the table below, choose three sentences from the passage and explain for each why it makes the reader feel sorry for Curley's wife. To help you, the first one has been done for you.

Quote	Why it makes us feel sorry for her
1. 'Whatta ya think I am, a kid?'	The men on the ranch do not treat her as an equal. She has no status; she is undervalued and looked down on.

6 In groups, discuss the suggestion: 'By the end of the book, Curley's wife is a sympathetic character'.

⟳ Taking it further

Use the information you have learned in this section to write:

> How does Steinbeck develop the character of Curley's wife in *Of Mice and Men*?

Start by writing three paragraphs explaining how the **D**escription and her **D**eeds and **D**ialogue make her out to be a 'tramp' at the start of the novel. Then write a second section of three paragraphs, beginning with the word 'However', and then explaining how the **D**escription and her **D**eeds and **D**ialogue make her appear more sympathetic by the end.

George's assessment of Curley's wife was:

'Ranch with a bunch of guys on it ain't no place for a girl, specially like her.'

Spend a little time talking with a friend about how this sums up the whole problem of Curley's wife.

! Essay tip

Use the 'Good writing techniques' listed on page 48.

13.3 Establishing a character on the stage

You will learn how a playwright uses **D**escription, **D**ialogue and **D**eeds to create a character for the stage. You will study the character of Mr Birling in J.B. Priestley's *An Inspector Calls*.

➲ For starters

An Inspector Calls, by J.B. Priestley, is set in 1912. It starts with the wealthy (and smug and snooty) Mr and Mrs Birling and their son Eric, who are celebrating the engagement of their daughter, Sheila, to Gerald, the son of another rich local family.

↑ *Inspector Goole*

The family is surprised when Inspector Goole comes to tell them that a poor girl named Eva Smith has killed herself. They claim to know nothing of the girl, but, one by one, Goole shows them how they all helped to cause her suicide – Mr Birling sacked her; Sheila got her sacked from her next job; Gerald had an affair with her then dumped her; Eric got her pregnant; and Mrs Birling persuaded the local Women's Charity Organisation not to give her any help.

The Inspector's point is the point of the play – that 'we are responsible for each other'. (It is important to realise that the play was written in 1945, at the start of the Welfare State.)

At the end, the traumatised family finds out with much relief that 'Inspector Goole' does not exist; only to be told that a girl has killed herself and the police are on their way …

Read the description of Arthur Birling and his home in the stage directions (right). Find TWO words Priestley uses which help to reveal Arthur Birling's character, and explain their effect on the audience.

Stage Directions:

The dining-room of a fairly large **suburban** house, belonging to a **prosperous** manufacturer … **substantial** and heavily comfortable, but not cosy and homelike …

The parlourmaid is just clearing the table, which has no cloth, of dessert plates and champagne glasses, etc. …

ARTHUR BIRLING is a heavy-looking, rather **portentous** man in his middle 50s with fairly easy manners but rather **provincial** in his speech. His wife is about 50, a rather cold woman and her husband's **social superior**.

> **Suburban**: out-of-town.
> **Prosperous**: wealthy.
> **Substantial**: wealthy.
> **Portentous**: important.
> **Provincial**: not from London (and therefore not posh).
> **Social superior**: she came from a posh family; he was a factory owner.

⊃ Task

1 At the start of the play, Arthur Birling makes these predictions:
  * there would be no more strikes
  * there would not be a war
  * the Titanic was unsinkable
  * by 1940 there would be peace and prosperity everywhere.

  Writing in 1945, Priestley knew that all these claims were nonsense – so why did he make Arthur Birling say them? What impression of Arthur Birling was he trying to create?

2 Working in groups, study (see right):
  * Arthur Birling's speech to Gerald about marrying Sheila
  * his statement to his son Eric about the meaning of life
  * his threat to try to get Inspector Goole to stop his questioning.

  For each speech:
  * Discuss what it tells you about Arthur Birling.
  * Find, and explain the effect of, two significant words.

3 Here are three of the things Arthur Birling does in the play:
  * he boasts to Gerald that he is expecting a knighthood
  * he sacked Eva Smith because she led a strike for higher wages
  * when he finds out that Eric has been stealing money from the firm, his first thought is to cover it up quickly.

  What do these things suggest about Arthur Birling's character?

4 Finally, thinking about what you have learned, share ideas about the possible reasons *why* Arthur Birling behaved and talked as he did. Does Arthur Birling's comment to Gerald (bottom right) about marrying into the Birling family give you any ideas?

⊃ Taking it further

Imagine you are the producer of a production of *An Inspector Calls*. Write a set of ***Guideline Notes*** on Mr Birling for the Director.

Organise your ***Notes*** under three headings:
* In J.B. Priestley's stage directions he is **D**escribed as:
* His **D**eeds (actions) show him as:
* The **D**ialogue (what he says) shows him as:

You should think of at least three ideas for each section.

Write your ideas as bullet points, which will begin (for example):
* He is …
* He should …
* Make sure he …

Remember to back up your points with facts and quotes from the play.

Arthur Birling's speech to Gerald about marrying Sheila

'You're just the kind of son-in-law I always wanted. Your father and I have been rivals in business for some time now … and now you've brought us together, and perhaps we may look forward to the time when Crofts and Birlings are … working together – for lower costs and higher prices.'

Arthur Birling's statement to his son Eric about the meaning of life

'A man has to make his own way – has to look after himself … the way some of these cranks talk and write now, you'd think everybody has to look after everybody else… – community and all that nonsense.'

Arthur Birling's threat to try to get Inspector Goole to stop his questioning

'Perhaps I ought to warn you that [the Chief Constable] is an old friend of mine, and I see him fairly frequently. We play golf together sometimes.'

Arthur Birling's comment to Gerald about marrying into the Birling family

'I have an idea that your mother – Lady Croft – while she doesn't object to my girl – feels you might have done better for yourself socially.'

13.4 Developing a character on the stage

> You will learn how a playwright uses **D**escription, **D**ialogue and **D**eeds to develop a stage character by studying the character of Mrs Birling in J.B. Priestley's *An Inspector Calls*.

↑ *Mrs Birling*

⊃ For starters

Discuss with a partner what Priestley tells us about Mrs Birling in the stage directions on page 131.

⊃ Task

Mr Birling, in *An Inspector Calls*, is a 'do-er' – he is characterised by his words and actions. Mrs Birling, by contrast, is *reactive*; her character is shown in the way she reacts to events and people.

Mrs Birling *speaks* mainly in short exclamations:

- When Sheila says Eric is 'squiffy' (drunk), she says:
  MRS B.   What an expression, Sheila! Really the things you girls pick up these days!

- When Arthur says that Gerald joining the family will be good for business:
  MRS B.   Now Arthur, I don't think you ought to talk business on an occasion like this.

- When the Inspector begins to question her, at first she says:
  MRS B.   That – I consider – is a trifle impertinent, Inspector.

- When Sheila suggests that the family had killed Eva Smith:
  MRS B.   (*sharply*) Sheila, don't talk nonsense.

- When Gerald says his relationship with Eva was not disgusting:
  MRS B.   It's disgusting to me.

One focus of the play is Mrs Birling's relationship with her son. Again, this is revealed in what she says:

- When Sheila and Gerald tell her that Eric is often 'squiffy':
  MRS B.   (*bitterly*) And this is the time you choose to tell me.
- When she realises that Eric was the father of Eva Smith's baby:
  MRS B.   (*with a cry*) Oh Eric – how could you?
- And when she finds out that he was stealing money:
  MRS B.   (*shocked*) Eric! You stole money?

1   Study each of Mrs Birling's five exclamations (left).
    What do they show about her character?

2   Working with a partner, practise saying each of these statements in the way you think Mrs Birling would have said them.
    Experiment with different tones and gestures, and decide which works best.

3   Study these three statements by Mrs Birling (left). What do they tell us about her feelings for her son?

4   Mr Birling said that Eric was spoilt; do you agree?

And it is Mrs Birling's adoration for her son which leads to the time in the play when she loses her self-control. In the following dialogue, Eric has just found out that his mother had refused to help Eva:

INSPECTOR	(*with calm authority*) I'll tell you. She went to your mother's committee for help, after she'd done with you. Your mother refused that help.
ERIC	(*nearly at breaking point*) Then – you killed her. She came to you to protect me – and you turned her away – yes, and you killed her – and the child she'd have had too – my child – your own grandchild – you killed them both – damn you, damn you—
MRS B.	(*very distressed now*) No – Eric – please – I didn't know – I didn't understand—

One thing Mrs Birling *did*, of course, was refuse to help Eva Smith, who:

- had called herself Mrs Birling ('impertinently made use of our name')
- had refused to marry the father ('she was claiming fine feelings and scruples that were simply absurd in a girl in her position')
- had refused money from the father because he was stealing it ('it sounded ridiculous to me').

By the end of the play, Mrs Birling is treating the Inspector's visit as a joke. The last thing she says in the play, when Eric and Sheila refuse to find it funny, is:

MRS B.	They're over-tired. In the morning they'll be as amused as we are.

5 Working with two partners, act out the scene between the Inspector, Eric and Mrs Birling. Experiment with different tones, voices and gestures, and decide which works best.

6 From pages 133–134, list all the stage directions given by Priestley about Mrs Birling. What picture of her do they create?

7 What can we learn about Mrs Birling from the fact that she refused to help Eva Smith?

8 Do you think Mrs Birling felt any guilt for Eva Smith's death? Did the events change her at all?

9 From her speeches on pages 133–134, choose three words or phrases Mrs Birling says, and explain how they make you feel about her.

➲ Taking it further

Playwrights, like authors, use three devices to establish a character:

- **Stage directions** – to paint an outline sketch of the person
- **Deeds** (their actions and reactions) – to show them 'in action'
- **Dialogue** – to reveal their inner thoughts and feelings.

List all your thoughts about Mrs Birling under these three headings.

Use these ideas to answer the question:

> How did J.B. Priestley develop the character of Mrs Birling in *An Inspector Calls?*

Remember, for each paragraph to:

- Start with a topic sentence stating the point.
- Provide evidence – in the form of facts or a quote – to back up your point.
- Explain and develop your idea, particularly explaining the effect on you as the audience.

! Essay tip

Write your essay in six paragraphs about:

1 The play's storyline and message.
2 What we can tell about Mrs Birling from Priestley's stage directions.
3 What we can tell about her from her actions.
4 What we can tell about her from the play's dialogue.
5 How her character changes as the play goes on.
6 A summary conclusion.

14 Genres and Form – Openings

14.1 *Romeo and Juliet* – exploring language and action

> You will work out what is happening in this scene and explore the aggressive language used to set the scene.

⟳ For starters

Has there ever been a time when you have argued or had a fight with someone else?

In pairs, tell each other about a time when you saw a memorable fight or argument on a recent soap or TV programme and explain what happened. Share some of your moments with the rest of the class.

Romeo and Juliet is about two families, the Capulets and the Montagues, who hate each other and are always getting into fights and arguments. This is what causes the tragedy of *Romeo and Juliet*.

➡ *An image from Baz Luhrmann's film of* **Romeo and Juliet**.

➲ Task

Romeo and Juliet opens, as Shakespeare's stage directions tell us, in 'Verona. A public place.' At first the scene is amusing – servants of the two warring families are mixing, boasting and swapping insults. But the atmosphere soon turns violent when Sampson (a Capulet) decides to bite his thumb at the Montagues ('which is a great disgrace to them if they bear it'). In Shakespeare's time, to 'bite your thumb' at someone was a great insult (like swearing at someone today). After this, the situation quickly turns violent:

Genres and Form – Openings

Enter ABRAHAM and BALTHASAR

ABRAHAM	Do you bite your thumb at us, sir?	39
SAMPSON	I do bite my thumb, sir.	40
ABRAHAM	Do you bite your thumb at us, sir?	
SAMPSON	[*Aside to GREGORY*] Is the law of our side if I say ay?	
GREGORY	No.	
SAMPSON	No, sir, I do not bite my thumb at you, sir, but I bite my thumb, sir.	45
GREGORY	Do you quarrel, sir?	
ABRAHAM	Quarrel, sir? No, sir.	
SAMPSON	But if you do, sir, I am for you. I serve as good a man as you.	
ABRAHAM	No better.	50
SAMPSON	Well, sir.	
GREGORY	Say 'better,' here comes one of my master's kinsmen.	
SAMPSON	Yes, better, sir.	
ABRAHAM	You lie.	55
SAMPSON	Draw, if you be men. Gregory, remember thy washing blow.	

They fight

Enter BENVOLIO

| BENVOLIO | Part, fools! Put up your swords, you know not what you do. | 59 |

Beats down their swords

In a group of four, act out this scene. Try saying the lines in different ways, so as to achieve different effects, for example:

- Say the words in a very angry and confrontational way, so that the atmosphere is very threatening and violent.
- Say the words in a very childish and exaggerated way, so that the affair seems trivial and the effect is to make the men look ridiculous.
- Say the words in a very 'smart-alec' and cocky way, so that the effect is to make the scene amusing and clever.

Which interpretation worked best?

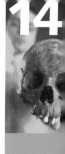
Taking it further

Based on your study of Act 1, Scene 1, lines 39–59, write a paragraph describing the mood of the scene. To prepare your ideas, think about:

- the way the scene gradually builds up
- the way aggressive and crude language is used during the conversation
- how the language gets more aggressive as the scene progresses
- how the scene climaxes with a fight, but not a fight like we might see in the street today – a fight with swords.

When you have written your paragraph, read it to a friend or group of friends. Ask for feedback on these points:

- Have you explained your ideas thoroughly?
- Have you supported your points with facts and quotes?

Grammar link

Short sentences – these can make a speaker's words seem to the point, harsh and aggressive, for example:

ABRAHAM   No better.

SAMPSON   Well, sir.

14.2 *Romeo and Juliet* – exploring atmosphere and excitement

> You will explore further the aggressive language and look at what the theatre was like when the play was first produced.

Concept bank

Speed of speech: how quickly a line in the play is said. The more quickly, the more aggressive a character will come across. Speaking too quickly, however, cannot be heard by the audience.

For starters

When Shakespeare wrote his plays, as well as including aggressive language and insults, he used a number of devices to create a sense of tension and aggression, including:

- short lines
- **speed of speech**
- the number of people speaking.

Working in a group, for each of the devices in the list, suggest how it might have helped to create a sense of tension and aggression.

In lines 60–74, therefore, the quarrel that started with Sampson biting his thumb at Abraham continues to escalate (get worse) until it involves high-ranking Capulets such as Tybalt, whole mobs of citizens, and eventually the Lords Capulet and Montague themselves.

⊃ **Task**

1 Find in lines 60–74 an example of Shakespeare using:
   - short lines
   - **speed of speech**
   - a large number of people speaking.

   What is the effect of this in the scene?

2 A good way to describe the first scene of *Romeo and Juliet* would be 'aggressive' and 'petty'. Having studied and acted the scene, list all the things which make the scene aggressive and petty. Remember to explain each idea, and to support it with a quote from the play.

Enter TYBALT

TYBALT	What, art thou drawn among these heartless hinds?	60
	Turn thee, Benvolio, look upon thy death.	
BENVOLIO	I do but keep the peace. Put up thy sword,	
	Or manage it to part these men with me.	
TYBALT	What, drawn and talk of peace? I hate the word,	
	As I hate hell, all Montagues, and thee.	65
	Have at thee, coward.	

They fight

Enter, several of both houses, who join the fray, then enter Citizens, with clubs

FIRST CITIZEN	Clubs, bills, and partisans! Strike! Beat them down!	
	Down with the Capulets! Down with the Montagues!	

Enter CAPULET in his gown, and LADY CAPULET

CAPULET	What noise is this? Give me my long sword, ho!	
LADY CAPULET	A crutch, a crutch! Why call you for a sword?	
CAPULET	My sword, I say! Old Montague is come,	70
	And flourishes his blade in spite of me.	

Enter MONTAGUE and LADY MONTAGUE

MONTAGUE	Thou villain Capulet! – Hold me not, let me go.	
LADY MONTAGUE	Thou shalt not stir one foot to seek a foe.	74

ⓘ **Concept bank**

Speed of speech: how quickly a line in the play is said. The more quickly, the more aggressive a character will come across. Speaking too quickly, however, cannot be heard by the audience.

↑ *When Tybalt enters, he sums up the whole aggression of the opening scene.*

⊃ **Taking it further**

Looking back on this section, write three paragraphs to answer the question:

> How does Shakespeare gain his audience's interest at the start of *Romeo and Juliet*?

- In the first paragraph, write factually about what happens in the scene.

- In the second paragraph, using quotes from the play, explain how Shakespeare uses language to create excitement.

- In the third paragraph, explain how he uses other devices (short lines, speed of speech and the number of speakers).

14.3 *Hamlet* – exploring mood and staging

You will work out what is happening and explore how Shakespeare creates mood and atmosphere in the very opening scene of *Hamlet*.

➲ For starters

⬆ *The Globe Theatre*

When *Hamlet* was first performed, there was no set and no lighting and the play had to be performed in an open-air theatre in the light of day.

Shakespeare's plays were performed at the Globe Theatre in London, which has been made as good as new and is still used for plays today. Think about what the theatre was like during the time when Shakespeare wrote this play. There was no lighting like we have today; instead there was just natural daylight and maybe the light of candles and torches (from flames). There was little in the way of **set**, with just the items of furniture needed for certain scenes. Sound would have been performed live as there were no facilities to play CDs or mp3s then.

1 How might the actors and the director get across key elements of the play with very limited scenery, sound effects and lighting?
2 How might the lack of sound, lighting or scenery affect the audience watching the play?
3 Looking at the picture of the Globe Theatre, list as many differences from a modern theatre as you can see.

ⓘ Concept bank

Mood and atmosphere: the emotional feeling that is created in the scene, such as sad, happy, depressed and tense.

Set: the backdrop, the use of scenery and fixed furniture on stage.

⊃ Task

1 The opening scene of *Hamlet* is set on the castle ramparts (the top section where soldiers would have aimed their weapons at invaders) in the dark at night. As you read the following extract from Act 1, Scene 1 (lines 1–14), think about what the mood and atmosphere of the scene is and how this is put across to the audience.

Elsinore. A platform before the castle

FRANCISCO at his post. Enter to him BERNARDO

BERNARDO	Who's there?	1
FRANCISCO	Nay, answer me: stand, and unfold yourself.	
BERNARDO	Long live the king!	
FRANCISCO	Bernardo?	
BERNARDO	He.	5
FRANCISCO	You come most carefully upon your hour.	
BERNARDO	'Tis now struck twelve; get thee to bed, Francisco.	
FRANCISCO	For this relief much thanks: 'tis bitter cold,	
	And I am sick at heart.	
BERNARDO	Have you had quiet guard?	10
FRANCISCO	Not a mouse stirring.	
BERNARDO	Well, good night.	
	If you do meet Horatio and Marcellus,	
	The rivals of my watch, bid them make haste.	14

On page 138, you learned a number of dramatic devices which Shakespeare used to create a sense of mood in *Romeo and Juliet*. Looking at Act 1, Scene 1 of *Hamlet*, look at the way Shakespeare uses:

- short lines
- speed of speech
- the number of people speaking

and suggest what effect they have upon the mood of the scene.

There is clearly something wrong as they are nervous. Shakespeare builds up this nervousness throughout the scene.

2 Look again at the opening five lines of the play. How has Shakespeare created tension at the start of the scene?

3 Say these lines in pairs. How is it best to say them? Try them slowly, then try them quickly. Which works best?

4 Lines 6–14 give the audience more information about the time of night. What clues are given as to what time of the day or night it is?

5 What do we learn about the atmosphere from 'Not a mouse stirring'?

⊃ Taking it further

1 In pairs, act out the opening section up to line 14. Imagine the tension of the moment. Think about the following:

- It is cold – what do you do to show this?
- It is dark so they do not immediately recognise each other – how can you show this?
- It is very quiet – how is this best shown?

2 How did you make your decisions on how to act the scene? Write a short answer.

⊟ Grammar link

Colon – this punctuation mark is often used before a list. In the extract above, what follows the colon is a list of two things – either an instruction:

'Nay, answer me: stand, and unfold yourself.'

or two feelings (the cold and being sick at heart):

'For this relief much thanks: 'tis bitter cold,
And I am sick at heart.'

14.4 *Hamlet* – exploring reactions and effects

You will look at the beliefs and superstitions of those in *Hamlet* and of the audience who watched *Hamlet* when it was first produced.

↑ *David Tennant as Hamlet*

⭓ For starters

1 With a partner discuss whether you believe in ghosts.
2 Tell each other a ghost story or a story full of tension and fear. If you know a local ghost story, retell it to your partner.

⭓ Task

1 Once the atmosphere has been set we now move on to the first key event in the story. Look at the lines on the right.
   • What do these lines tell us about what they have seen?
   • What does another line 'Tush, tush, 'twill not appear' (line 38) from Horatio tell us about his attitude to it?

The audience would have believed very strongly in ghosts when the play was first performed in about 1601. They were very **superstitious** and would have taken this very seriously.

   • What do people tend to think about ghosts now?
2 Read the following extract from the scene:

'has this thing appeared again tonight?' *(line 29)*
'this dreaded sight' *(line 33)*
'this apparition' *(line 36)*

Enter ghost

MARCELLUS	Peace, break thee off. Look, where it comes again!	50
BERNARDO	In the same figure, like the king that's dead.	
MARCELLUS	Thou art a scholar. Speak to it, Horatio.	
BERNARDO	Looks it not like the king? Mark it, Horatio.	
HORATIO	Most like. It harrows me with fear and wonder.	
BERNARDO	It would be spoke to.	55
MARCELLUS	Question it, Horatio.	
HORATIO	What art thou that usurp'st this time of night,	
	Together with that fair and warlike form	
	In which the majesty of buried Denmark	
	Did sometimes march? by heaven I charge thee, speak!	60
MARCELLUS	It is offended.	
BERNARDO	See, it stalks away!	
HORATIO	Stay! speak, speak! I charge thee, speak!	63

ⓘ Concept bank

Superstitious: to believe something so much that you change your behaviour because of it: for example, not walking under a ladder.

What does the ghost look like? Use these lines to help you:

> 'it harrows me with fear and wonder' *(line 54)*
>
> 'fair and warlike form' *(line 58)*
>
> 'majesty of buried Denmark' *(line 59)*
>
> 'like the king that's dead' *(line 51)*

- Pick out a few words and phrases that tell us about its appearance.
- What does the ghost do? These lines may give you some clues:

> 'See, it stalks away!' *(line 62)*
>
> 'Stay! speak, speak! I charge thee, speak!' *(line 63)*

- How do the others react to it? The following line may help you:

> 'it harrows me with fear and wonder' *(line 54)*

3 The audience would know what the mood and atmosphere was by how Shakespeare uses language and words and how the actors deliver the lines of the play.

- Act out the whole scene in groups of about four (some of you will have to play more than one part). Remember to think about how Shakespeare creates tension in this scene.
- A good way to describe the mood of the first scene of *Hamlet* is 'menacing'. Having studied and acted the scene, list all the things which make the scene menacing. Remember to explain each idea, and to support it with a quote from the play.

⊃ Taking it further

Write an essay in three sections to compare how the opening scenes of *Romeo and Juliet* and *Hamlet* gain their audiences' interest. What are the main similarities and differences?

- In the first section, compare the scenes of the two plays – writing about such issues as Where? Who? And What?
- In the second section, compare how Shakespeare uses language to create the mood and atmosphere for the play. Remember to support your ideas with quotes from the play, and to explain the effect that his words have on an audience.
- In the third section, write about how Shakespeare uses other devices (such as short lines, speed of speech and the number of people speaking) to make the scene powerful and interesting.

⟳ Grammar link

Repetition – used to emphasise a point or an instruction. In the line:

'See, it stalks away!'

'Stay! speak, speak! I charge thee, speak!'

the word 'speak' is repeated three times as Horatio urges the ghost to stay and speak to them.

! Essay tip

In a 'compare' essay, you need to split each paragraph into two halves, which are joined by a discourse marker such as 'Similarly …' or 'By contrast …'

For example:

- In *Romeo and Juliet*, Shakespeare … Similarly, in *Hamlet*, he …

or

- *Romeo and Juliet* is … By contrast, *Hamlet* is …

15 Attitudes to Spoken Language

Learning aim

In this unit you will think about how we speak. You will learn some of the important terms we use to describe language, and gain the skills you will need for your Controlled Assessment Task investigating spoken language.

ⓘ Concept bank

Accent: the way in which words are pronounced.

⬆ *Steven Gerrard has a Scouse accent and Cheryl Cole has a Geordie accent.*

15.1 Introducing accent

You will investigate the ways in which different groups of people pronounce words differently.

↺ For starters

Some people have an **accent** that depends on where they were brought up. Do you think you have this kind of accent? How would you describe it?

Everybody has an accent (often more than one!) which depends on a number of things: where we live or were brought up; the way our friends speak; our surroundings; what we feel about ourselves.

Are there people in your class with a different accent from you? (Do not forget your teacher!) What words are pronounced differently? For example, some people pronounce the word 'laugh' with a short 'a' like 'laff' some people pronounce it with a long 'a' like 'larf'.

↺ Task

Many people are proud of their regional accent.

1 Make a list of regional accents (for example: Scouse/Liverpudlian, Glaswegian, Geordie/Newcastle). Who do you know who speaks like this? Remember to include people on TV! Share your answers with a partner.

2 Try this quick quiz.

> How do you pronounce the following words?
>
> GARAGE   (to rhyme with LARGE or RIDGE?)
>
> GLASS   (with a short A to rhyme with MASS or a long A to rhyme with FARCE?)
>
> ENVELOPE (with EN or ON at the beginning? Or as EM-VELOPE?)
>
> HOTEL   (with an H at the start or an O? Do you say 'AN OTEL' or 'A HOTEL'?)
>
> SANDWICH (SAND-WICH, SAN-WICH, or SAM-WICH?)

Compare your findings with your partner. Are they the same or different? Why? Make a note of your findings.

'**Received Pronunciation**' is a term used to describe an accent that is often called 'BBC English'. Some people think that people who speak with an RP accent have more power, have better jobs and are better educated than people who have a regional accent.

3 With your partner, make a list of people you think have power – in your school, in society and in the media. Do they speak with an RP accent, or do they have a regional accent?

4 Discuss this with your partner. Do you think this shows that RP has '**high prestige**'? Do you think it is fair to judge people by how they speak?

↻ Taking it further

1 Give one or two older people (perhaps your parents or grandparents) the same quiz as above. Show them the words. Listen carefully to the way they say them. Make some notes. Is there any difference between the ways people of your age and older people pronounce these words? Why might this be?

2 Prepare a short presentation on this quiz. You will need to:

- show the list of words and say who you asked to do the quiz
- explain what you discovered about the way you and your partner pronounced the words
- explain what you discovered about the way the older people pronounced the words
- say what you discovered in your research. Did the results surprise you?

Ask your family to complete the quiz ➔

> **ⓘ Concept bank**
>
> **Received Pronunciation (RP):** a non-regional English accent that is often used for serious television and radio programmes and in formal contexts. Some people regard it as having 'high prestige'.
>
> **High prestige:** describes an accent or dialect that some people think is spoken by people who have power and status in society.

15.2 Introducing dialect

You will look at the way you and other people use **dialect**.

⊃ For starters

People from different parts of the country often use words that other people find unusual. Here are some examples of **non-standard dialect** words in speech:

A

We was fishing in the rain. If thou seed the line twitch thou'd pull he in

C

Ah'd say gan yam, but tha'll tek nee notice any road!

D

Mi Mam caught me waggin school and went mental at me

B

Ay up mi duck, ow art?

1   Write down the words that come from non-standard dialects, and try to work out their meanings (for example, 'yam' in C – in some Cumbrian dialects, 'yam' means 'home').

2   Some dialect forms use non-standard grammar. Can you find any in example A?

3   Rewrite the four examples in **Standard English**. (Example A might be: 'We were fishing in the canal. If you saw the line move, you would pull it in.')

⊃ Task

Read the local news article below on dialect. (It is taken from *The Great Harwood Mercury* by Joan White.)

DEAD AS A DODMAN?

Joan White talks about the near extinction of the rural Essex dialect

Ever done a pitch-a-pennie-pie? Seen a dodman? Eaten ingons? You probably have, but if you're a furriner, you won't know it. But when I was young, you only had to 5 walk through any Essex village to hear these words – and many more.

My old Nan were an Essex gal. Although it's many years since she was 'laid by the wall', I still 10 remember the dialect words she used: 'Don't be afeard'; 'Do you need the dunnekin?' (Nan had a ferociously clean outside toilet!); 'Don't goffle your food'. 15

Accents and dialects remind us that although we are all called 'British', our country is a mixture of different regions and groups, and that's a real strength. 20

But now regional dialects seem to be dying. It might be because people move around a lot more nowadays. It might be because we have radio and television to let us 2 hear how other people speak. It might be because school teachers insist that children 'Talk properly'. Whatever the reason, I think it's a shame. 3

So, if you have a grandmother who uses odd words, don't laugh at her. Instead, why not persuade her to keep them alive by recording them? After all, this means that your 3 grandmother – like dialect – will become a national treasure!

1 Read the first two paragraphs. Make a list of the dialect words here.
2 What do you think these dialect words mean?
3 Find an example of non-standard grammar in the first sentence of paragraph 2.
4 Why does Joan White think dialects are important (paragraph 3)?
5 In paragraph 4, what *three* reasons does Joan White give to explain why regional dialects are dying?

⊃ Taking it further

Joan White thinks that dialects are dying out.

Write a letter to *The Great Harwood Mercury* in which you argue that dialects are not dying out, and that there are still interesting words being used today. Think about:
• words that you and people in your area use
• words used by young people and not by older people; for example, words used by young people to describe something as good, or words to describe skipping school
• words from modern technology.

Remember to use paragraphs for each new topic you introduce. If you use the ideas from the bullets above, then you will need a paragraph for each. Remember to start your letter 'Dear Editor', and to finish with the words 'Yours faithfully' and your name.

⊙ Grammar link

Paragraphs are an important feature of writing: they allow the reader to follow your ideas more easily. It is important to remember the need to give each separate point its own paragraph – especially in the exam, because the examiner will be looking to see that you can use paragraphs!

15.3 Attitudes to accent in the media

You will look at the ways that accents are used in TV programmes.

⟳ For starters

Radio and television can be important in reinforcing our attitudes to accent.

List TV programmes which show different accents. You might want to start with soaps, and move on to chat shows, cookery shows and the news. What accents are being used (for example, Scouse, Cockney)? Compare your list with a partner.

⟳ Task

The two letters below have been read out on a viewer feedback show on the BBC. They show two different attitudes to non-standard accents. Read the letters, and then answer the questions on page 148.

↑ *The chef Jamie Oliver has an Essex accent.*

Dear BBC

Well done, BBC! If you intend to 'dumb down' your service until it has lost the little respect it used to have, you've certainly succeeded!

I was shocked when I listened to the *6 o'clock News* last night. The newsreader had such a strong accent I was totally distracted from what she was saying.

I'm not saying I couldn't understand the newsreader, but it's a question of standards. The BBC has a duty to preserve correct 'BBC English', and this is especially important for the *News*. Accents are not suitable for serious broadcasting.

Harold Timmins, Potters Bar

Dear BBC

I am amazed and angered by the bigoted views of Mr Timmins. What's wrong with having newsreaders talking in their own accents?

Millions of people watch and enjoy soaps like *EastEnders* and *Coronation Street*. Accents here are no problem, so why should it be different for the *News*?

Britain is made up of 60 million people, and most do not have a middle-class Southern 'BBC accent'. Let's show that we value everybody, not just Mr Timmins and his like. Otherwise, you're saying that people like me who are proud of our accents can't be trusted with serious things like the *News* or current affairs.

Let's have <u>more</u> regional accents on the *News* – then we might really become an equal society!

David Bruce, Aberdeen

1 Write out one sentence from each letter that you think shows the attitude of the writer to non-standard accents.

2 Write down two words from each letter that show the emotions the writer feels.

3 Using your own words, what is Mr Timmins arguing in his letter?

4 Using your own words, what is the main argument in Mr Bruce's reply?

5 Write a letter to the viewer feedback show explaining your own feelings on this issue. You should start your letter 'Dear BBC' and write a short paragraph for each of the following points.

- Say which writer you disagree with.
- Show why you think his argument is wrong.
- Explain why you agree with the other writer.
- Say what you want the BBC to do about it.

⟳ Taking it further

1 Think about the way accents are used on television. Make a list of tonight's TV programmes that show strong non-standard accents. Identify what kind of programmes these are (soap operas, comedy, sports, music …).

2 Do newsreaders also use a variety of accents, or only one? Try to see part of at least two different news programmes to answer this question.

3 Do your answers to the above two tasks suggest anything about the attitudes to accent held by the television companies? Write a paragraph that sums up your findings.

Tom Leonard's famous poem (right) is a protest about the way the news is usually read by someone speaking with an RP accent. The poem is ironic – the newsreader makes negative comments about people who speak with a strong accent … whilst speaking in a strong Scottish accent himself.

4 Which lines show that people tend to look down on people who speak with a strong regional accent?

5 Which lines show that the poet is violently angry about this?

6 Try to read the poem in a strong Scottish accent. Try to read it with an RP accent. Does the use of an accent make the poem more, or less effective?

'Unrelated Incidents' - No.3

```
this is thi
six a clock
news thi
man said n
thi reason          5
a talk wia
BBC accent
iz coz yi
widny wahnt
mi ti talk         10
aboot thi
trooth wia
voice lik
wanna yoo
scruff. if         15
a toktaboot
thi trooth
lik wanna yoo
scruff yi
widny thingk       20
it wuz troo.
jist wanna yoo
scruff tokn.
thirza right
way ti spell       25
ana right way
to tok it. this
is me tokn yir
right way a
spellin. this      30
is ma trooth.
yooz doant no
thi trooth
yirsellz cawz
yi canny talk      35
right. this is
the six a clock
nyooz. belt up.
```

15.4 Understanding sociolect

You will investigate how different groups of speakers of English use language in different and distinctive ways for different purposes.

○ For starters

People who share the same interest, profession, background or belong to the same social group often have their own variety of language. Different groups of people will use specialist terms that other groups will not use; for example, rock-climbers might talk about 'pitons', 'pitches', 'routes' and 'harnesses', as well as terms for different grades of climb such as 'VS' or 'E5'. This shared language is called a **sociolect**.

What special words or phrases might some of the following groups use?
- Football fans
- Teachers
- Drummers (or other musicians)
- Skateboarders
- Doctors

Discuss your ideas with your partner.

(i) Concept bank

Sociolect: a variety of language used by people with shared interests or belonging to a particular group.

○ Task

1 Here Michael is writing about his hobby, canoeing. What specialist terms does he use in his description?

My favourite sport is kayaking. A kayak is a sort of canoe in which you sit and use a double-ended paddle, and you have a spraydeck that goes around your waist to keep the water out of the cockpit. We go on rivers like the Dee up to about Grade 4, which means large waves called stoppers and some little waterfalls, but nothing really dangerous.

2 You will belong to a number of groups that have their own words or sociolect. How many can you identify? You might think about your sporting interests, hobbies, part-time job or intended career.

3　Write a short paragraph about one of the activities you listed in task 2. Your audience should be someone who is *not* part of that grouping, so you will need to explain specialist words that you use, as Michael has done.

4　What do you think might be the purposes of different sociolects? One purpose is to help people feel part of a group, because they share the same language. Can you think of any others? You might want to think about how you feel when you talk to people who share your interests, and how you feel when you hear people talking about a subject that you do not enjoy.

➲ Taking it further

Look back at the paragraph you have written. If your audience were people who shared your interest, they would understand your sociolect (specialist terms) without you explaining them. How would you write for this audience?

Here is some writing aimed at a specialist audience – motorbike riders – from a Harley-Davidson weblog written by Head Hog.

HOG HEAVEN!

It don't come better than this: cruisin' down Route 66, helmetless, sunshine highlighting the silver flakes in the Electra Glide's Arctic White glacier-deep paint, accompanied by the iconic throb of the monster Twin Cam powerplant. Forget your Japanese crotch-rockets: Harley, America, the Mother Road – motorbikin' suddenly makes perfect sense again.

HOG: a Harley-Davidson motorcycle or motorcyclist.

1　What specialist words show the writer's use of sociolect? Write them down.

2　Write your own 'blog' entry for a specialist audience about your chosen topic. Choose a specialist topic – a hobby or a personal interest.

- Perhaps using an Internet search on the topic to help you, make a list of specialist terms, jargon and slang words used by people who share the sociolect for this activity – for instance, terms they use to refer to each other, or words they use to describe the activity.

- Imagine you were doing the activity yesterday. Write a short account of what you did, including as many specialist terms as possible.

- Give yourself an appropriate 'username' (a name you give yourself online to preserve your privacy).

- Be prepared to read it out loud for others to listen to.

Learning aim

In this unit you will gain the skills and knowledge you will need to do an investigation of spoken language for the Spoken Genres Controlled Assessment Task. You will learn about some of the factors which influence spoken language.

16.1 Words in context

You will learn about the factors that influence the way we speak.

⊃ For starters

In pairs, make a list of 'things that teachers say'. When do they say these things? Share your list with other students.

⊃ Task

Scenario: Mr Layton stops a fight between Matthew Miles and another boy. Mr Layton is angry and frustrated – Matthew is often in fights and he has spent a lot of time trying to help him. He sets off to the staffroom to phone Matthew's mother but, before he makes the call, he tells one of the other teachers in the staffroom what has happened.

Confrontation	Apologise for
Contact	Parent
Punish	Endangering
Guess what?	Incident
Lads	Out of control
Matthew	Mother
Losing patience with	Pain in the backside
Right troublemaker	Put him on report
Required to	Students
Scrap	Sick of it
Thug	Typical of him
Bully	Matt
Detention	Mum
Getting stuck in	Continuing problems
Intimidating	Regret
Ring up	Terrorise
Yob	Disappointing

1 Draw a table with two columns: **Words he used when talking to the teacher** and **Words he used when talking to the mother on the phone**. Now look at the word bank on the left. Are there any words in the word bank that you can definitely put in one column or the other?

2　Are there any words that you are not sure about, or words that you could put in either column? Explain why (and leave them out of your table).

3　Using the words in the first column of your table, perform a short drama of Mr Layton telling the member of staff about the fight. Make sure you get the tone and gestures right, as well as the words.

When we speak, there are four factors which influence what we say and how we say it:

Role	Context
In the staffroom, he was Mike the friend and colleague.	He was talking privately in the staffroom.
Purpose	**Audience**
To talk about an event which had annoyed him.	He was talking to one person who was a friend.

4　Looking at these four factors, explain how each might have affected the way Mr Layton talked to the other teacher about the fight.

5　Mr Layton is the Head of Year. He goes into his office and phones Matthew's mother. How might what he says, and how he says it, be affected by:

- the **role** he is in when he makes the call (Head of Year, representing the school)
- the **context** (a phone call which may be recorded)
- the **purpose** of the call (to complain about Matthew)
- the **audience** (Matthew's mother – what kind of woman might she be, and how would this affect how he talks to her)?

6　Using the words in the second column of your table, perform a short drama of Mr Layton phoning the mother about the fight. Make sure you get the tone and gestures right, as well as the words.

⟳ Taking it further

Write an analysis in four paragraphs of how Mr Layton speaks to Matthew's mother. For each paragraph:

- identify the factor which influences him (the context and audience, his role and purpose)
- provide examples of things he might say where he was being influenced by that factor
- explain how the factor leads him to say those things.

The following template will help you answer this question:

> One factor which influenced Mr Layton was his role – he was …
>
> This was why he …
>
> He said this because …

ⓘ Concept bank

Role: the status, actions and behaviours given to or expected of a person in a particular situation. For example: team captain, brother or teacher. Roles carry expectations of behaviour and of language use.

Context: the situation, purpose or audience for a text. For example, talking privately to your teacher is a different context to talking to a group of friends in the canteen.

16.2 Voices and choices

> You will learn that speech varies according to whether it is planned or **spontaneous**, and according to how familiar speakers are with each other.

⊃ For starters

1 You greeted four people when you came to school this morning. Match what you said to the people you met (the first one has been done for you).

Greeting		Person
'Hiya, mate!'		The Headteacher
'Morning!'		Your best friend
'Hello, Miss!'		A classmate
'Good morning, how are you?'		Your form teacher

Below are six statements made by Mrs Marianne Chadwick, Deputy Headteacher and Chemistry teacher at a school in London.

2 Choose one extract and suggest:
- what Mrs Chadwick's role is at the time
- what the context is for what she is saying
- what her purpose is
- who the audience is for what she is saying.

3 Discuss how these factors seem to influence what she says and the words she uses.

A Hi, Joan. Yeah, sorry … Can I just grab you for a quick minute about Toni Arthur in your form? Won't be a sec … promise … Can I just move your bag?

B Jonty Neville! Don't look away when I'm talking to you. Didn't we have words about this yesterday? Back in line now!

C 8N, quiet, please. Come on … That's it … We, we need just to … to have a look again at yesterday's objectives … that business on atoms and molecules off the whiteboard. Can … Who can remember the difference between a compound and a molecule? Javinder, you?

D Firstly, welcome. It's wonderful that so many of you have turned out to support the school! As you know from newsletters, we've been raising money now for well over 12 months, and it's truly excellent that we're only just a little short of our target.

E I'm expecting nothing but the best behaviour from you all. You are ambassadors for the school, and if there's any nonsense you'll be having a word with me when we get back. Is that clear? I said, is that clear? That's you too, Frances …

F Hello … Mrs Marler? It's Mrs Marianne Chadwick from Midbridge School. Nothing to worry about … Natalie wasn't in registration this morning … I'm phoning to see if there's anything we need to know …

⊃ Task

You should now be familiar with the effect of role, context, purpose and audience on speech. Another influence on speech is the amount of planning. For example, at one end of the scale is a thoroughly planned speech which is then read out; at the other end of the scale is a casual chat between friends in a **spontaneous** way.

1 Look at Mrs Chadwick's six statements on page 153. Working with a friend, for each statement:
   - consider whether it is planned or spontaneous
   - suggest one way this affects the way she speaks
   - decide where you would place it on the line below
   - explain your decision.

| Very prepared and planned | Somewhere in between | No thought – spontaneous |

A further influence on speech is how familiar you are with the person you are talking to – you speak in a very different way to your best friend than you do to a complete stranger.

2 Look again at Mrs Chadwick's six statements on page 153. Working with a friend, for each statement:
   - consider how well she knows her audience
   - suggest one way this affects the way she speaks
   - decide where you would place it on the line below
   - explain your decision.

| Very familiar | Somewhere in between | Very unfamiliar |

You now know six influences on speech:
- What role is the speaker in?
- What context are they speaking in?
- What is their purpose in speaking?
- Who are the audience?
- How planned is their speech?
- How familiar do they feel with the person they are speaking to?

ⓘ Concept bank

Spontaneous: without planning or warning.

➲ Taking it further

Read the two **transcripts** below which show Miss Powell, a young English teacher, speaking in two different contexts.

Text 1: In class, teaching

People: Miss Powell [P] – teacher, mid 20s; Chelsea [C] – one of the students. The group are about to start writing.

P   Right [.] if you need a pen come and
get one from the box on my table [*1*]
gentlemen at the back [*2*] can I have your
attention please [*3*] [*while the students settle
down*] OK right once you have got this   5
written down from the board you can start
looking for the quotes [.] Chelsea will you
please sit down

C   But Miss [.] you said I could get a pen

P   OK but hurry up [.] I want all this finished   10
by the end of the lesson [*3*] Rob [.] Shaun
[.] is there any danger of you two getting
some writing done this side of Christmas
[.] you've done nothing but talk since I told
you to get writing   15

ⓘ Concept bank

Transcript: the written text that is made when a speech is recorded and then written out or transcribed. The symbols in a transcript show how the conversation sounds: [.] is a very short pause; [*2*] is a pause of two (or however many) seconds.

Text 2: At a parents' evening, talking to Chelsea's parents

People: Miss Powell [P], Mr Wright [Dad] and Mrs Wright [Mum]

P   Hello [*1*] you must be Chelsea's mum and dad
[*shakes hands*] [*2*] it's really nice to meet you
[*2*] please sit down [*3*] Chelsea's doing really
well you know [.] especially in her speaking
and listening we did an assessment last week   5
and hers was one of the best in the group

DAD   No surprise there [*1*] she's been good at
talking ever since she was a little girl [*2*]
never shuts up

P   And her last piece of writing [*1*] a   10
description of a place that she knows well
was excellent [.] very imaginative and full of
excellent descriptive vocabulary [*2*] at this
rate she should at least get a B in her GCSE

---

1   For each of the six influences on speech (role, context, purpose, audience, planning and familiarity), make notes on Miss Powell's speech in Text 1. For each influence, find a word or phrase she said which was directly affected by that factor. Do the same for Text 2. Use a table like this one to help you:

Influence	Text 1	Text 2
1 Role	Can I have your attention please?	
2 Context		

2   Compare the way Miss Powell talks in Texts 1 and 2. Write a paragraph on each of the six influences on speech. In each paragraph:
   • firstly mention how it affects how she speaks in class
   • then use a discourse marker such as 'Similarly' or 'By contrast'
   • next mention how it affects how she speaks *to the parents*
   • finish with a sentence suggesting *why* her speech was similar or different in the two texts.

16.3 Represented speech and real speech

> You will look at the way speech is represented in a TV drama and compare this with how you speak in real life.

➲ For starters

Read this extract from *Waterloo Road*, a TV drama set in an English comprehensive school. In the scene Mr Treneman, the English teacher, has been joined in the classroom by a trainee teacher on teaching practice, an ex-policeman called Mr Millen. Mr Treneman has been teaching an English class about nouns.

SCENE 13: ANDREW TRENEMAN'S CLASS, PERIOD ONE, 09:25

Teachers: ANDREW TRENEMAN, RUSSELL MILLEN. **Year 7s:** ARON, REST OF CLASS

Mr Treneman and Mr Millen are checking on the pupils' work. Mr Millen picks up Aron's jotter.

MR MILLEN	'Loyalty – stick.' Stick? How did you come up with that?
	There are a few titters.
ARON (*offended*)	When you're loyal, you stick by somebody, don't you?
	Mr Millen isn't sure how to react but pretends to be on top of things and reads another of Aron's suggestions. 5
MR MILLEN	'Anger – kettle'.
ARON	You can boil with anger like a kettle. *And now the class is laughing a bit. Aron is mortified.*
MR MILLEN	I don't think Aron's quite got what you were on about, Mr Treneman. *Andrew tries to encourage Russell to help Aron – after all, this is what Russell wanted.* 10
MR TRENEMAN	Perhaps you could explain, Mr Millen?
MR MILLEN	Yeah, yeah sure … You see what it is, that you're … looking for here, Aron, is a word that isn't … too far away from the words on the board. For example, anger is a word that comes from inside you … it's a feeling like when your mum doesn't allow you to watch your telly in your bedroom … 15
ARON	You mean like 'minging'? *Aron hasn't really understood.*
MR MILLEN	Exactly. Good. *This is not at all good, but Andrew does not want to correct Russell.*
MR TRENEMAN	Although 'anger' is a noun. An abstract noun. *It is obvious Russell's never heard of them.* As Mr Millen says it's about a feeling. Things you can't touch or see or smell or hear. *(To Aron)* Try to think of a word you would substitute for 'anger' in a 20 sentence, Aron. He felt 'anger'. *Aron has a good think.*
ARON	Fury? *Russell gives him a condescending pat on the back.*
MR MILLEN	Give the boy a gold star. *The class laughs perhaps because of Russell's comment. We see a hint of a flicker cross Andrew's face.*

We are familiar with TV dramas and say they are 'realistic', but if you listen carefully (even to 'soaps' like *EastEnders*), you will realise that none of the characters talk like we do in everyday life. The speech is scripted – this **script** is called **represented speech**.

↑ *Speech in soaps is not representative of real speech.*

↺ Task

When a scriptwriter writes a TV script, realism is one of the last things they are concerned about. Here are some of the more important concerns:

- To tell a story which has impact, which will grab the audience's interest (real life can sometimes be boring).
- To keep the story moving along at a good pace (things can go much more slowly in real life).
- To expose the character's personality and feelings (in real life people can try to keep their real feelings hidden).
- To get a message across which the writer wants the audience to understand (real life teaches us things, but it never makes its meaning clear – you have to work that out for yourself).

This episode of *Waterloo Road* is about a trainee teacher who turns out not only to be a useless teacher, but an alcoholic who is unsuitable to be in a school. The script is dramatic but does not reflect real life in most schools – the speech and situation are not very realistic. Read the script extract again on page 156, concentrating only on Mr Millen.

1   Working with a friend, make a list of ways in which the script is not realistic; for example, you could start by looking for things that would never happen in a real classroom.

2   In the extract, find one thing that Mr Millen says or does which shows that the scriptwriter is:
   - trying to grab the audience's interest
   - keeping the story moving along at a good pace
   - showing Mr Millen's personality
   - showing that Mr Millen is unsuitable to be a teacher.

3   In the final line of the extract, Mr Millen says: 'Give the boy a gold star.' How realistic is this compared with real speech? Think about:
   - Mr Millen's role as a student, trying to do well – would he speak like that?
   - The context – would Mr Millen speak like that in front of the normal teacher in his own classroom?
   - The purpose – for what reason would any teacher say this?
   - The audience – would anyone speak like that to Year 7 pupils?
   - The planning – how long does Mr Millen have to think of an answer?
   - The familiarity – would you speak like that to someone you had never met before?

   Give this speech a score out of six for realism. What *would* a trainee teacher say in real life?

⊃ Taking it further

Here is a **transcript** of a real teacher talking to a real pupil.

Text 3: In class, teaching

People: Miss Powell [P] and Rachel [R] – Year 7 pupil in P's tutor group.
They are the only people in the room.

P   Now then Rachel [.] what was it that you wanted

R   Miss [.] well [.] er Miss [.] it's just that I've got er maths next and I
     I I'm not sure how to get there

P   What are you like. [.] didn't you get a map on the first day of term
     [.] and we did a walk round and went to all the rooms didn't we   5
     [1] can't you remember where maths is

R   I've left it at home miss [.] I didn't | think

P   isn't there someone else in the
                                             form in the same maths group
                                             [1] Ellie's your friend isn't she   10

R   yes [.] but she's gone ahead with the others [.] | and

P   well hurry along
                                             after her [.] they're
                                             not long gone and
                                             you'll soon catch   15
                                             them up

R   Yes miss [1] | thanks miss

P   see you later

R   See you miss

> ### ⓘ Concept bank
>
> **Transcript:** the written text
> that is made when speech is
> recorded and then written out
> or transcribed. The symbols
> in a transcript show how the
> conversation sounds: [.] is
> a very short pause; [2] is a
> pause of two (or however
> many) seconds. The vertical
> line shows when the two
> speakers speak at the same
> time.

1   Working with a friend, compare this transcript of real speech with
    the written TV script of *Waterloo Road* on page 156. Find four
    differences, and add these to your list of ways in which the TV script
    is not realistic.

2   Write an essay with three sections to answer the question:

> How realistic is Mr Millen's speech in the TV script extract
> from *Waterloo Road*?

   • Section 1: comment on how realistic the script is compared with
     real speech. Look back at your list of ways in which the script is
     not realistic.
   • Section 2: use your notes on role, context, purpose, audience,
     planning and familiarity to help you explain why or why not
     what Mr Millen says is realistic.
   • Section 3: explain why a TV script such as *Waterloo Road* is
     intentionally unrealistic, remembering to give examples from
     the script.

Impact of Technology on Language Use

Learning aim

In this unit you will find out how language is changed by the use of technology. You will think about text messaging and email so that you can find out what is unusual about these texts. You will learn how to present what you discover as a written response.

17.1 What is the difference between speech and writing?

> You will learn how technology is making the difference between spoken and written texts less clear.

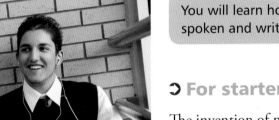

⊃ For starters

The invention of new technology such as mobile phones and computers is making language change. For a start, new words linked to technology are coming into the language.

Look at the list of words below. Do you know what each one is?

- Internet
- CD-Rom
- Wi-fi
- Modem
- Blog
- Facebook

Were there any you did not know? Why might this be the case? If you looked these words up in a 10-year-old dictionary you would probably find very few of them. Why do you think this is?

⊃ Task

1 Now you are going to think about the differences between spoken and written language. You will need to work in groups of three. One of you will watch the other two and make notes on how you do the task.
   - Tell your partner the way from your classroom to the canteen.
   - Write down directions from your classroom to the canteen.

2 What are the differences between the spoken and written directions?

3 Fill in the gaps in your version of the table below which explains the differences between speech and writing.

Features of spoken language	Features of written language
Sounds are used	
	Planned
	Usually done alone
You can use your voice in many ways like whispering, shouting, speaking fast	
It is unusual for a person not to be able to speak	
Lots of different things are talked about	
	The writing must be completely clear. The reader cannot ask for help
	Parts of sentences are joined with 'and'
	Usually permanent – can be read again
Facial expressions help show meaning	
	Full sentences are used

4 Sometimes it is easy to decide if a text is spoken or written. Looking at the 'Ten methods of communication' on the right, it would be easy to place a conversation at one end of the line below, and a novel at the other. But where would a chat-room conversation go?

5 Working with a friend, for each method of communication:
- use the table to consider how far it is 'speech' or 'writing';
- decide where on the line below you would place it.

Speech ⟵――――――――――――――⟶ Writing

⟲ Taking it further

Find a chat-room conversation. Does it have the same features as a face-to-face conversation? Answer the following questions and think about the way technology is changing language.

1 How many things do people talk or write about?
2 Do they interrupt each other? How?
3 How do people take turns?
4 Is the vocabulary chatty or formal?

Ten methods of communication

1 A conversation
2 A novel
3 A chat-room conversation
4 A formal written speech
5 A transcript of a telephone conversation
6 An email
7 A message left on an answerphone
8 An audiobook
9 Twitter or Facebook
10 Subtitles on the TV

⟲ Grammar link

You would use formal language when you want to make a good impression, for example, if you were talking to your Headteacher. You would not use slang and would think about the way you say things.

17.2 Texting

> You will explore the features of text language.

⊃ For starters

Make a list of all the text messages you have sent over the last few days. Look at your list with a partner. What do you use texting for? Who do you text? How long are your messages? If your parents made a list, would it be different?

⊃ Task

The ways in which we use our mobile phones have changed a lot since they were first produced. Call charges used to be very high and quite often people would use texting to save money. A lot of people found texting difficult to use and very slow! As a result, people changed the language they used to speed things up. The invention of predictive text made sending a message easier, although people still use shortcuts.

1 Turn these messages into texts:

> **A** Dear Manjeet,
>   I will not be able to come to the cinema tomorrow evening. I
>   must stay at home to finish my homework.
>   Yours sincerely,
>   Ben

> **B** Mum,
>   Please note I will be late home as I will be spending
>   approximately one hour looking at the clothes in Primark.
>   Love,
>   Emma

> **C** Chris,
>   Could you please remember to feed the cat?
>   Dad

What changes did you make? You probably began by changing the length. You may have changed some of the words and missed out punctuation. Did you use capital letters?

2 Text messaging has many special features which are not used in ordinary writing. Look at the list. Think of two more examples of each one.

Initialisms	you put the first letter of each word	brb
Modified acronyms	using letters or numbers in place of words or a phrase	F2F
Emoticons	symbols	☺
Number homophones	using a number as the word it sounds like	8
Letter homophones	using a letter as the word it sounds like	b
Omission of letters	missing out letters	gd
Substitution of letters	using as few letters as possible	wot
Lower case letters	not using many capitals	
No punctuation	not using any full stops or commas	

3 In pairs, write a message using as many features of text language as possible. Stick it onto a large piece of paper. Label it to show how you used text language.

4 Where would you place texting on the speech and writing line? Why?

Speech ←——————————————————→ Writing

⊃ Taking it further

Write an advice sheet for your grandparents of 'Five Tips for Writing a Modern Text Message'.

1 Think carefully about *who* you are writing for and *what* they need to know.

2 From the table above, choose the five easiest to learn texting techniques then write five paragraphs, in each:
   • explaining what the technique involves
   • giving examples to make it clear
   • explaining why it is useful, quick and easy.

3 Finish with a paragraph recommending texting as a method of communication.

↑ *Think carefully about your grandparent and what language they will understand*

> ### ! Essay tip
>
> In this advice text, include the writing techniques you learned on page 60, such as:
> • appropriate register, including modal verbs ('you should')
> • direct address ('you')
> • clear explanations, including connectives
> • authoritative tone, including facts, examples and specialist words
> • enthusiastic adjectives to persuade
> • reassurance
> • specific suggestions and instructions.

> ### ⓘ Concept bank
>
> **Acronym:** word made up from the first letters of a group of words.
>
> **Homophones:** words which sound the same but mean different things.

17.3 Attitudes to technology

You will think about how people feel about texting and language change.

ⓘ Concept bank

Grammar: the way words are linked together to make a language.

➲ For starters

Some people feel that technology is having a negative impact on our language and **grammar**. Read the following two texts and discuss with a friend what you feel about them:

TXTZ RNT GUD 4U – OFFICIAL

Aptly-named Professor Speak, Head of English at Mercia College, believes that texting harms children's writing.

'Text messages teach wrong writing technique,' Professor Speak told *The Advertiser*. 'They omit punctuation. They misspell words. Repetition turns these errors into habits, and suddenly we have undergraduates using text-speak in academic essays … so texting undermines 'appropriateness' – the ability to use the right words in the right place.'

'Moreover, young people who use emoticons to identify their feelings, get worse at expressing those feelings in words.'

Professor Speak claims that his research is a wake-up call to educated England. 'We are getting swamped by the language of the street,' he warns. 'We need to act now, before this lazy way of communication takes away altogether our ability to write in proper English.'

Article in a local newspaper

Dear Editor

May I contradict the old-fashioned twaddle that text messages are ruining language skills? In fact exactly the opposite is the case.

Text messaging helps spelling because abbreviations such as 'txt' and 'wot' force children to think about the structures and sounds of words. And you've *got* to be able to spell accurately to use predictive texting.

At the same time, is not abbreviation a skill we teach pupils to help them make notes; how is it 'wrong' to be able to get down three ideas in 12 letters?

Above all, texting is inspiring youngsters, who previously refused to pick up a pen, to churn out thousands of words of written communication. Texting is teaching us how to write again!

Language changes all the time, n txt MSGs R takN us N2 d fucha.

Yours truly,

Alan Widge

Letter to a magazine for young mothers

⟳ Task

Some people feel that texting is having a bad effect on our language. Other people think that texting is really useful and can be **creative**.

1 Using the articles on page 163 to help you, work with a partner to think of as many arguments as you can for and against texting. Use a table like the one below to organise your ideas.

Texting is the future!	Texting is destroying the language!
Quick and easy, faster than normal writing	Only lazy people use it

2 Look at the ideas you discussed. Use some of your ideas to write a letter to a newspaper making your views on texting clear. You could do further research on the Internet. You will find lots of articles and websites which give people's views. They often feel strongly about technology and how it is changing language. You might like to start your letter like this:

> Dear Sir,
> I am really concerned about the amount of time young people spend sending each other text messages. Have they forgotten how to read and write normally?

⟳ Taking it further

1 Ask five people how they feel about texting. Try to get a range of different people. Find out if they think texting is a useful shorthand or if they believe it is ruining the language. Use a table like the one below to record their answers, but add at least two extra statements of your own.

	Agree strongly	Agree	Disagree	Disagree strongly
Texting is lazy				
Texting leads to poor spelling				
Texting is destroying English				
Texting is new and exciting				
Texting is quick and convenient				

2 Write a few sentences on what each person tells you. What conclusions can you draw?

17.4 Email

> You will think about how emails are written.

⊃ For starters

We have a wide choice of ways to communicate with other people. You could choose email, a letter, a text or even a phone call. Discuss with a partner which you would choose for the messages below. Think about why you would make each choice. Make brief notes explaining why.

- A message from the bank to tell you that you are overdrawn.
- A message to a parent or guardian to let them know you missed the bus and will be late for tea.
- A message to invite a lot of friends to a party.
- A party invitation to someone you don't know well.
- A message to a wide audience advertising something for sale.

⊃ Task

Do you think there is a special language of email? Most emails do have things in common, but they can be very different because of their audiences and purposes.

> ### ⓘ Concept bank
>
> **Closing:** the words used to end a letter or email, for example 'Yours sincerely'.

1 Write a short email to your form tutor from your parent or guardian to explain why you missed school.

2 Write a short email from yourself to your friend explaining why you missed school.

3 In pairs, compare the two. Use your version of the table below to help you. Were they different? One should have been much more friendly and chatty than the other!

	Email to friend	Email to tutor
Planned?		
Formal or friendly?		
Opening?		
Closing?		
Paragraphs?		
Punctuation?		
Normal spelling?		

4 Investigate the features of email.

Sunday 14th January 2010, 10:42	Inbox | Sent | Junk | Draft

Hi Sam,

Lovely to hear from you! Thanks for emailing me. Can you get there for 6.30 to 7ish? I'll wait for you at the entrance – what film do you want to see? Really looking forward to seeing you and catching up on the goss. Should be kinda fun!

Love, Han xx

- Who is sending it? Audience?
- Is there a **header**? What information is given? For example: date, time, sender.
- Is there a **greeting**? For example: Hi, Dear.
- What kind of vocabulary is used? Friendly or formal?
- Is it in full sentences?
- Is it in paragraphs?
- How does it close? For example: Best wishes.

5 Where would you put email on the speech and writing line? Why?

Speech ←——————————————————→ Writing

⊃ Taking it further

1 Collect five interesting emails you and your family get over the next week. Fill in a table like the one on page 165.
2 Present your results in a diagram to show the features of emails.

⫘ Grammar link

A full sentence is a sentence which has a subject, verb and object or adverbial.

ⓘ Concept bank

Header: information put at the top of a page, for example the date, a title.

Greeting: the words used to open a letter or email, for example, 'Dear Joe'.

Doing Well in the English and English Language Exam

Introduction

This unit will give you information and advice about your English and English Language exam paper. It will help you to answer these four questions:

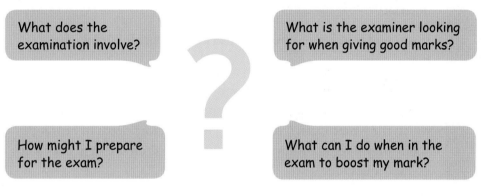

What does the examination involve?

What is the examiner looking for when giving good marks?

How might I prepare for the exam?

What can I do when in the exam to boost my mark?

The English and English Language exam

What does the examination involve?

Here are some facts:

- The exam is called *Unit 1: Understanding and producing non-fiction texts* and is worth 40 per cent of your GCSE. It is a two-hour examination split into two sections. Both sections are worth the same marks.
- Section A tests how well you can read non-fiction texts. You will be given texts such as magazine or newspaper articles. You will also be given texts such as diaries, letters or autobiographical writing. Do not be surprised if you see adverts or parts of leaflets or web material – you will be given images and other visual items to write about. In Section A, you will be asked five questions based on four pieces of writing.
- Section B tests how well you can do your own writing. You will be asked to produce two pieces. One is worth fewer marks than the other. Expect to write things such as letters, articles, speeches, essays or leaflet material.

What is the examiner looking for when giving good marks?

There are two sections to the English and English Language examination.

Section A – Reading

In Section A, the examiner is looking to see how well you can read and understand the texts you are given. They will test you by asking a set of five questions.

The first few questions will be 'retrieval' questions. These ask you to **find** specific pieces of information in the texts. Imagine a newspaper article about why dogs should not be kept as pets in a town or city. The article gives a series of reasons, some facts and opinions, about why it is wrong to keep dogs. Question 1 on the right shows an example question.

If you find four reasons from the text you will get full marks for this question!

The next two questions will follow a similar model, but the examiner will leave the questions more open-ended. Imagine an article in which the writer Dean Connolly argues that more needs to be done about stray dogs in his town centre. Question 2 on the right shows an example question.

Again, find what is asked for, present your ideas clearly and in detail, and you get all the marks.

An answer heading towards a C grade might begin as the example on the right.

This detail and depth made in several further comments too is likely to get high marks.

Question 4 will dig deeper into how well you have understood and can think about the language in one of the texts. Imagine one of the texts is a letter to a newspaper. Someone has angrily written to the editor about how the streets and centre of their town are 'no-go areas' because of all the stray dogs 'prowling around in packs'.

There is an extract from the letter below:

> **Question 1**
>
> Give four reasons from the article about why it is wrong to keep dogs as pets in a town or city.

> **Question 2**
>
> What does the writer in the article think about the problem of stray dogs in his town centre?

> Connolly is angry about the dogs. This is obvious when he calls the dogs 'packs'. His anger is even clearer when he refers to 'horror films' saying that is what it is like at night because of strays... Later he says more should be done to rid the streets of strays and and it is the town council 'desk jockeys' who should sort it out.

Dear Editor

I want to raise an issue that is driving me mad, and I'm sure is driving your readers crazy too! Dogs. Not pets. Not dogs smartly walking on a lead. Strays!

The streets and centre of our town are no-go areas because of all the stray dogs prowling around in packs. Dogs, dogs and more dogs! Some of them are like small horses. Others snarl and growl as if they have somehow arrived in our country straight off the plane from some dog-infested desert country where dingos and jackals eat anything that moves. Others are those dog-monsters that scared us when as children we sneaked down to watch bad horror films, and beautiful women were chased through forests by howling hounds. But this isn't a horror film is it? It is Britain in the 21st century and I'm heartily sick of it.

The examiner could ask you Question 4 (on the right).

The examiner is now asking for more. This is not just about finding information. You are being asked to explain and analyse the use of language in the letter. For best marks the examiner will expect you to:

- find good examples
- quote them
- explain how the language is working for effect.

Here is part of a student's answer that was given full marks:

> You can tell the writer is angry because of how he writes the letter. At the start the writer uses single-word or two-word sentences: 'Dogs. Not pets.' This makes him sound abrupt and angry, so this is effective in showing how he feels. He also describes the streets as 'no-go areas' and this is the kind of language used when writing about a war zone or places where something really bad has happened. This is exaggeration because you probably can go there, but it makes it sound like you cannot. Later in the letter the writer compares the dogs to ones in horror films, like 'howling hounds'. This is emotive language and shows you how strongly the writer is feeling. There is alliteration in 'howling hounds' and this is effective because we notice it more.

This is a good answer because it answers the question. It finds relevant examples to show the examiner and explains them.

The last question in the section will ask you to compare presentation in two of the texts.

Let us imagine one text is the front of a leaflet produced for a charity trying to persuade you to give money to a rescue dogs kennel. This is a place where stray or abandoned dogs are taken and cared for. You can visualise what that leaflet would contain – the droopy-looking dog; big sad eyes; an appealing caption and headline; a logo for the charity.

Let us imagine the other text is part of an article about training a new puppy. Again, you can visualise what the leaflet would contain – a clear title; a picture of a happy puppy; bright cheerful colours throughout; bold lettering to show the main advice.

A possible question is on the right.

Top marks will again go to you if you:

- identify several presentational features in each text
- describe them
- compare them.

Question 4

Choose three examples of language use in the letter. Write them down and explain why each is effective.

Question 5

Compare the presentational devices in the charity leaflet with the presentational devices in the puppy training article.

Here is part of a top-mark answer:

> Both texts use pictures but in different ways. The leaflet uses a picture of a miserable-looking dog. It is a close-up of its face so you can see how sad its eyes are. The picture of the puppy is different. It is a longer shot and shows the puppy on a lead, looking happy. This creates an impression of why you should train your dog. These differences are because the texts are trying to do different things.

Section B – Writing

Let us think now about Section B – Writing. Here it is easier to work out what the examiner is looking to give marks for. You will be asked to do two pieces of writing. Both will be some sort of non-fiction text. You must do both tasks.

One task will be worth fewer marks than the other, so the examiner will expect the piece of writing to be shorter. This shorter task is likely to have you informing or advising someone about something. For an example of a shorter task, keeping to the dog theme, see Question 1 on the right.

For an example of a longer task, see Question 2 on the right.

In both tasks the examiner will want to see certain skills being used well in order to give high marks for the writing:

- ✔ The writing should be detailed and include a range of ideas – lots of information, a variety of reasons. This is most likely to happen if you plan before you start to write.
- ✔ It should be obvious that the writing is doing the job asked for. So, it should contain information; it should offer advice; it should give reasons and be persuasive. Using language that is persuasive, or informative, or offers advice gets you marks for writing for purpose.
- ✔ The writing should be structured, with some sense of beginning, middle and end. Use of paragraphs or sections instantly lets the examiner give you marks for structure.
- ✔ Interesting words should be used that show a good vocabulary.
- ✔ The writing should be in well-punctuated sentences. Use of a **range** of punctuation gets you extra marks.
- ✔ Spelling of most words should be accurate.

How might I prepare for the exam?

Some people say:

- You can't revise for English!
- True, but you can **prepare** – so no excuses!

Question 1

Write a letter to the manager of a local dog rescue kennel. In the letter, introduce yourself and advise the manager on how he or she might persuade more young people to do voluntary work at the kennels.

(16 marks)

Question 2

Write an article for a school magazine in which you persuade students at the school to get involved in charity work. In your article you should:

- inform them about the kind of work they might do
- explain why it is a good thing to get involved
- use language that appeals to the readers' thoughts and feelings.

(24 marks)

There are a number of things you can do in the weeks before you sit the English and English Language exam paper that will make a difference to your marks on the day. Here are 10 tips:

Ten tips for exam success

✔ Reread this unit to revise the exam paper, and what the examiner wants.

✔ In bursts of 20–30 minutes each time, review Units 2, 3, 4 and 5 of this book. If it gets you that all-important C grade, it is worth it. If there is anything you do not remember, or understand, have a word with your teacher.

✔ Flick through the Grammar unit on pages 173–181 – this will help you with any bits and pieces of grammar you still do not get.

✔ Check out the key words in the Concept Bank on pages 182–184.

✔ You will have plenty of notes you made whilst working in class in the past year or so. Remind yourself what is on the exam paper, and have a look at the relevant notes.

✔ If you did a mock exam, or any practice questions, look again at what you wrote, and at any comments your teacher made. Do this to help you spot your strengths and areas for improvement. Then ask for help with what you are most unsure of.

✔ Have a go at a practice paper or a section or two from one. Units 2–7 of this book give you some exam-style questions to work on.

Your teacher will have some more. The AQA website http://www.AQA.org.uk definitely does.

✔ Share your answers with your teacher. Ask your teacher: 'What can I do that would improve my performance by 3 marks next time?' Listen to what they say!

✔ Come up with some planning memory-joggers – like FOREST on page 172. Ask your teacher if they might do this with the whole class to get more ideas for memory joggers.

✔ Do some honest self-analysis. Ask yourself: 'What do I still find tricky in English?' Here are some prompts. Is it:

- writing in sentences
- using punctuation
- using paragraphs
- reading stuff quickly
- explaining how language is used
- writing about pictures and visual material
- doing a quick plan before you start writing
- writing about something in detail?

Find **one** thing that you think you could improve on, and book a five-minute chat with your teacher to talk about it.

So there are 10 things you can do before the exam to help you. Say you did just six of them. Imagine that doing each one improved your English skills by 1 per cent. That would add up to 6 per cent and could easily be the difference between a D and a C!

What can I do when in the exam to boost my mark?

The exam room will feel like a scary place to be. Rows of desks, invigilators walking up and down, the demand that you are silent. Not a nice place to spend two hours. But an important two hours, so what can you do in the exam room itself to improve your mark?

There are some more tips on page 172. If you act on them it could make the difference of another few marks – they all add up! Read the checklists now, and again on the day of the exam.

Tips for planning your time

As soon as you open the exam paper, write yourself a quick timetable. Remember:

✔ Section A and Section B should **each** take about **1 hour**.

✔ Section A is divided into **at least five** questions, but they will not all be worth the same number of marks. Look at the end of each question and find out how many marks it is worth. Then make sure you spend the right proportion of time on each question depending on what it is worth. So if the examiner has, say, just 4 marks to give for Question 1 and 8 marks for Question 2, you should spend twice as long on Question 2.

✔ Section B has two questions, one worth fewer marks than the other. You are advised to spend 60 minutes altogether on this section. So you obviously need to spend a few minutes less than 30 minutes on the question with fewer marks, and a few minutes more than 30 minutes on the question with more marks. Stick to this timetable and you will not run out of time.

Tips for Section A

✔ Read the question **first** so you know what you are looking for.

✔ Then read the passage. But do not **just** read it! Read it with your pen in your hand and be ready to put some letters in the margin when you find things in the text that answer the question. For example, if the question asks for 'four reasons' put the letter R next to where you find a reason. Or put an L for language next to any bits of language you might use when answering about language.

✔ Quickly read the question again, and then answer it using your notes to help you.

✔ With any question worth 8 marks or more, spend a minute doing a quick plan of key ideas you aim to put in the answer.

Tips for Section B

✔ Section B answers **must** be planned before you start to write unless you want to risk messing up the structure, or running out of time. Spend about three minutes thinking about what you are going to write, scribbling a few words and ideas down. Maybe each one will become the main point of a paragraph.

✔ Examiners often see strange words like FOREST with a few words next to them in students' exam plans. These will be checklists to help remind them what to do.

For example, FOREST might help you remember that in a newspaper article that tries to persuade someone about something, you should include:

F Facts

O Opinions

R Rhetorical questions

E Emotive language

S
  Structure Triplets.
T

Before the exam, see if you and your class can come up with your own. Some plans are lists of words or phrases; sometimes plans can look like brainstorms or thought showers.

✔ Last but not least, save time at the end to check your Section B answers. Imagine you correct three spelling mistakes. Imagine you sort out three punctuation slip-ups – missing capital letters, for example, or an apostrophe in the wrong place. That's at least two lost marks saved.

Grammar

The word 'grammar' is used to describe the way in which the words in our language can be combined to communicate meaning. Some people describe it as a system of 'rules'.

There are a number of reasons for studying grammar. For example:
- Knowing about grammar will give you more control of your writing and make it more effective.
- Knowing about grammar can help you see how texts work and describe how their messages and effects are created.

Word classes (parts of speech)

The most basic part of our reading and writing is the **word** – words are the building blocks of our language. If you are to be able to understand and use language in an effective way, you need to be able to recognise the job that each type of word does in the texts that you write and the ones that you read. Ideally, you should be able to recognise what **word class** (or **part of speech**) each individual word in a piece of writing belongs to. On the right is a traditional rhyme which gives a brief summary of the main word classes in English.

Every name is called a **NOUN**,
  As **field** and **fountain**, **street**
  and **town**.

In place of noun the
  PRONOUN stands,
  As **he** and **she** can clap their
  hands.

The **ADJECTIVE** describes a
    thing,
  As **magic** wand and **bridal**
  ring.

The **VERB** means action,
  something done –
  To **read**, to **write**, to **jump**,
  to **run**.

How things are done, the
  ADVERBs tell,
  As **quickly**, **slowly**, **badly**,
  well.

The **PREPOSITION** shows
    relation,
  As **in** the street, or **at** the
  station.

CONNECTIVES join, in many
    ways,
  Sentences, words, **or** phrase
  and phrase.

Find out about nouns

Question	Answer	Examples
What do nouns do?	Nouns identify people, places and things.	Mr Bean; teacher; London; market
How do nouns work in sentences?	Nouns can be preceded by such words as *a*, *the*, *some*, *this*, *that*, etc. which provide more information about them.	some *money*; a *child*; the *teapot*; this *girl*; that *boy*
	Nouns can change their form to show how many they are (singular or plural) or to show possession.	*teapots*; the *girl's clothes*; the *children's toys*
What are the different types of nouns?	• **Common nouns** are non-specific people, places and things.	*man*; *woman*; *children*; *town*; *car*; *drink*
	• **Proper nouns** are particular people, places and things.	*Cheryl*; *Kings of Leon*; *Birmingham*; *Pepsi*
	• **Concrete nouns** are those people and things that you can physically experience with your senses.	*chair*; *fish*; *teacher*; *train*; *rain*
	• **Abstract nouns** relate to emotions, qualities and concepts that you can experience mentally or emotionally.	*happiness*; *fear*; *speed*; *trust*; *love*

How will knowing about nouns help my reading and writing?

Reading: If you are given a passage to read, and you identify a number of **concrete nouns**, you could conclude that the writer is trying to appeal to the reader through the senses (things that readers could see, feel, smell or hear themselves). If, on the other hand, you identify more **abstract nouns**, perhaps the writer is trying to appeal to the readers' emotions?

Writing: If you have a writing task to complete (especially a descriptive piece), you can add variety and interest to it by making sure you use a combination of concrete and abstract nouns. Concrete nouns can make your description detailed and convincing, while abstract nouns can help your readers share your thoughts and feelings about a topic.

Find out about pronouns

Question	Answer	Examples
What do pronouns do?	Pronouns are used to take the place of nouns.	*I*; *you*; *they*; *him*; *herself*; *mine*
How do pronouns work in sentences?	Whenever a noun is used in a sentence, it can be replaced by a pronoun.	'*Maria borrowed Katie's iPod*' could become: '*She borrowed her iPod*' or '*Maria borrowed it*'
What are the different types of pronouns?	There are many types of pronoun in English. The most familiar and probably the most useful type for your reading and writing are the **personal pronouns**.	These are words that can be used in place of people and things, such as: *I*; *me*; *you*; *he*; *she*; *it*; *we*; *us*; *they*; *them*. If the personal pronouns refer to *I*, *me*, *we* or *us*, they are called *first person pronouns*. If they refer to *you*, they are called *second person pronouns*. If they refer to *he, she, him, her, it, they* or *them*, they are called *third person pronouns*.

How will knowing about pronouns help my reading and writing?

Reading: If you are given a passage to read which is designed to persuade or to advise, it is often interesting to look at the choice of personal pronoun(s) that the writer has made. For example, the use of the first person has the effect of identifying the writer's point of view, while the use of the second person addresses the reader directly. The use of the first person plural makes the reader feel included and the use of the third person makes the text feel like a statement of fact.

Writing: If you are asked to produce writing to persuade or advise, you could use the above techniques. You could choose to use one pronoun style throughout your text, or change at different times in order to give variety to your writing and to show a range of persuasive techniques!

Find out about adjectives

Question	Answer	Examples
What do adjectives do?	Adjectives are words which give you more information about nouns.	a *good* man; a *fast* car; a *long* life; *beautiful* music; *modern* buildings
How do adjectives work in sentences?	Adjectives can go immediately before the word that they are describing, or following it and a part of the verb 'to be'.	*loud* music or The music was both *loud* and *modern*.
What are the different types of adjectives?	There are many different types of adjective in English, for example, adjectives relating to: • age • colour • personality.	 *old*; *new*; *young* *red*; *white*; *blue*; *pink*; *purple* *angry*; *happy*; *sad*; *calm*

How will knowing about adjectives help my reading and writing?

Reading: Since adjectives are used to give the reader more information about the subject that is being written about, they can also be used to emphasise the opinion of the writer. Some adjectives such as 'beautiful' carry positive suggestions about whatever it is they are describing, while others, like 'miserable', have negative suggestions. Understanding this can help you explain how writers use language to be persuasive, or to influence the reader.

Writing: You can enrich and improve your own writing by using adjectives carefully. You can use adjectives to provide more information, and by selecting adjectives with strong positive or negative suggestions, you can subtly persuade your readers to agree with your point of view.

Find out about verbs

Question	Answer	Examples
What do verbs do?	Verbs denote an action, a feeling, an occurrence or a state of being.	*Action* – She *danced* all night. *Feeling* – I *wanted* to watch the match. *Occurrence* – It *rained* all week. *State of being* – You *are* my best friend.
How do verbs work in sentences?	Verbs tell you *what* is happening in a sentence, and also *when* it happens, happened, or will happen.	*Present* – He *is watching* the game. *Past* – He *watched* the game. *Future* – He *will watch* the game.
What are the different forms of verbs?	Verbs sometimes have a different form depending on who is performing the action in the sentence.	I *go* to town on Saturdays. She *goes* to town on Saturdays. He *likes* football, but you *like* rugby.

Reading: A verb is a very important word class as no sentence is complete without a verb. The most important aspect of verbs is the type of verb that writers use. Have they selected verbs because they have strength or express a particular feeling? For example, think about the difference between the verbs *like*, *love*, and *adore*. They all have the same basic meaning, but some are stronger than others.

Writing: In your own writing, if you want to show how strongly you feel, or if you want your readers to share these feelings, you could use **emotive verbs**; you could choose stronger alternatives to commonly used verbs such as *say*, *go* and *get*. For example, 'The teacher *said*, "Stop talking now"' is much less powerful than 'The teacher *bellowed*, "Stop talking now."'

Find out about adverbs

Question	Answer	Examples
What do adverbs do?	Adverbs give more information about (or modify) verbs, adjectives or other adverbs.	I *completely* agree; a *totally* awesome experience; *quite* loudly
How do adverbs work in sentences?	Adverbs normally go next to the word that they give more information about. In most cases this is before the word – but occasionally afterwards for emphasis.	I *distinctly* heard you speak. That is *completely* unacceptable. I will support you *totally*, whatever happens.
What are the different types of adverb?	The most widely used types of adverb are adverbs of: • **Manner** which answer the question **how**? • **Place** which answer the question **where**? • **Time** which answer the question **when**? • **Frequency** which answer the question **how often**? • **Degree** which answer the question **how far**?	She sings *beautifully*. We saw you *there*. I can't find them *anywhere*. I've been there *before*. He is *still* at school. I *often* miss the bus. You *always* give me a hard time. We *almost* won the lottery. The weather was *quite* good.

Reading: Since adverbs are used to give the reader more information about the subject that is being written about, they can also be used to suggest the opinion of the writer and to influence the reader. Using adverbs such as *obviously* or *clearly* suggests that the writer is sure that what they are saying is true, while the use of adverbs such as *perhaps* or *possibly* casts doubt upon it.

Writing: You can enrich and improve your own writing by using adverbs carefully. You can suggest additional information about people, places and actions by selecting suitable adverbs. As with adjectives, you can influence your readers without being too obvious about it.

Grammar

Find out about prepositions

Question	Answer
What do prepositions do?	Prepositions are words that express a relationship between nouns or pronouns and other words in a sentence.
How do prepositions work in sentences?	The most common prepositions are small words related to: • **Direction** – They are going *to* the match. • **Location** – He hid *under* the bed. • **Time** – She left for work *after* her breakfast. • **Possession** – The Queen *of* England.
What are the different prepositions? (a detailed but not complete list)	**Simple prepositions:** *above; after; at; before; below; by; for; from; in; near; on; over; round; since; till; to; under; until; with* **Prepositional phrases:** *according to; ahead of; apart from; as well as; because of; except for; in addition to; in favour of; in spite of; near to; on behalf of*

Find out about connectives

(For an explanation of terms marked with an asterisk, see page 178.)

(For an explanation of terms marked with an asterisk, see page 178.)

Question	Answer
What do connectives do?	Connectives are words that join two or more words, phrases* or clauses*.
What are the different types of connectives?	**Coordinating connectives** The most common of these are *and*, *but* and *or*. They join words, phrases or clauses when all of the parts being joined together are equally important. For example: The Long *and* the Short *and* the Tall. (single words) Football shorts *or* a pair of swimming trunks are necessary. (phrase) She locked the door *but* left the window open. (clause) **Subordinating connectives** These help to show connections in meaning between main clauses* and dependent (or subordinate) clauses*. • **Simple subordinating connectives** include such words as: *although; as; because; before; if; since; though; unless; until; when; whenever; while*. • **Complex subordinating connectives** are made up of more than one word and include: *assuming that; in case; in order that; insofar as*.

How will knowing about connectives improve my writing?

As connectives are the main way in which words, phrases, clauses and sentences can be joined, knowing about them allows you to choose the length and complexity of your sentences. This allows you to vary the effects that your writing can have on your readers.

Phrases, clauses and sentences

This section looks at how you can put words together to get your meaning across to your readers or listeners. You can put words together to make **phrases** and **clauses**, and put words, phrases and clauses together to make **sentences**. The table explains the process.

You can combine		
words	**phrases**	**clauses**
word: the representation of a sound in writing which communicates a meaning	phrase: a group of words which belong together but do not contain a verb	clause: a group of words which go together and contain a verb
to make **sentences**.		

What is a sentence?

A sentence is a piece of language which generally starts with a capital letter and finishes with a full stop, an exclamation mark or a question mark, and which makes sense. In order to make sense, it has to follow the accepted rules of grammar.

What are the different types of sentence?

There are two ways of looking at types of sentence.

1 Consider the *sort of meaning* a sentence puts across:

Statement (also known as **declarative**) This type of sentence gives information.	This is a statement.
Is this a question?	**Question** (also known as **interrogative**) This type of sentence asks for information.
Command (also known as **imperative**) This type of sentence gives instructions.	Look at this sentence.
What a great sentence!	**Exclamation** (also known as **exclamatory**) This type of sentence expresses strong feelings.

2 Consider *how complicated* the sentence is:

Simple This type of sentence is made up of a single part (usually called a **main clause**).	This is a simple sentence.
This is a compound sentence but it is not very long.	**Compound** This type of sentence is made up of two or more main clauses, joined together with *and*, *but* or *or*.
Complex This type of sentence is made up of at least one main clause and at least one other clause starting with such words as: *if; when; where; because; that; unless; as; while*, etc. These are called **subordinate** or **dependent clauses**.	This is a complex sentence, because I have added this extra clause to it.

How will knowing about sentences help my reading and writing?

Reading: Writers use different types of sentences depending on the purpose of their writing. They will use *statements* when they are writing to *inform*; *questions* when they are trying to *involve* the reader (and perhaps to *persuade* them); *commands* when they are providing *instructions*; and *exclamations* when they *feel strongly* about the subject (and perhaps as part of a description in a piece of writing to *entertain*).

A writer may choose to use a mixture of simple, compound or complex sentences for a number of reasons. A writer might choose to use mostly simple or compound sentences to make sure important points are very clear to the reader. If a writer wants to appear well educated and well informed, they might choose to use a series of complex sentences, in order to sound like an expert! If a writer wants to emphasise a point, they might write a series of long and complex sentences and then finish with a short, simple one. The contrast will draw attention to the final, short, sentence.

Writing: You can use any of the techniques (or all of them) in your own writing. Variety is a good way of keeping your readers' attention.

Punctuation

Another important weapon in the writer's armoury is **punctuation**. Punctuation can be defined as 'the use of marks and signs in writing to divide words into sentences, clauses and phrases in order to make their meaning clear to the reader'.

Punctuation mark		Function	Examples
.	**Full stop**	• A full stop indicates the end of a sentence. • A full stop is sometimes used to show that a word or phrase has been abbreviated.	*We arrived in New York in the afternoon.* *Dr. Lewis O.B.E.; Mrs. Doyle*
?	**Question mark**	• A question mark is used to show that a sentence is a question. • Sometimes the sentence might look like a statement, but the question mark shows that it is meant to sound or act like a question.	*'Will that be everything, madam?'* *'So that is the best you can do?'*
!	**Exclamation mark**	• An exclamation mark shows that a sentence is carrying some form of strong feeling.	**Anger** – *'Get out of my sight!'* **Forcefulness** – *'Never again!'* **Surprise** – *'I don't believe it!'* **Strong dislike** – *'That's gross!'* **Commands** – *'Do it now!'* **Joy** – *'That's fantastic!'*
,	**Comma**	• A comma is used to separate words, clauses or phrases in a sentence. These could be parts of a list. (Note that just before the last item of the list *and* is used instead of a comma.) • Commas are used when there is extra material in a sentence which is not part of the main clause. • If a sentence includes some information before the main clause, there is normally a comma after that information. • In written speech, commas usually separate the words that are spoken from the person who is speaking them. • A comma is used if you start a sentence with the name of the person or people you are talking to.	*He asked for bacon, egg, sausage, hash brown, mushrooms and baked beans.* *It was, without doubt, the best day of her life.* *Even though he hated maths, Mike passed his GCSE.* *'That will be £17.99,' said the shop assistant, 'would you like a bag?'* *'Lucy, have you handed in your homework?'* *'Year 11, please lead out first.'*
,	**Apostrophe**	The apostrophe has two main uses: • To show that something belongs to something else (possession).	To show that something belongs to a noun that is singular, put the apostrophe *before* the s: *Peter's dog; the teacher's pen*

				To show that something belongs to a noun that is plural, put the apostrophe *after* the s: *Footballers' Wives*; *the passengers' luggage* **EXCEPTION:** if a plural word does *not* end in an *s*, you must treat it like a singular noun and put the apostrophe *before* the *s*: *a children's story*; *men's clothing* **Note:** the words that mean 'belonging to her, us, you and them' (possessive pronouns) do *not* have apostrophes. They are written as: *hers*; *ours*; *its*; *yours*; *theirs* *The monster raised its ugly head.*
			• To show that a letter or a group of letters have been missed out (omission).	This usually occurs when you are writing speech, or writing in an informal way, trying to make your writing sound like the actual words that people say. The apostrophe goes in the place where a letter or group of letters have been left out: *I am* becomes *I'm* *She will* becomes *She'll* *You could have* becomes *You could've* *It is* becomes *It's*
" " • • •	**Speech marks**		If you use speech (the exact words that people say) in your writing, it is important that you use speech punctuation accurately: • The speaker's exact words are placed inside speech marks (they are also known as *quotation marks* or *inverted commas*). • When the speaker changes, start a new paragraph. • There should always be a punctuation mark at the end of a piece of speech. • Each new piece of speech should start with a capital letter. • If a phrase such as 'asked Jane' or 'she asked' appears in the middle of a piece of speech, the 'a' of 'asked' or 's' of 'she' is not a capital letter, even if the piece of speech before ended with a question mark or exclamation mark.	*"Where are you going?" she asked.* *He replied, "I'm going to the paper shop, if that's OK with you."* *"Fine," she said, "Pick me up a pint of milk while you're there, please."* *"Is that the one with the green top?" she asked, "Because that's what I usually have."*

Concept Bank (Glossary)

Accent: the way in which words are pronounced.

Acronym: word made up from the first letters of a group of words.

Adjective: a word which describes a noun (a thing, object or person).

Alliteration: repeating the first letters of words, as in 'Peter Piper picked a peck of pickled pepper'.

Analysis: thinking about a text and explaining how it is written, and how it tries to influence the reader.

Anecdote: a short personal story used to make or illustrate a point.

Argument: a logical statement in support of a point, backed up with relevant facts and figures.

Argument text: presents different sides to a debate and comes to a conclusion.

Audience: the intended readership of a particular piece of writing.

Balanced: where the approach is unbiased and based on the facts.

Biased: where the text is affected by the author's personal feelings and beliefs.

Closing: the words used to end a letter or email, for example 'Yours sincerely'.

Colloquialisms: informal words or phrases, including slang.

Compare: to examine people or things for similarities and differences.

Connectives: linking words such as 'because', 'which' or 'although'.

Context: the situation, purpose or audience for a text.

Connotation: the idea or meaning suggested by a word, image or colour.

Creative: inventing new ways of doing things.

Deeds: what the character does.

Description: what the character is like physically.

Dialect: the choice of words and grammatical construction in speech and writing. Everyone has a dialect.

Dialogue: what the character says, and how he or she interacts with other characters.

Discourse marker: a word or phrase which helps the reader understand how a writer's argument is organised in a text. For example: 'Firstly' or 'In addition'.

Editing: changing a photo, film or text to modify the impact of it.

Emotive language: words or phrases which describe the writer's emotions and/or make the reader feel a certain way.

Evidence: a piece of information used by a writer to make a point.

Explanation: saying why something happened or describing its effects. Texts that explain often contain facts and figures, like information texts, but they can also give personal opinions and be biased.

Extract: find and state information from a text.

Fact: a statement that can be checked and proved to be true or false.

Figurative language: descriptions in which one thing is compared with another to create interesting or powerful images. Examples include similes, metaphors and personification.

First person: 'me' and 'I', or 'us' and 'we'.

Form: the way in which the subject matter is presented; the shape of the text on the page.

Formal text: uses academic English as in a text book.

Genre: style or type. There are genres of fiction, like detective stories, and non-fiction, such as newspapers.

Grammar: the way words are linked together to make a language.

Greeting: the words used to open a letter or email, for example, 'Dear Joe'.

Half rhyme: where the rhyme is suggested but is not obvious.

Header: information put at the top of a page, for example, the date, a title.

High prestige: describes an accent or dialect that some people think is spoken by people who have power and status in society.

Homophones: words which sound the same but mean different things.

Hyperbole: exaggeration.

Image: using words in a way which creates a picture in the mind's eye of the reader.

Impersonal: where the language of a text is dispassionate, as though the author is completely detached from the subject.

Infer: to read 'between the lines'

Informal text: uses everyday words, as in a telephone conversation.

Lists of three: when a writer or speaker repeats an idea three times in slightly different ways. Politicians are very good at using lists of three in their speeches to persuade their audience that what they are saying is right.

Metaphors: compare one thing with another more directly.

Modal verbs: suggest that the reader does something. Examples: 'could', 'would', 'should', 'might'.

Mood and atmosphere: the emotional feeling that is created in the scene, such as sad, happy, depressed and tense.

Non-standard dialect: dialect that is different Standard English and which contains words and grammatical constructions not found in Standard English.

Pathetic fallacy: where the weather or surrounding landscape reflects the mood of the scene.

Persona: where poets write as if they are characters, not themselves.

Personal: where the author is emotionally involved – the opposite of 'impersonal'.

Personal pronouns: words which indicate the person/people being spoken about: 'I', 'me', 'my' – first person pronouns; you', 'your' – second person pronouns; 'they', 'their' – third person pronouns.

Persuasive language: emotive or engaging language that convinces you of something. For example: 'Choosing to stay at the resort can truly turn a weekend break into a magic experience' uses 'magic experience' instead of 'good experience' to show the reader that it is worth going on this holiday.

Pitch: a short speech where you try to persuade someone to buy a product. Often given to a group of people from businesses.

Presentational devices: features of presentation, design and organisation that help a text communicate its information, ideas and feelings.

Received Pronunciation (RP): a non-regional English accent that is often used for serious television and radio programmes and in formal contexts. Some people regard it as having 'high prestige'.

Register: the way a text sounds to its readers or listeners. This could be formal or informal, bossy, amusing, friendly or cold ... or many other registers.

Represented speech: speech which scriptwriters or authors include in their work.

Review: a critical report and evaluation of a film, book, play, performance or concert, often found in newspapers, in magazines or on the Internet.

Rhetorical devices: language tricks writers use to have an emotional effect on the reader.

Rhetorical language: very persuasive language that uses emotional words.

Rhetorical questions: questions that are addressed to an audience but do not require an answer. The questions are used for dramatic effect and/or designed to make an audience think. For example: 'Would you jump off the edge of a cliff just because someone asked you to?'

Rhythm: the 'beat' of a poem.

Role: the status, actions and behaviours given to or expected of a person in a particular situation.

Script: the written text of the lines the actors say, together with directions for the set and the action in the scene.

Set: the backdrop, the use of scenery and fixed furniture on stage.

Shot: how a photographer chooses to show the subject in a photo.

Sibilance: repeating S sounds, in the middle as well as the beginning of words.

Similes: compare one thing with another using 'as' or 'like'.

Slogan: a catchy phrase that everyone will remember.

Sociolect: a variety of language used by people with shared interests or belonging to a particular group.

Spoiler: where a review reveals enough of the film to spoil it for viewers who have not seen it.

Speed of speech: how quickly a line in the play is said. The more quickly, the more aggressive a character will come across. Speaking too quickly, however, cannot be heard by the audience.

Spontaneous: without planning or warning.

Standard English: writing or speaking that is generally accepted as grammatically correct.

Stanza: a group of lines arranged together in a poem, sometimes called a verse.

Style: the choices about words and sentences that a writer or speaker makes, such as the level of formality of a text.

Summarise: state a text's main ideas in a concise way, using a small number of words.

Superstitious: to believe something so much that you change your behaviour because of it: for example, not walking under a ladder.

Text: What we think of as a text is changing. Once, the word 'text' meant simply longer writing such as novels. Now we have all kinds of texts, including images and film as well as written and spoken texts. Some texts do not have words at all.

Transcript: the written text that is made when a speech is recorded and then written out or transcribed.

Visual aid: an object, poster, image, film clip or prop that will help you to present information in a visual way so that others can **see** what you are talking about.